VIZ GRAPI

Di Gi Charat™

VOL. 4

Di Gi Charat ™
Volume 4

English Adaptation by
Gerard Jones

Translation/Mari Morimoto
Touch-up & Lettering/Andy Ristaino
Cover & Graphic Design/Yuki Ameda
Editor/Eric Searleman

Managing Editor/Annette Roman
Editor-in-Chief/William Flanagan
Director of Licensing & Acquisitions/Rika Inouye
Sr. VP of Editorial/Hyoe Narita
VP of Sales & Marketing/Liza Coppola
Publisher/Seiji Horibuchi

© Broccoli 2001 and all respective creators: Nemuro-No-Hisayoshi, Strike-Heisuke, Aruto Suzuki, Akira Hojo, Akari Kita, J-ta Yamada, Towa Ozora, Kiro Hanehane, Aya Shouoto, Yuzuru Asahina, Kurumi Morisaki, Yuya Kuruma, Marumi Yamamoto, Kazuki Shu, Hina, Koge-Donbo and Kawaku.

First published in 2001 by Media Works Inc., Tokyo, Japan. English translation rights arranged with Media Works Inc.

New and adapted artwork and text © 2003 VIZ, LLC

Printed in Canada

Published by VIZ, LLC
P.O. Box 77064
San Francisco, CA 94107

10 9 8 7 6 5 4 3 2 1
First printing, October 2003

  store.viz.com

get your own vizmail.net e-mail account
register for the weekly e-mail newsletter
sign up for VIZ INternet
voice 1 (800) 394-3042 fax (415) 546-7073

CONTENTS

CHARACTERS

DI GI CHARAT

NAME: DI GI CHARAT
AGE: 10

THE CROWN PRINCESS OF PLANET
DI GI CHARAT, CURRENTLY "STUDYING"
ON EARTH. WHILE WORKING AT A
STORE CALLED **GAMERS** SHE
SCHEMES TO BECOME AN ACTRESS.
DESPITE HER ADORABLE EXTERIOR,
HER TRUE SELF IS DECIDEDLY
ARROGANT AND INSENSITIVE.
HAS A HABIT OF ADDING "MEOW" TO HER
WORDS, AN ODD ACCENT LEFT OVER
FROM PLANET DI GI CHARAT.

PETIT CHARAT

NAME: PETIT CHARAT
AGE: 5

CAME WITH DIGIKO FROM PLANET
DI GI CHARAT. USUALLY A GIRL OF FEW
WORDS, SHE ACTUALLY POSSESSES
QUITE A VENOMOUS TONGUE. SHE'S
ALWAYS STICKING TO DIGIKO, BECAUSE
(OR SO THE STORY GOES) SHE FEELS
INDEBTED TO DIGIKO FOR SAVING HER
FROM A DEADLY TRAP.

RABI EN ROSE

NAME: USADA HIKARU
AGE: 14

SHE ALSO WORKS AT GAMERS
AND YEARNS TO BE A STAR. OUT-
WARDLY DIGIKO'S RIVAL, SHE IS
SECRETLY A LONELY SOUL WHO
WISHES SHE COULD BE DIGIKO'S
FRIEND.
HATES HER REAL NAME, SO
USUALLY CALLS HERSELF "RABI
EN ROSE," MEANING (SORT OF)
"PINK RABBIT."

PYOCORA ANALOG III

NAME: PYOCORA ANALOG III
AGE: 8

BOSS OF THE DARK GEMA GEMA
GANG. IN ORDER TO REBUILD HER
EVIL ORGANIZATION'S TROUBLED
FINANCES, SHE SCHEMES TO KIDNAP
DIGIKO FOR RANSOM.
UNFORTUNATELY, SHE'S A GULLIBLE
IDIOT, SO DIGIKO IS ALWAYS
ESCAPING FROM HER CLUTCHES.
HER NICKNAME IS "PIYOKO."

RIK HEISENBERG

NAME: RIK HEISENBERG
AGE: 26

GENERAL OF THE DARK GEMA GEMA
GANG, HE SPEAKS COOLLY OF THE
MOST WICKED DEEDS. BUT HE ALSO
LOVES ANIMALS, AND PROUD OF THE
FACT THAT THEY LOVE HIM—EVEN
THOUGH HE'S A VET.

KY SCHWEITZER

NAME: KY SCHWEITZER
AGE: 17

LIEUTENANT GENERAL OF THE DARK
GEMA GEMA GANG. WITH HIS POWERFUL
SENSE OF RESPONSIBILITY, HE ALWAYS
PUTS PIYOKO'S NEEDS BEFORE HIS OWN.
HE'S ALSO A BRILLIANT DENTIST, AND
MAKES IT HIS DUTY TO CHECK PIYOKO'S
TOOTH-BRUSHING MORNING AND NIGHT.

COO ERHARD

NAME: COO ERHARD
AGE: 13

MAJOR IN THE DARK GEMA GEMA
GANG, HE THINKS OF HIS
CHILDHOOD FRIEND PIYOKO AS A
LITTLE SISTER. OF THE THREE, HE
IS THE CLOSEST TO HER.
HIS STUFFED PANDA IS HIS PRIZE
POSSESSION.

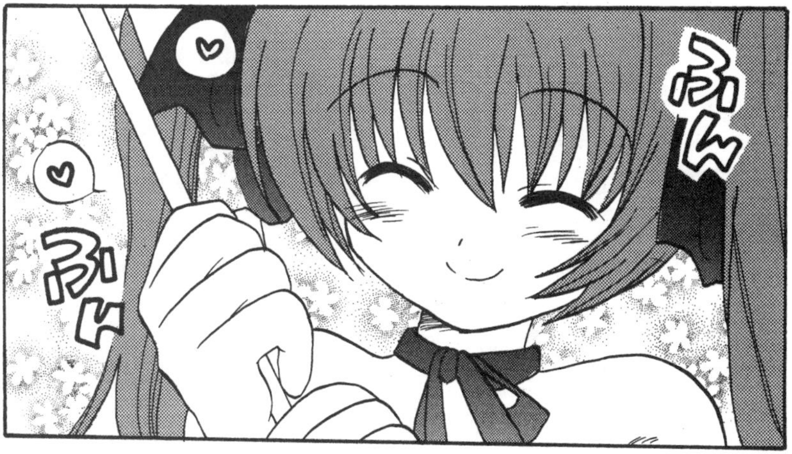
ふん
ふん

GET RABI!!

●●● ARTIST: NEMURO-NO-HISAYOSHI
ORIGINAL CONCEPT: STRIKE-HEISUKE ●●●

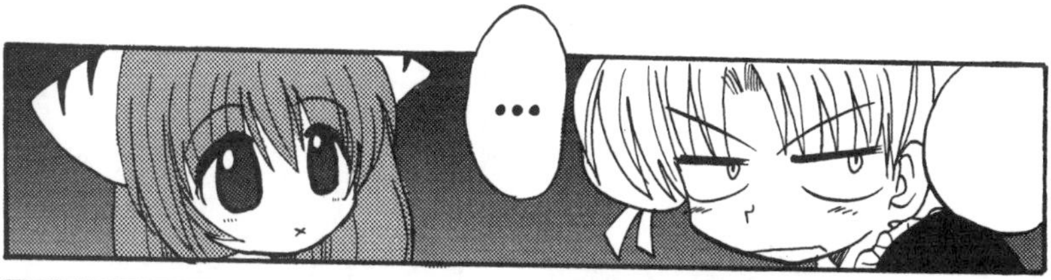
...

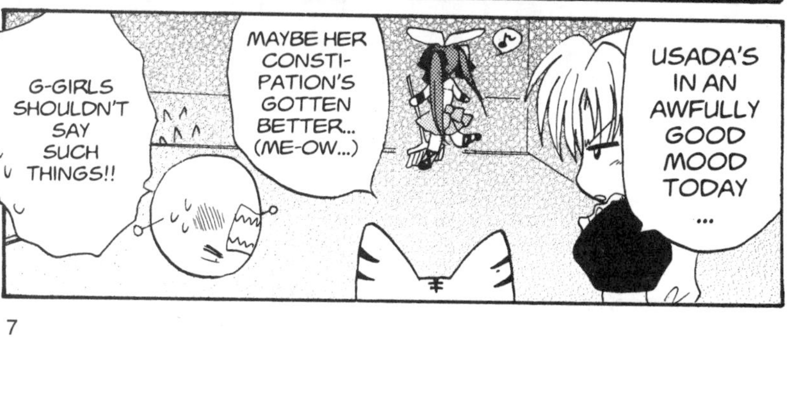
USADA'S IN AN AWFULLY GOOD MOOD TODAY ...
MAYBE HER CONSTI-PATION'S GOTTEN BETTER... (ME-OW...)
G-GIRLS SHOULDN'T SAY SUCH THINGS!!

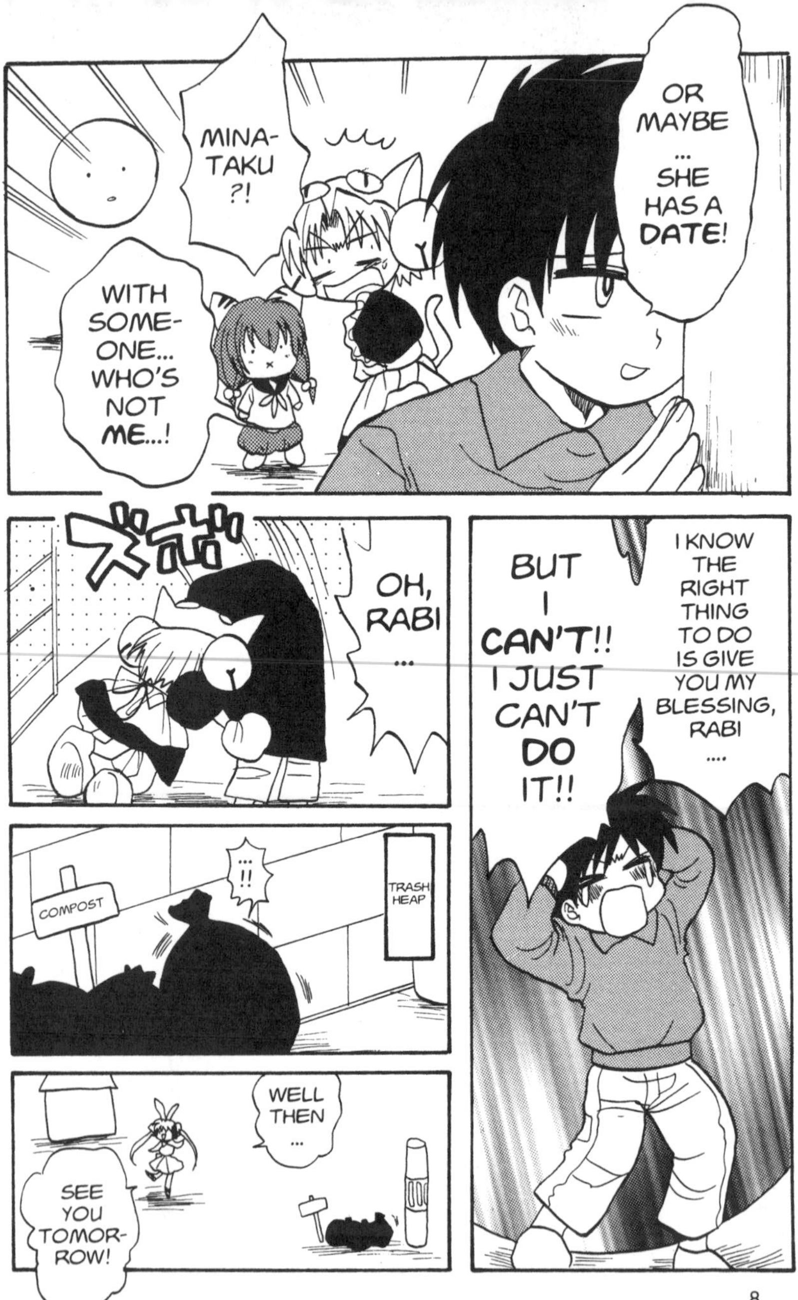
OR MAYBE ... SHE HAS A DATE!
MINA-TAKU ?!
WITH SOME-ONE... WHO'S NOT ME...!
I KNOW THE RIGHT THING TO DO IS GIVE YOU MY BLESSING, RABI ....
BUT I CAN'T!! I JUST CAN'T DO IT!!
ズボ
OH, RABI ...
...!!
TRASH HEAP
COMPOST
WELL THEN ...
SEE YOU TOMOR-ROW!

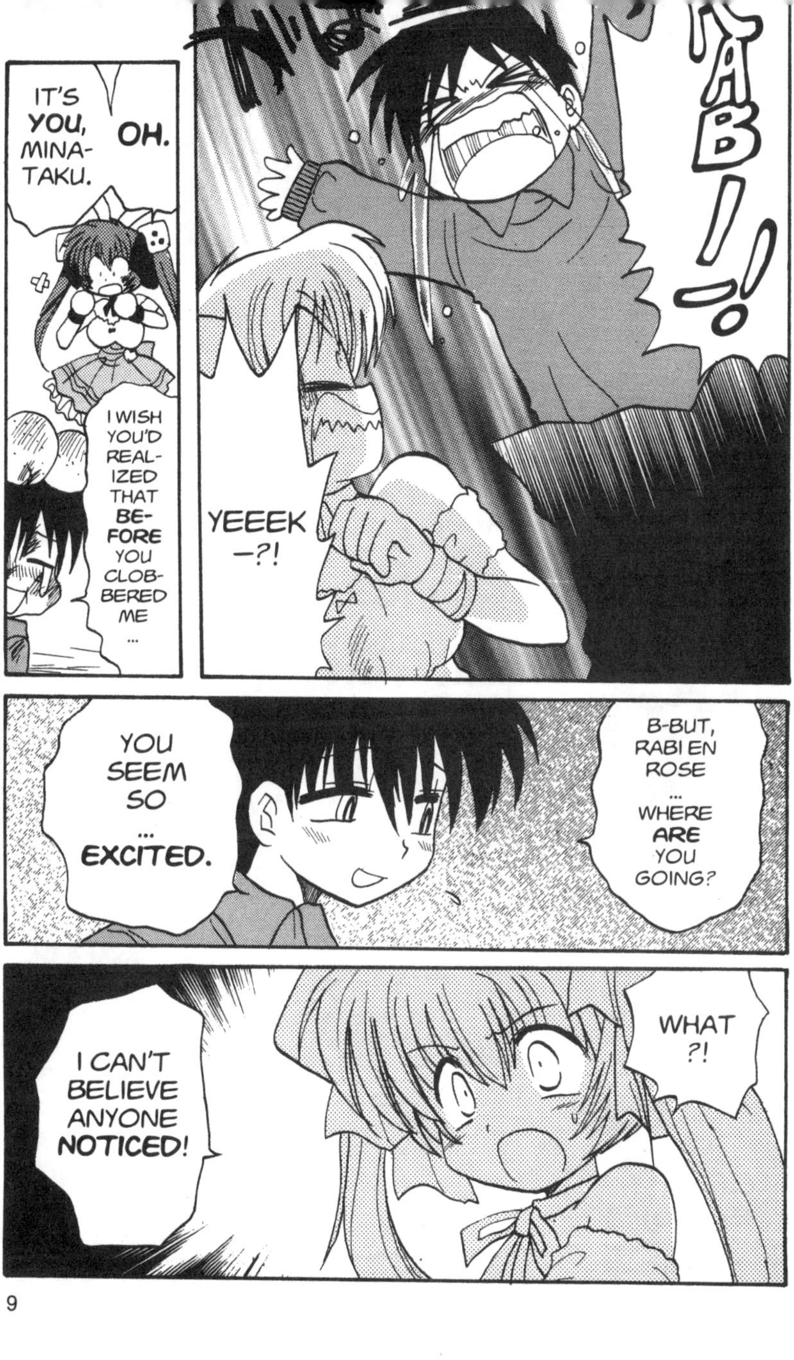
ABI—!
YEEEK—?!
OH.
IT'S YOU, MINA-TAKU.
I WISH YOU'D REAL-IZED THAT BE-FORE YOU CLOB-BERED ME ...
B-BUT, RABI EN ROSE ... WHERE ARE YOU GOING?
YOU SEEM SO ... EXCITED.
WHAT ?!
I CAN'T BELIEVE ANYONE NOTICED!

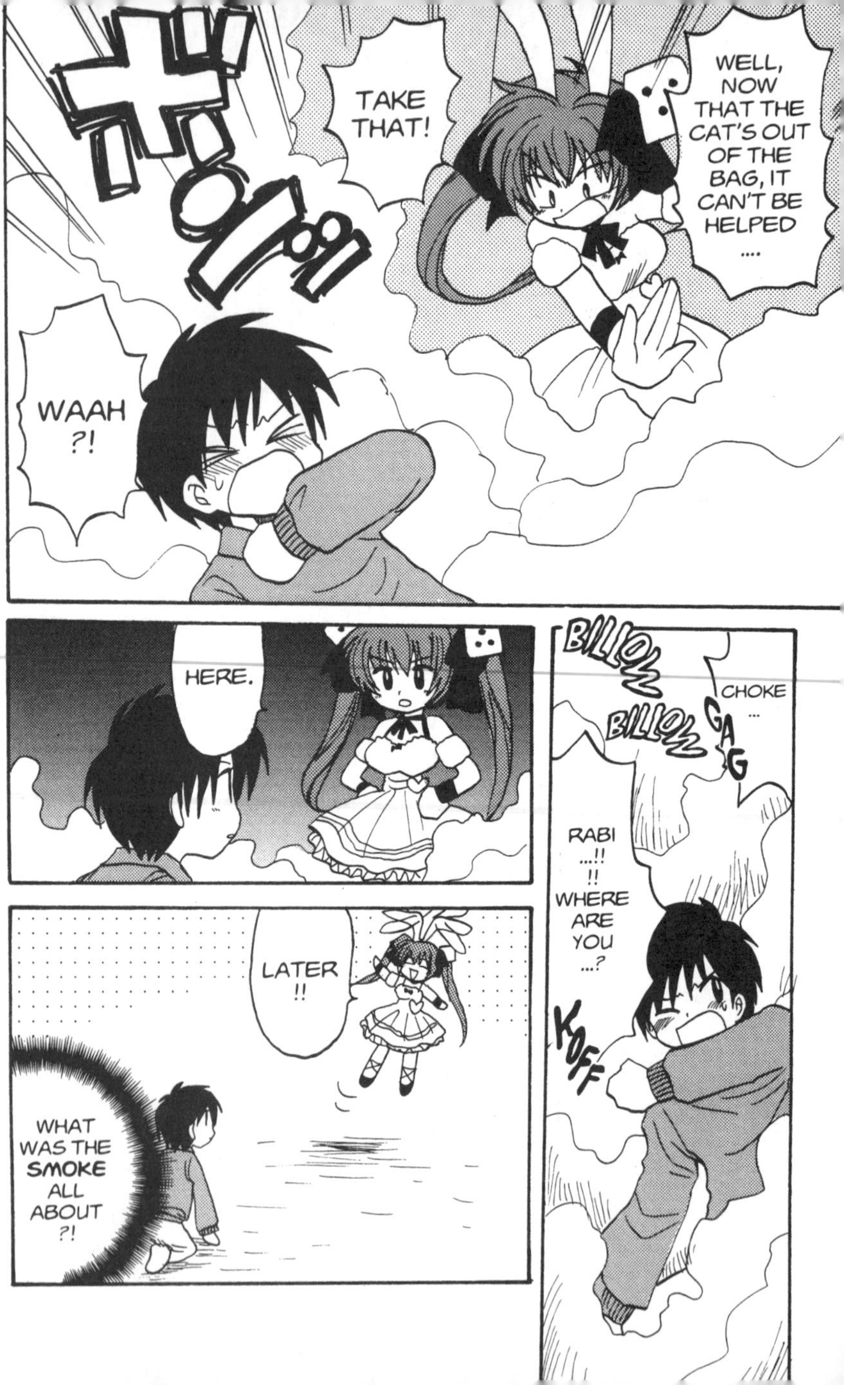
WELL, NOW THAT THE CAT'S OUT OF THE BAG, IT CAN'T BE HELPED ....
TAKE THAT!
WAAH ?!
BILLOW
BILLOW
CHOKE ...
GAG
RABI ...!! !! WHERE ARE YOU ...?
KOFF
HERE.
LATER !!
WHAT WAS THE SMOKE ALL ABOUT ?!

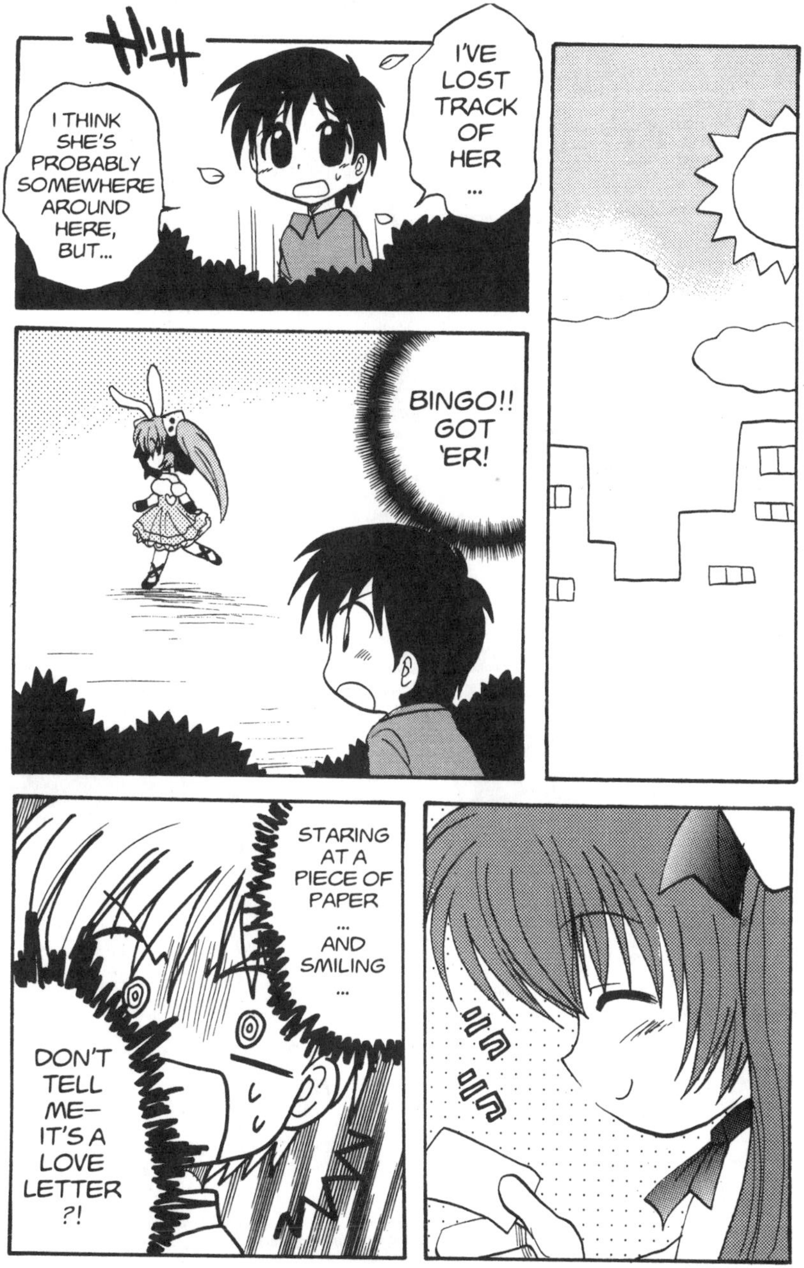
I'VE LOST TRACK OF HER ...
I THINK SHE'S PROBABLY SOMEWHERE AROUND HERE, BUT...
BINGO!! GOT 'ER!
STARING AT A PIECE OF PAPER ... AND SMILING ...
DON'T TELL ME— IT'S A LOVE LETTER ?!

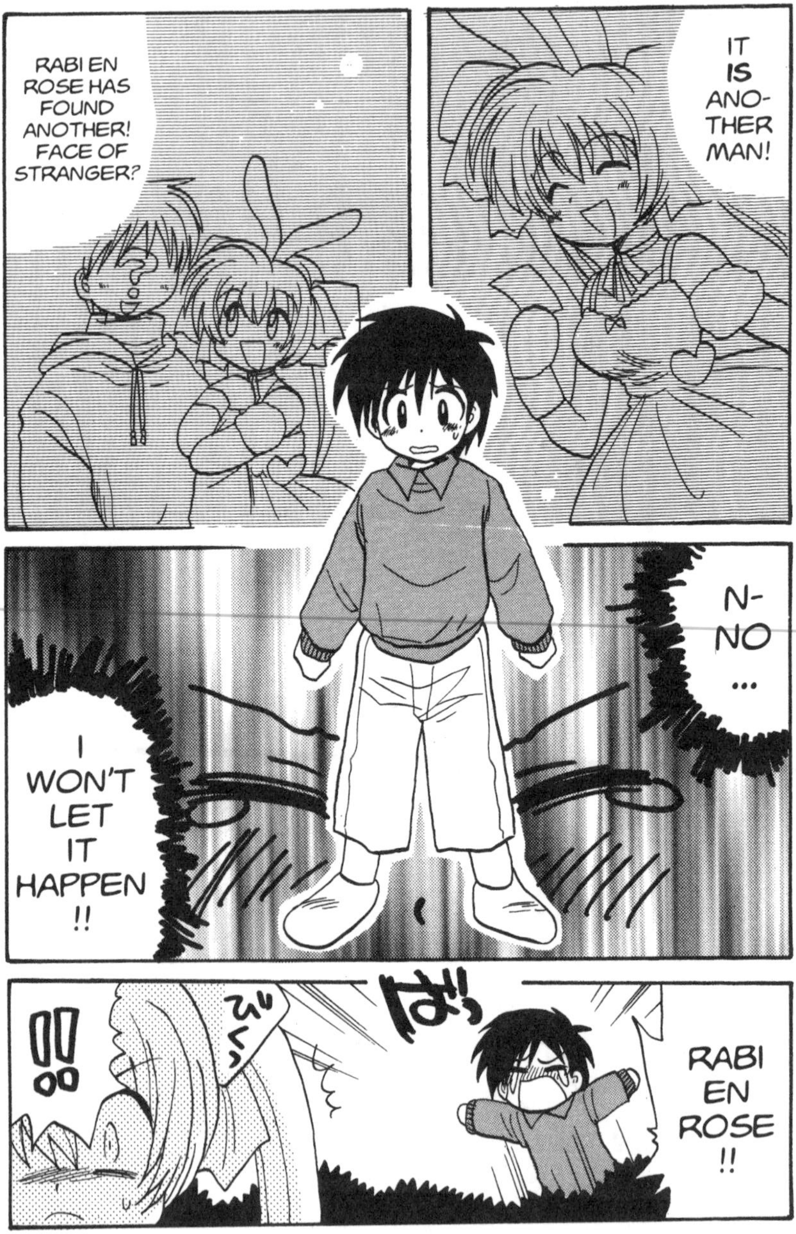

IT IS ANOTHER MAN!
RABI EN ROSE HAS FOUND ANOTHER! FACE OF STRANGER?
N-NO ...
I WON'T LET IT HAPPEN !!
RABI EN ROSE !!

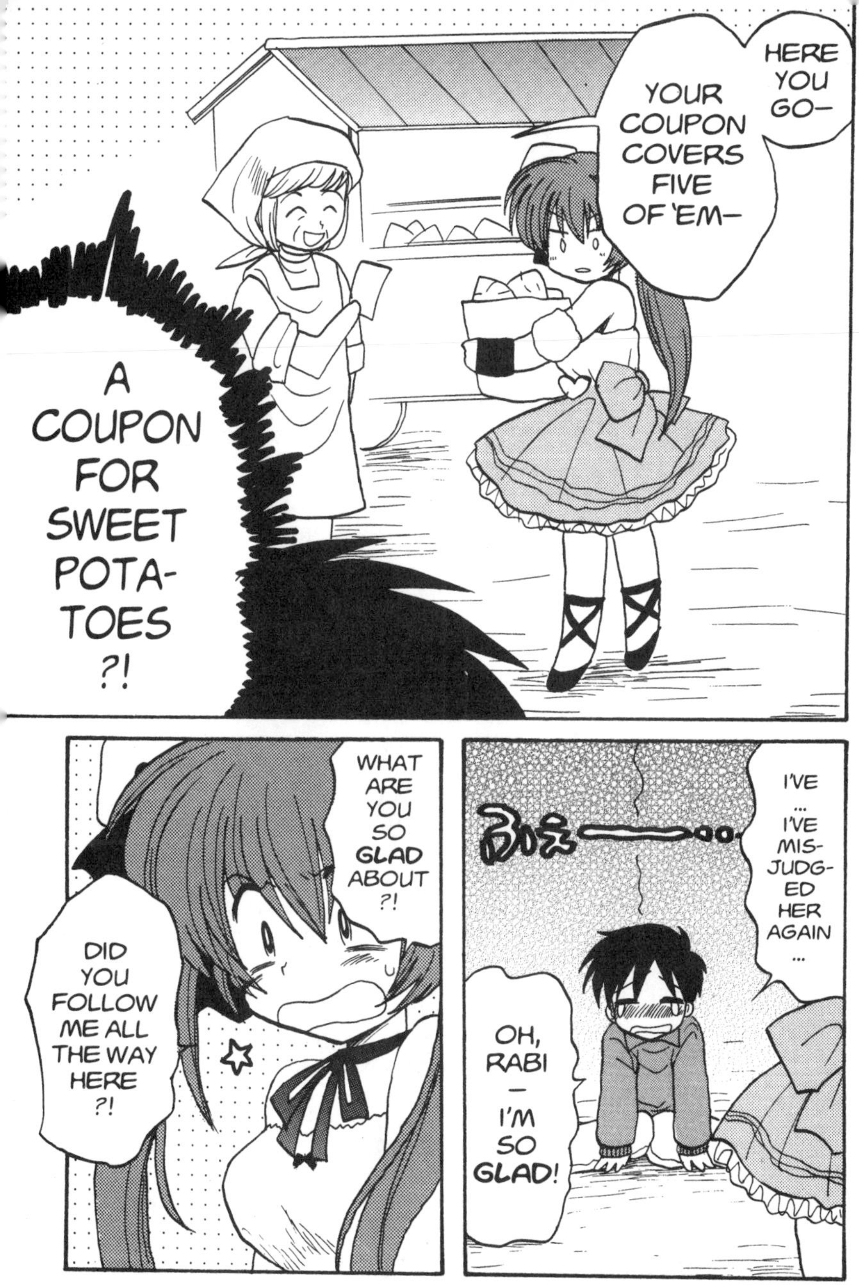
HERE YOU GO—
YOUR COUPON COVERS FIVE OF 'EM—
A COUPON FOR SWEET POTA-TOES ?!
I'VE ... I'VE MIS-JUDG-ED HER AGAIN ...
OH, RABI — I'M SO GLAD!
WHAT ARE YOU SO GLAD ABOUT ?!
DID YOU FOLLOW ME ALL THE WAY HERE ?!

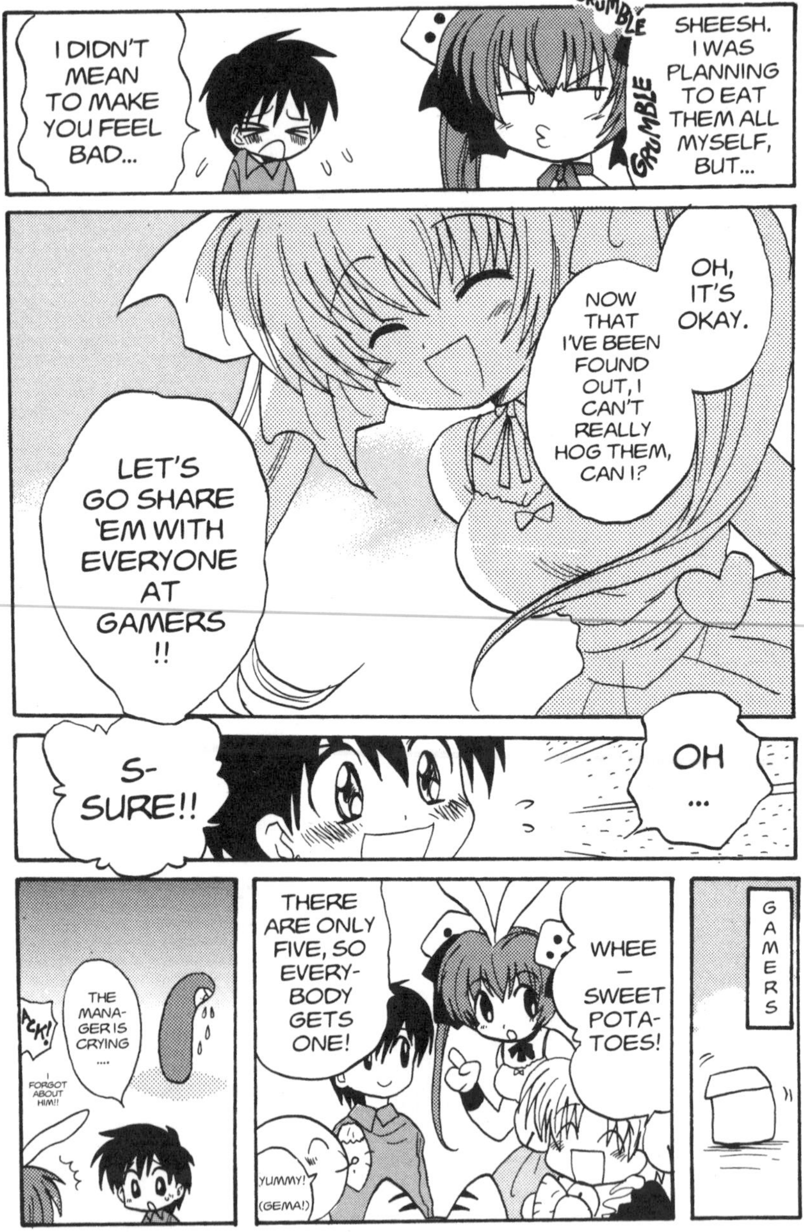
GRUMBLE
SHEESH. I WAS PLANNING TO EAT THEM ALL MYSELF, BUT...
GRUMBLE
I DIDN'T MEAN TO MAKE YOU FEEL BAD...
OH, IT'S OKAY.
NOW THAT I'VE BEEN FOUND OUT, I CAN'T REALLY HOG THEM, CAN I?
LET'S GO SHARE 'EM WITH EVERYONE AT GAMERS !!
OH ...
S-SURE!!
GAMERS
WHEE – SWEET POTA-TOES!
THERE ARE ONLY FIVE, SO EVERY-BODY GETS ONE!
YUMMY!
(GEMA!)
THE MANA-GER IS CRYING ....
I FORGOT ABOUT HIM!!

END ♡

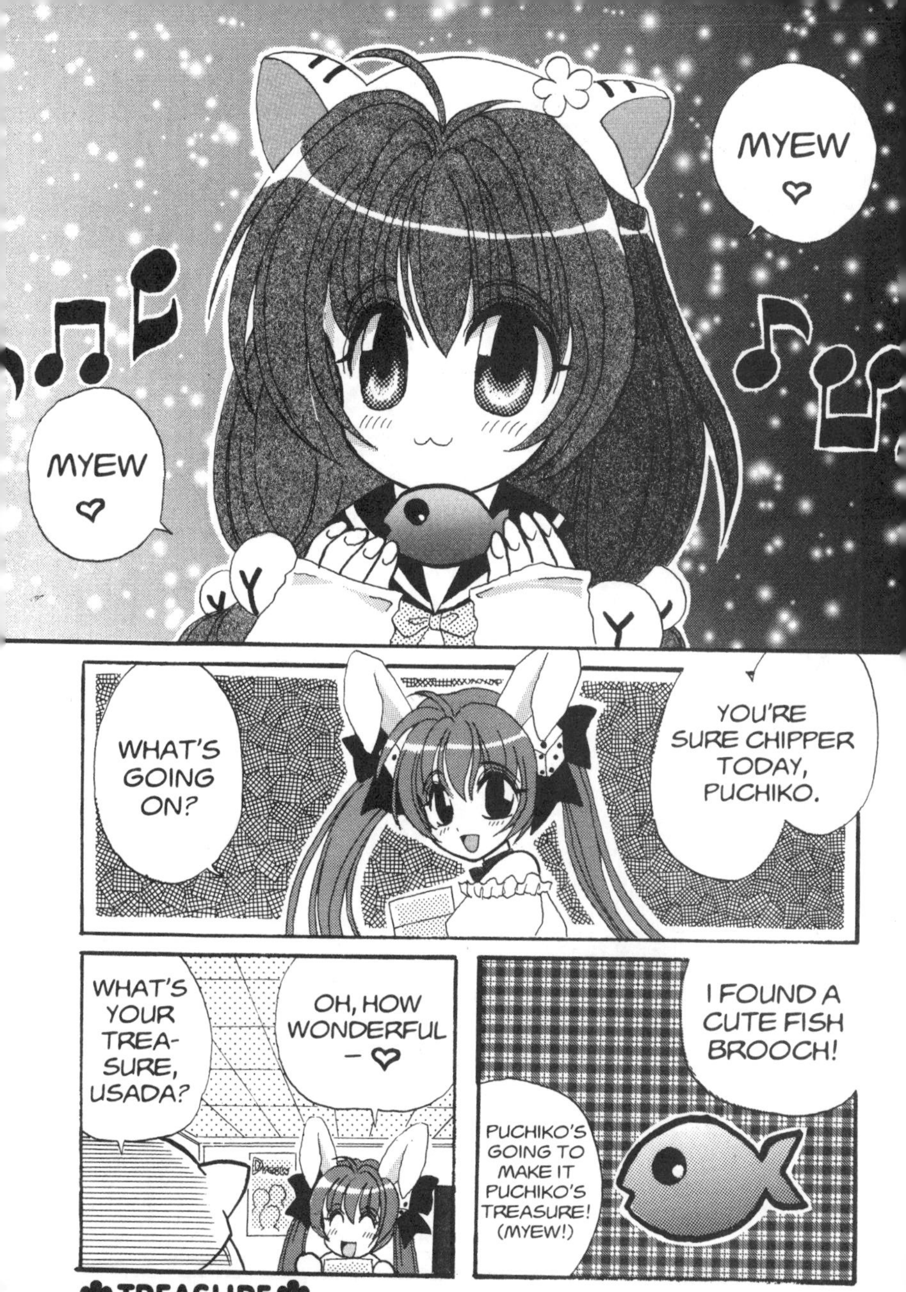
MYEW ♡
MYEW ♡
YOU'RE SURE CHIPPER TODAY, PUCHIKO.
WHAT'S GOING ON?
I FOUND A CUTE FISH BROOCH!
PUCHIKO'S GOING TO MAKE IT PUCHIKO'S TREASURE! (MYEW!)
OH, HOW WONDERFUL —♡
WHAT'S YOUR TREA-SURE, USADA?

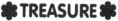

❀TREASURE❀

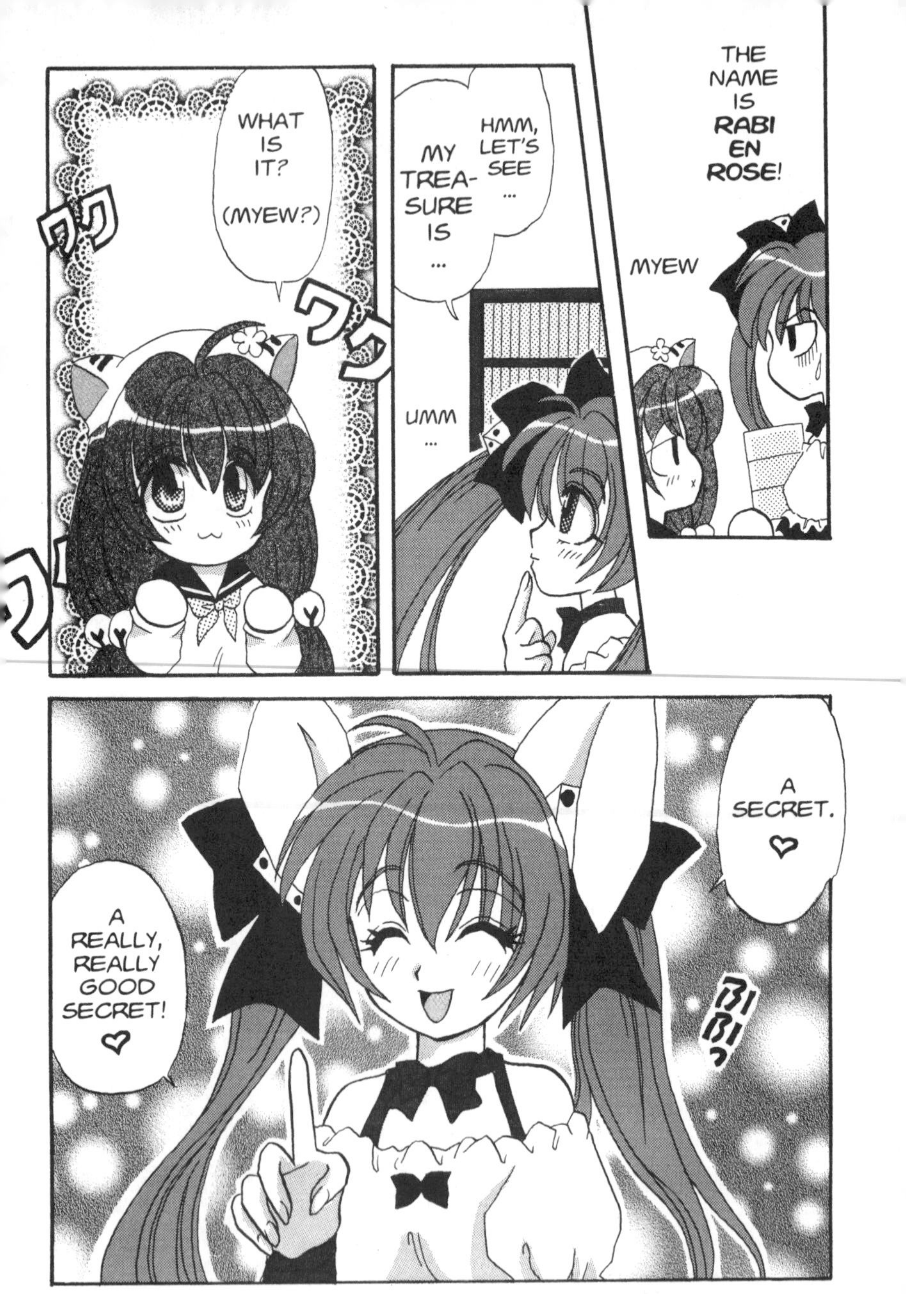
THE NAME IS RABI EN ROSE!
MYEW
HMM, LET'S SEE ...
MY TREA-SURE IS ...
UMM ...
WHAT IS IT?
(MYEW?)
ワク
ワク
A SECRET. ♡
A REALLY, REALLY GOOD SECRET! ♡

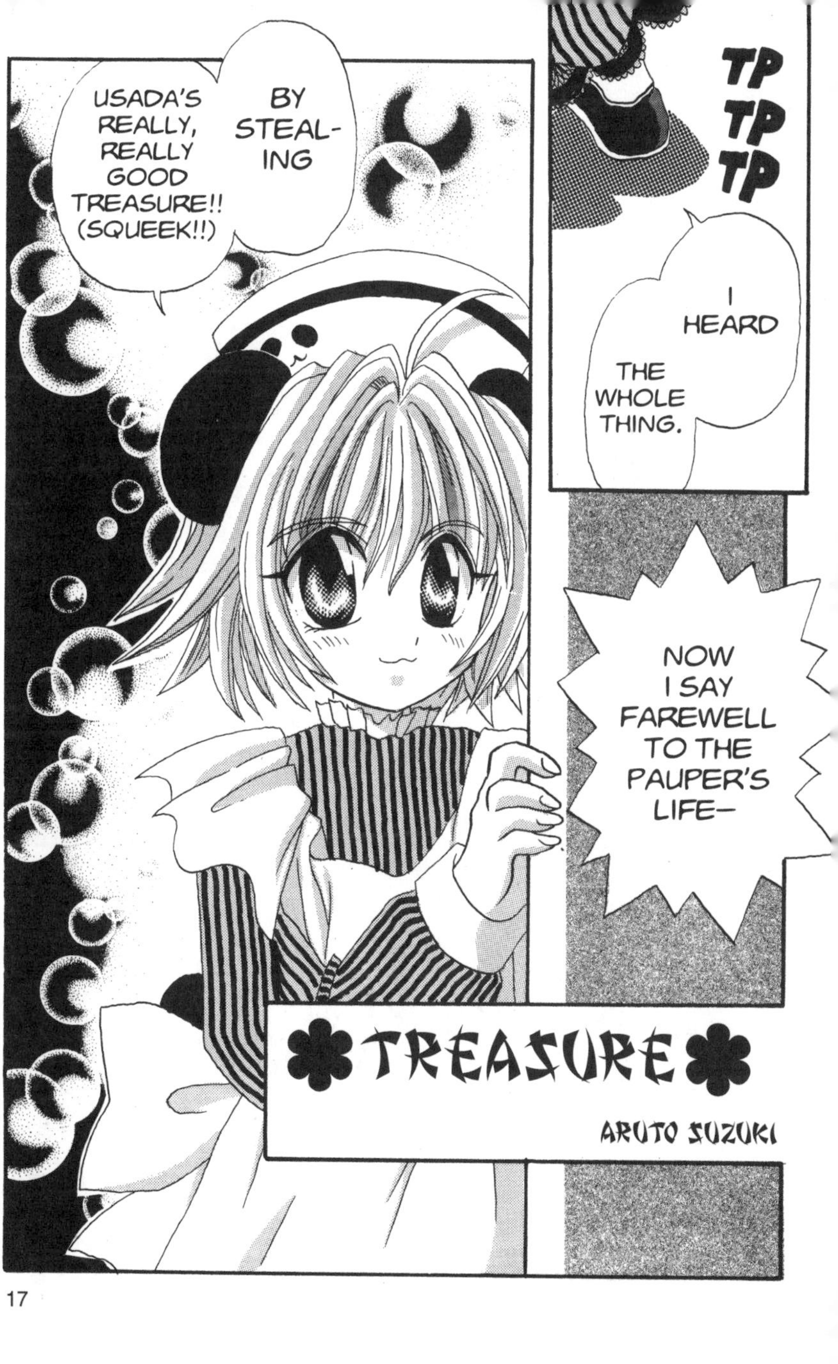
TP TP TP
I HEARD THE WHOLE THING.
NOW I SAY FAREWELL TO THE PAUPER'S LIFE–
BY STEAL-ING
USADA'S REALLY, REALLY GOOD TREASURE!! (SQUEEK!!)
TREASURE
ARUTO SUZUKI

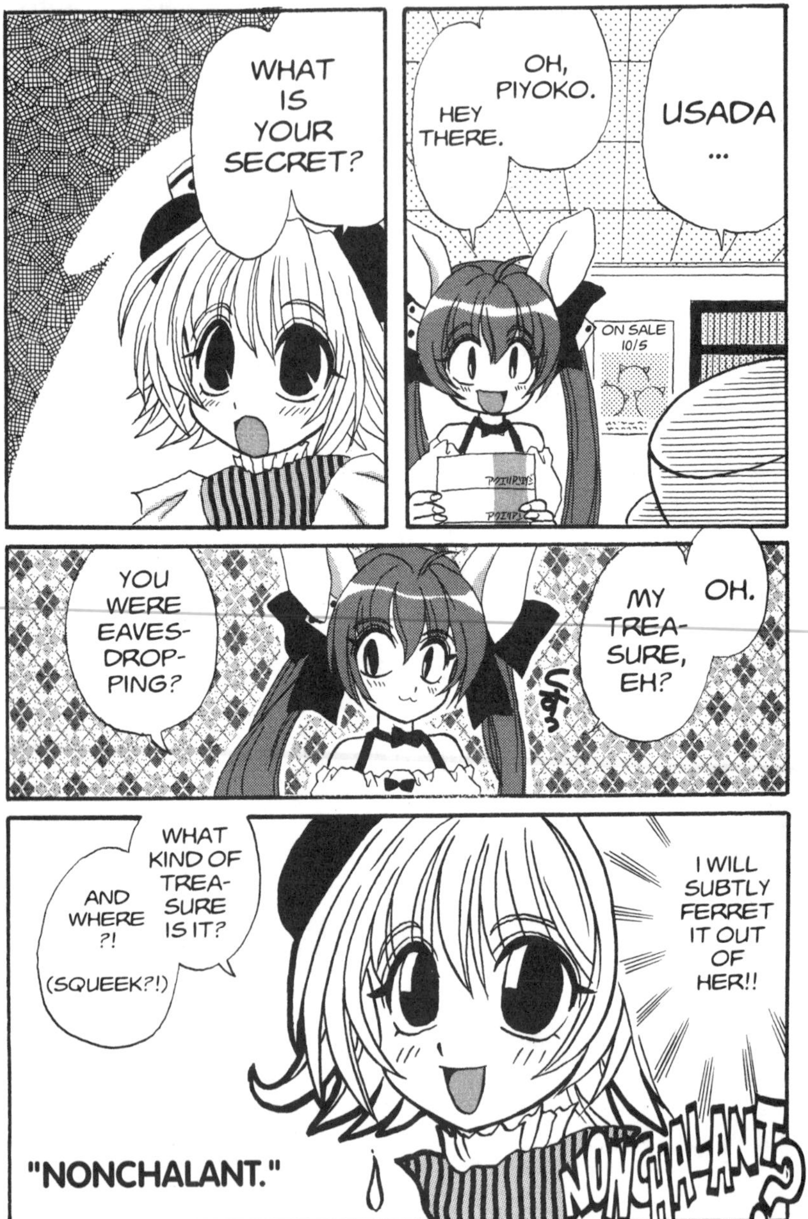
USADA ...
OH, PIYOKO.
HEY THERE.
ON SALE 10/5
WHAT IS YOUR SECRET?
OH.
MY TREA-SURE, EH?
YOU WERE EAVES-DROP-PING?
I WILL SUBTLY FERRET IT OUT OF HER!!
WHAT KIND OF TREA-SURE IS IT?
AND WHERE ?!
(SQUEEK?!)
NONCHALANT?
"NONCHALANT."

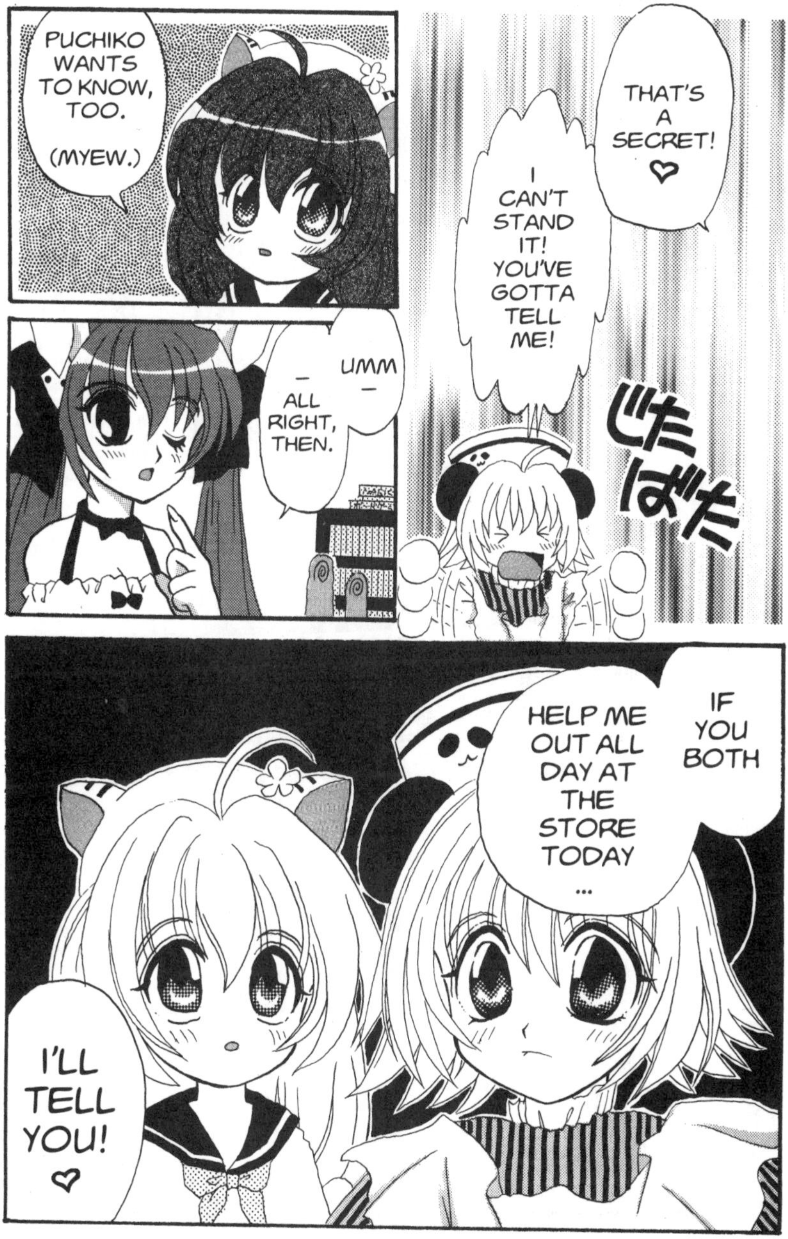
THAT'S A SECRET! ♥
I CAN'T STAND IT! YOU'VE GOTTA TELL ME!
じたばた
PUCHIKO WANTS TO KNOW, TOO.
(MYEW.)
—UMM— ALL RIGHT, THEN.
IF YOU BOTH
HELP ME OUT ALL DAY AT THE STORE TODAY ...
I'LL TELL YOU! ♥

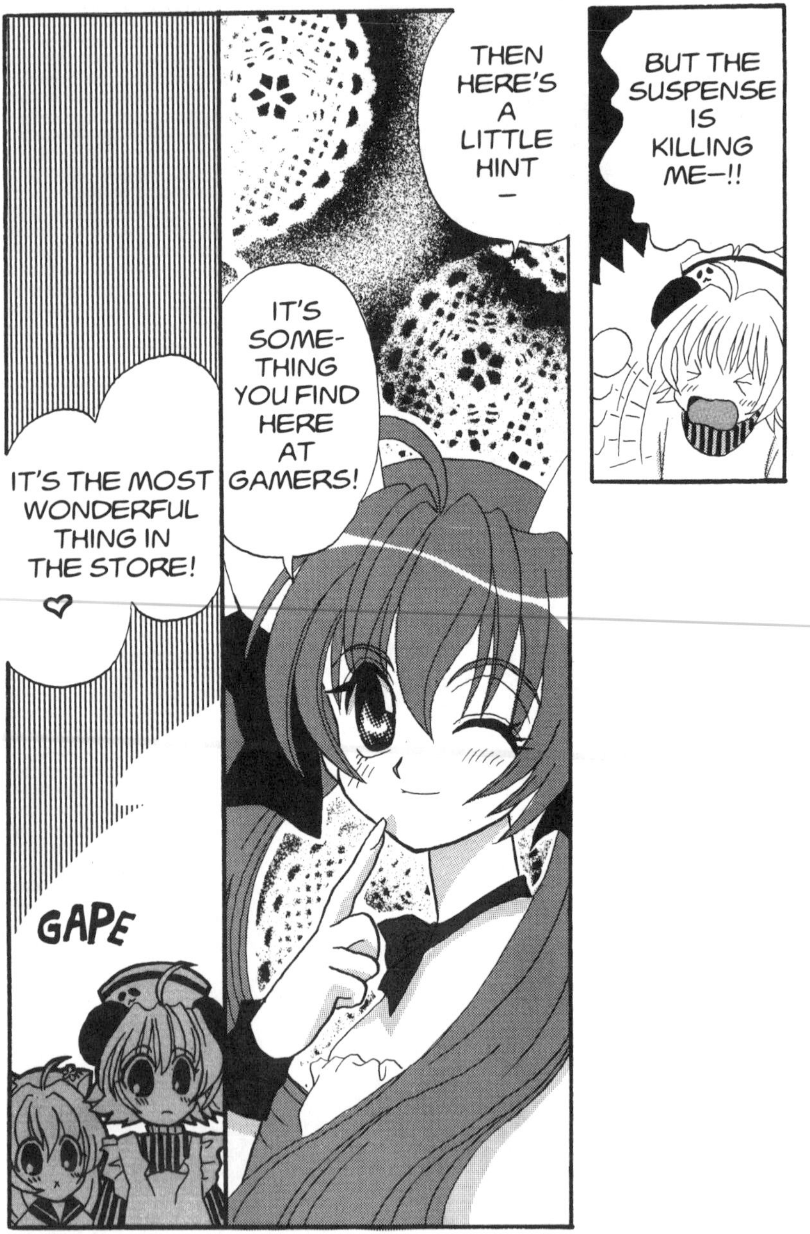
BUT THE SUSPENSE IS KILLING ME–!!
THEN HERE'S A LITTLE HINT –
IT'S SOME-THING YOU FIND HERE AT GAMERS!
IT'S THE MOST WONDERFUL THING IN THE STORE! ♡
GAPE

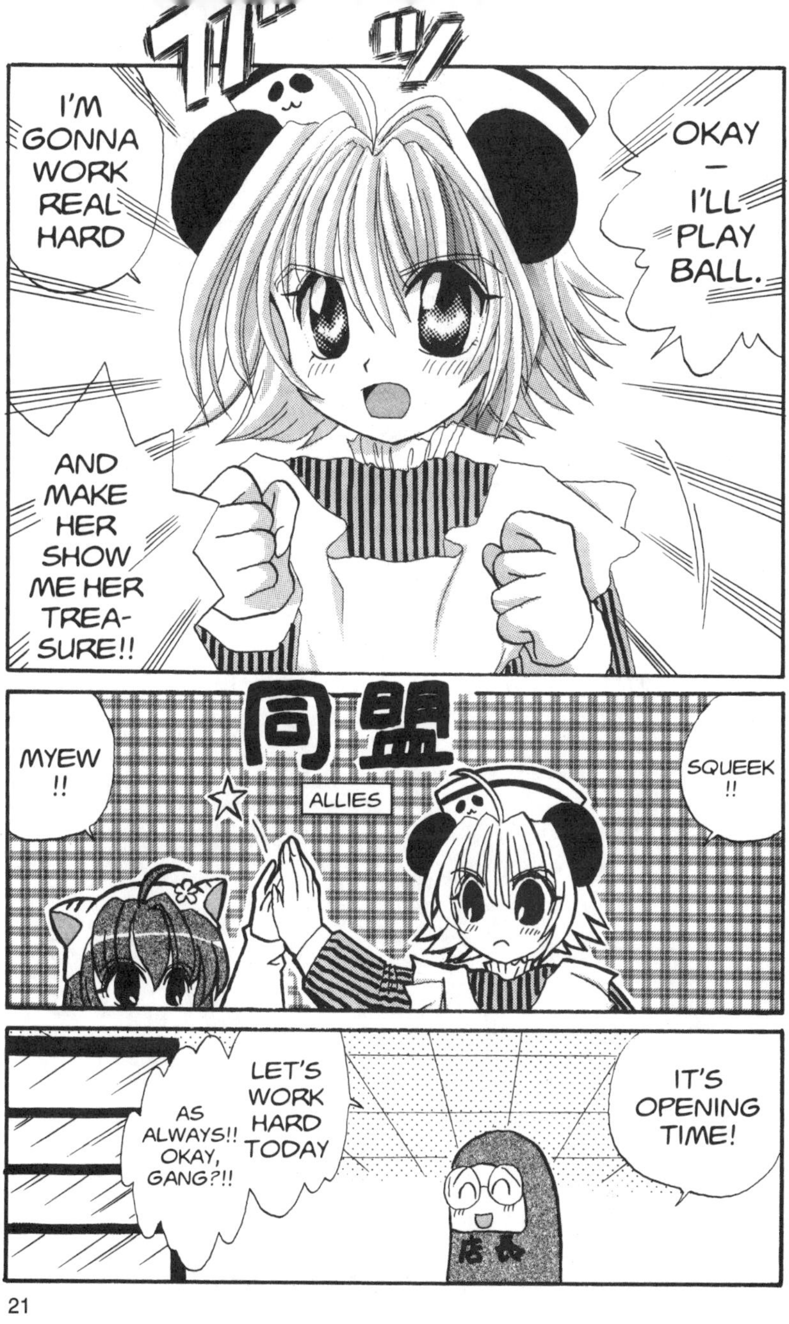
OKAY — I'LL PLAY BALL.
I'M GONNA WORK REAL HARD
AND MAKE HER SHOW ME HER TREASURE!!
SQUEEK !!
同盟
ALLIES
MYEW !!
IT'S OPENING TIME!
LET'S WORK HARD TODAY
AS ALWAYS!! OKAY, GANG?!!

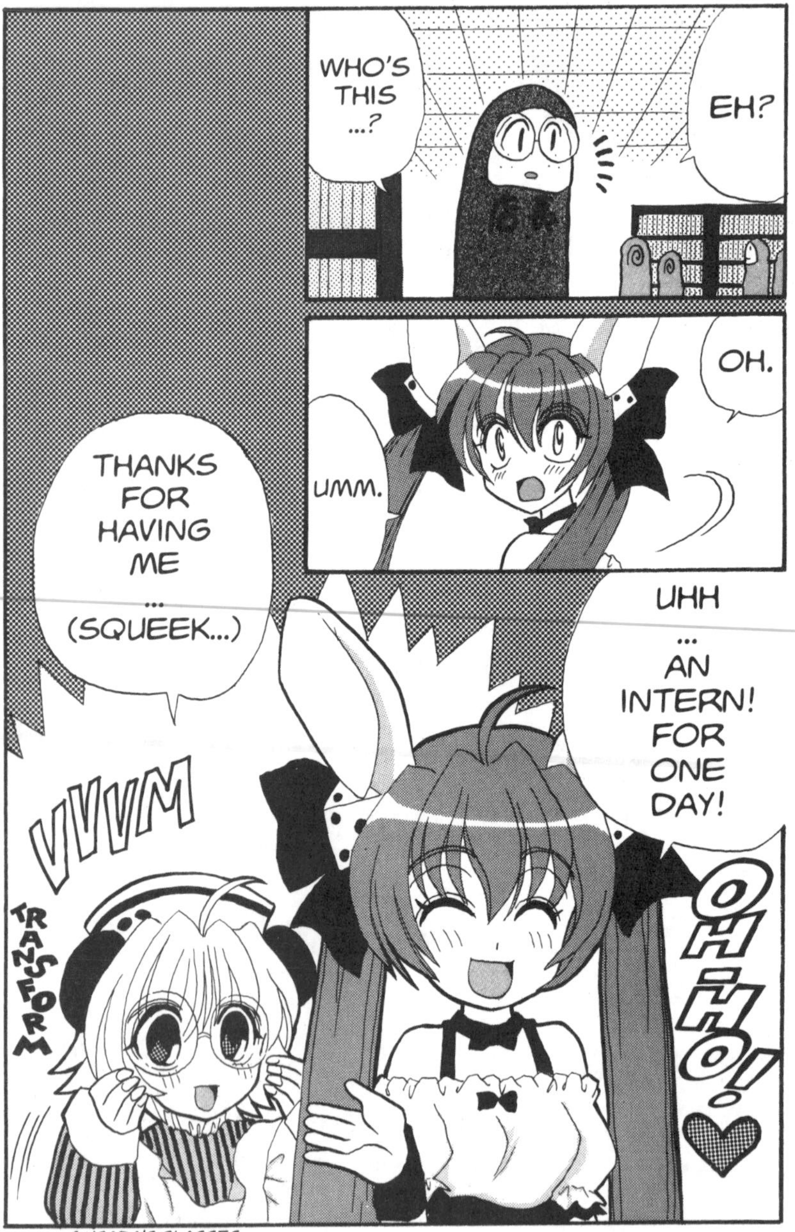
EH?
WHO'S THIS ...?
OH.
UMM.
UHH ... AN INTERN! FOR ONE DAY!
OH-HO-HO!
THANKS FOR HAVING ME ... (SQUEEK...)
VVVM
TRANSFORM

▲USADA'S GLASSES

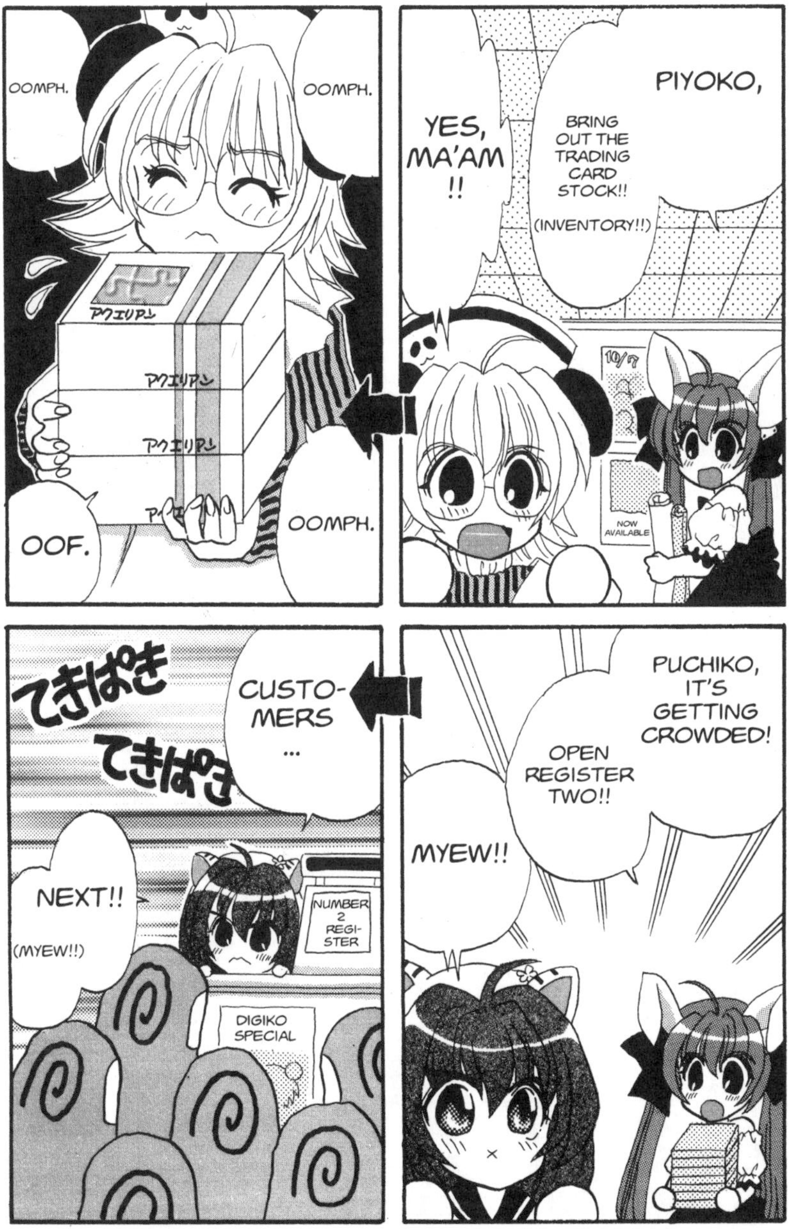
PIYOKO,
BRING OUT THE TRADING CARD STOCK!!
(INVENTORY!!)
YES, MA'AM !!
10/7
NOW AVAILABLE
OOMPH.
OOMPH.
アクエリアン
OOMPH.
OOF.
PUCHIKO, IT'S GETTING CROWDED!
OPEN REGISTER TWO!!
MYEW!!
CUSTO- MERS ...
てきぱき
てきぱき
NUMBER 2 REGI- STER
NEXT!!
(MYEW!!)
DIGIKO SPECIAL

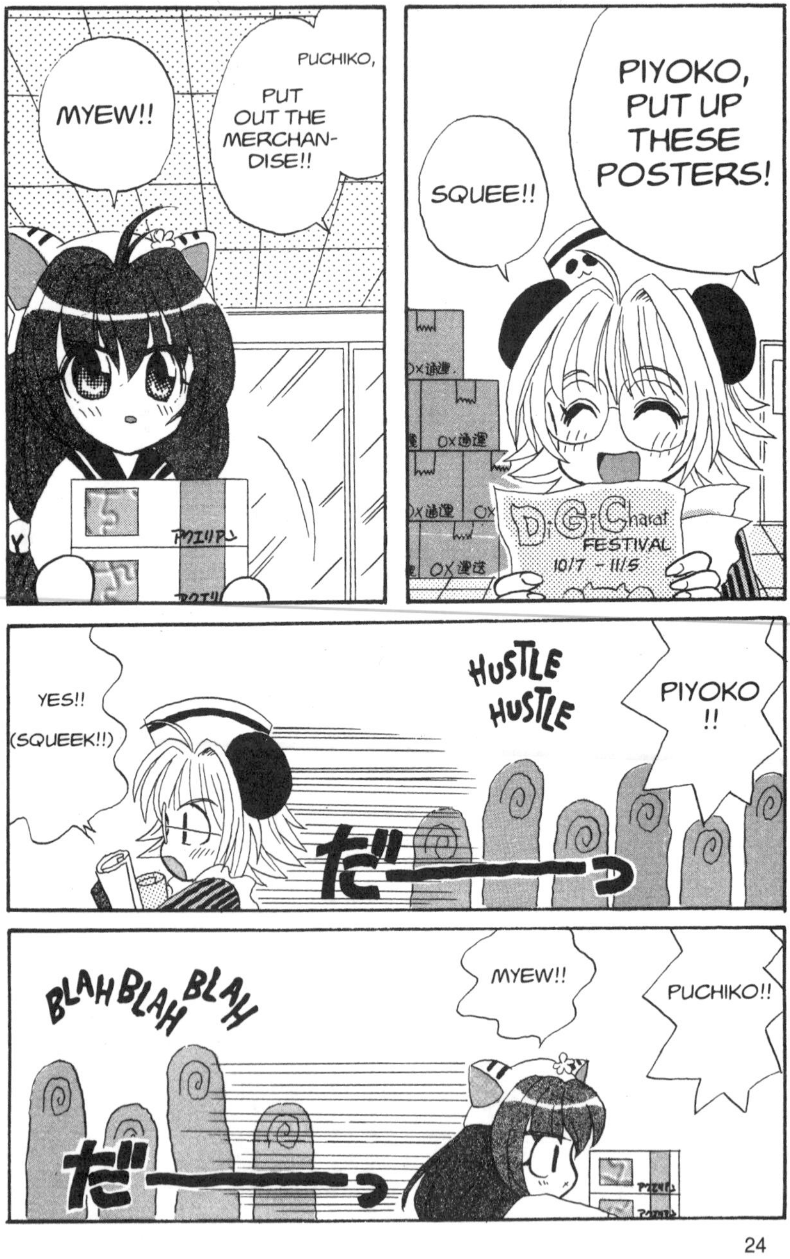
PIYOKO, PUT UP THESE POSTERS!
SQUEE!!
Di Gi Charat FESTIVAL 10/7 - 11/5
PUCHIKO, PUT OUT THE MERCHANDISE!!
MYEW!!
PIYOKO!!
HUSTLE HUSTLE
だーーーっ
YES!! (SQUEEK!!)
PUCHIKO!!
MYEW!!
BLAH BLAH BLAH
だーーーっ

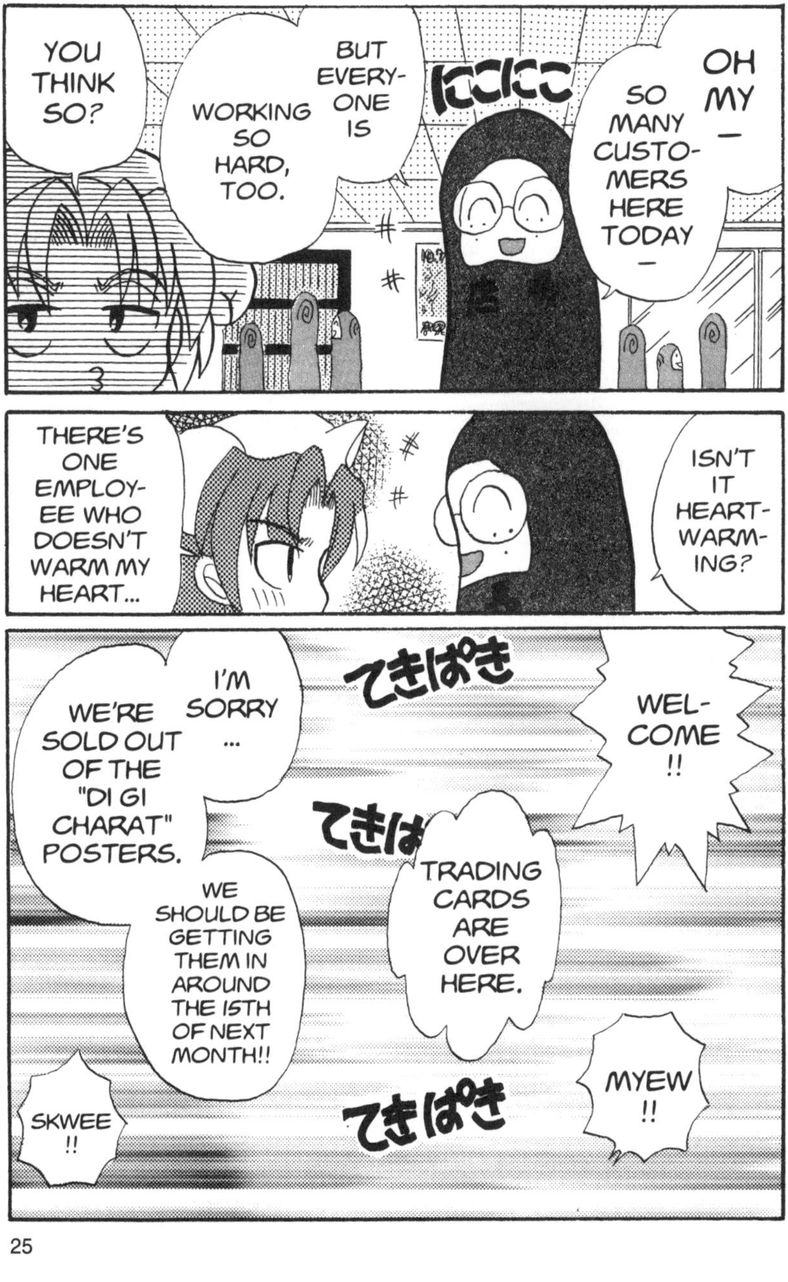
OH MY —
SO MANY CUSTOMERS HERE TODAY —
にこにこ
BUT EVERYONE IS
WORKING SO HARD, TOO.
YOU THINK SO?
ISN'T IT HEART-WARMING?
THERE'S ONE EMPLOYEE WHO DOESN'T WARM MY HEART...
WELCOME!!
てきぱき
I'M SORRY...
WE'RE SOLD OUT OF THE "DI GI CHARAT" POSTERS.
てきぱ
TRADING CARDS ARE OVER HERE.
WE SHOULD BE GETTING THEM IN AROUND THE 15TH OF NEXT MONTH!!
MYEW!!
てきぱき
SKWEE!!

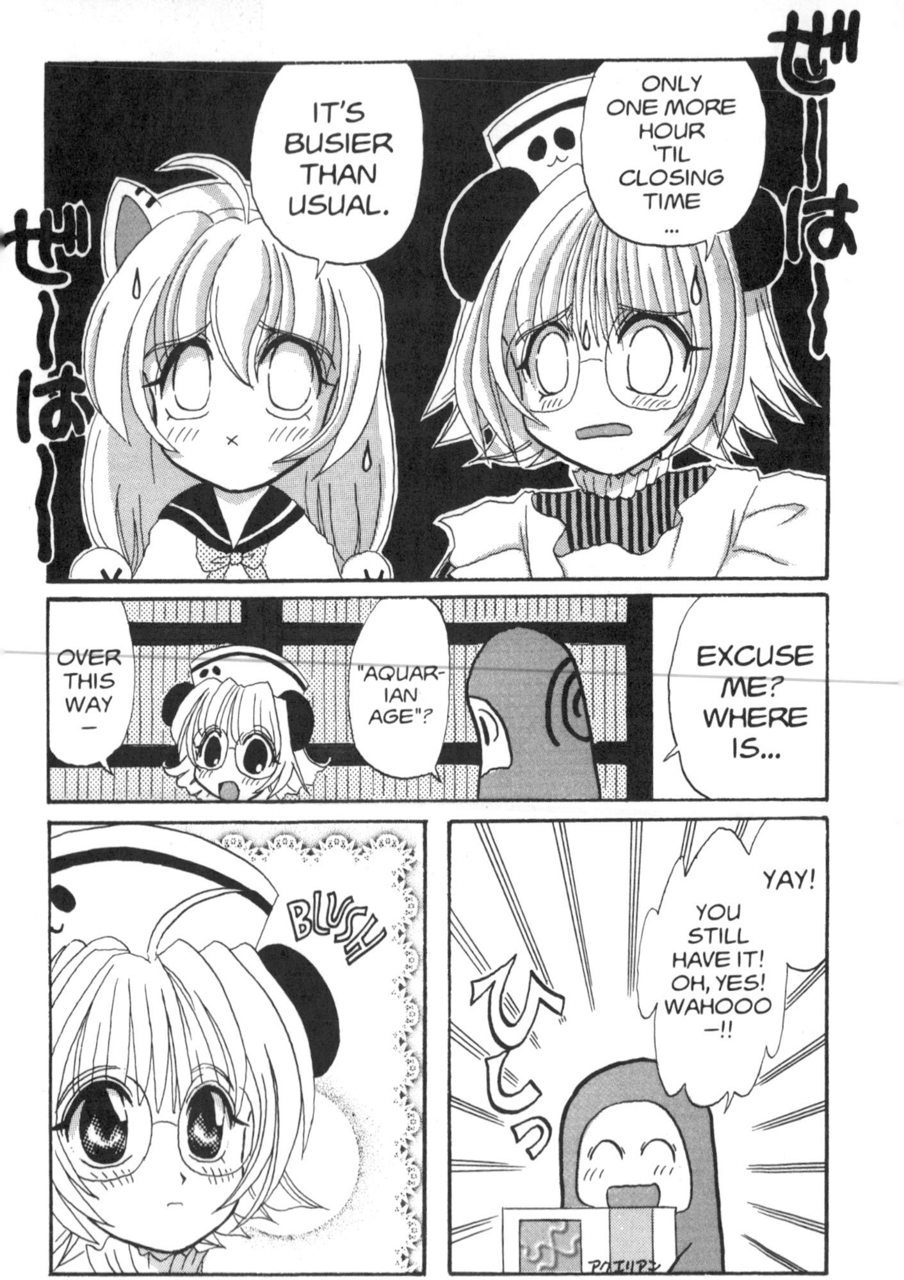
ぜーはー
ONLY ONE MORE HOUR 'TIL CLOSING TIME ...
IT'S BUSIER THAN USUAL.
ぜーはー
EXCUSE ME? WHERE IS...
"AQUARIAN AGE"?
OVER THIS WAY —
YAY! YOU STILL HAVE IT! OH, YES! WAHOOO —!!
ひしっ
アクエリアン
BLUSH

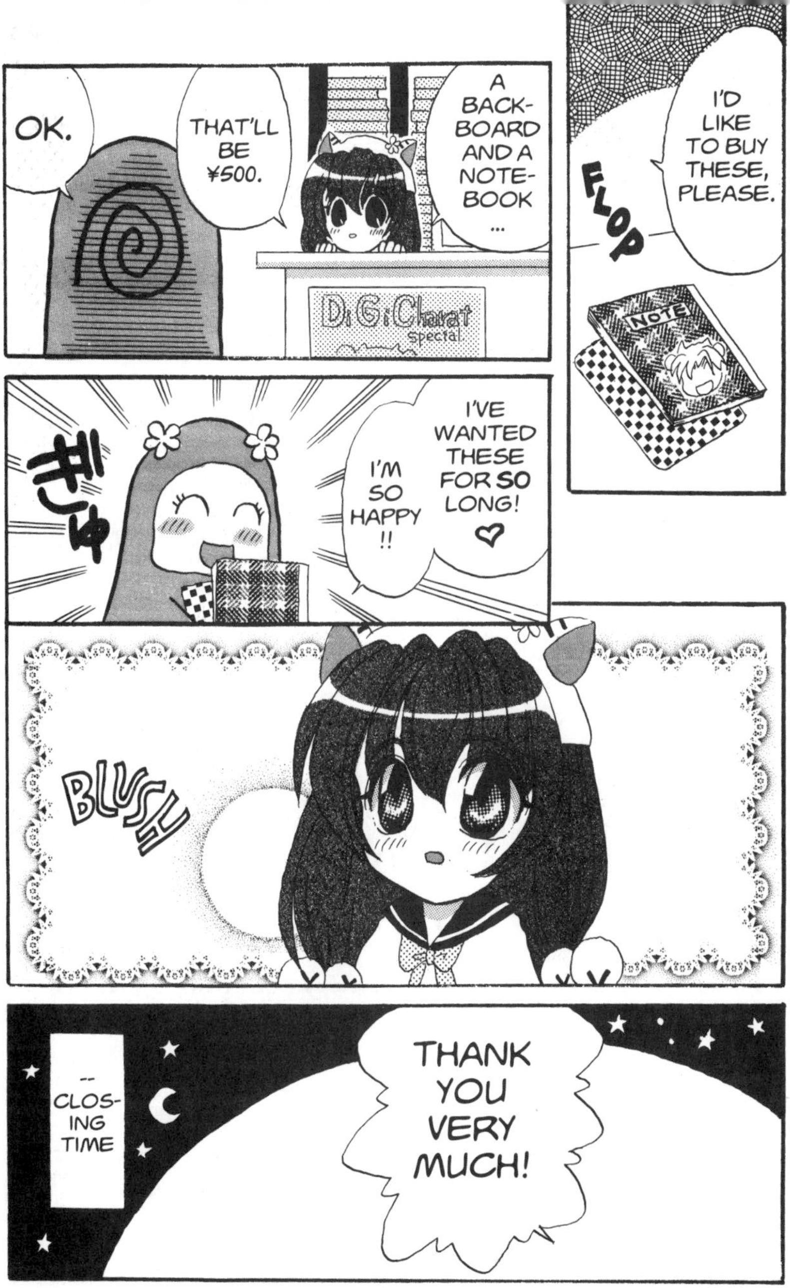

I'D LIKE TO BUY THESE, PLEASE.
FLOP
NOTE
A BACKBOARD AND A NOTEBOOK ...
THAT'LL BE ¥500.
OK.
DiGiCharat special
I'VE WANTED THESE FOR SO LONG! ♡
I'M SO HAPPY !!
ぎゅ
BLUSSH
THANK YOU VERY MUCH!
-- CLOSING TIME

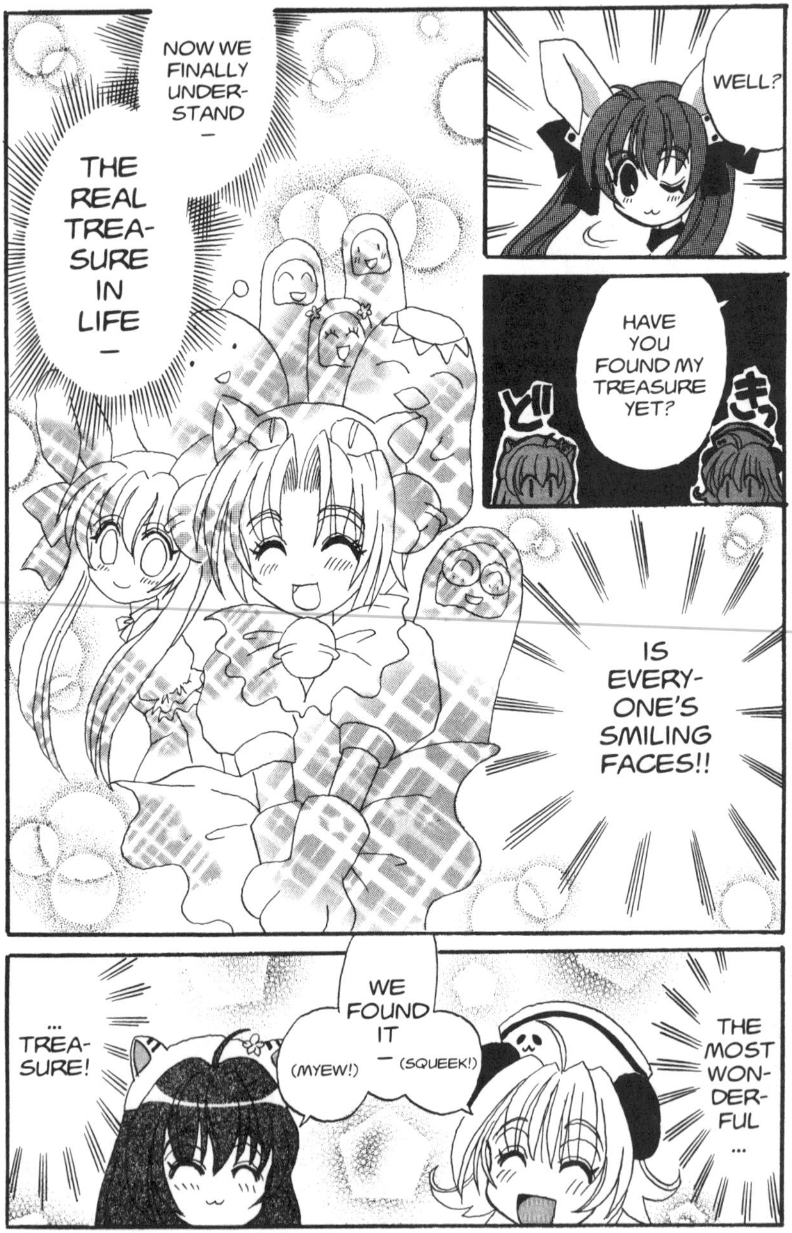
WELL?
HAVE YOU FOUND MY TREASURE YET?
NOW WE FINALLY UNDER-STAND —
THE REAL TREA-SURE IN LIFE —
IS EVERY-ONE'S SMILING FACES!!
THE MOST WON-DER-FUL ...
WE FOUND IT —
(SQUEEK!)
(MYEW!)
... TREA-SURE!

END

A WORD ABOUT "DI-GI-CHARAT"!

TOPIC:
A MESSAGE FOR DIGIKO.

"YOU ARE CUTE! ❤"

AND WE LOVE YOU—❤❤

OF COURSE YOU DO! (MEOW!)

...SORRY FOR THE BORING PAGE

NEMURO-NO-HISAYOSHI & STRIKE-HEISUKE

A WORD ABOUT "DI-GI-CHARAT"!

I LIKE USADA... ER, RABI EN ROSE. I LIKE PIYOKO AND RIKOKYO COO. I LIKE PUCHIKO. ...BUT I THINK I LIKE THE MANAGER THE MOST. HE'S SUCH A NICE GUY! ♪ IF THEY WERE ALL REALLY THERE, I'D LOVE TO WORK AT GAMERS TOO!!

FOR INTRODUCING ME TO DIoGIoCHARAT, AND EVEN MORE, FOR ALLOWING ME THE OPPORTUNITY TO DRAW IT LIKE THIS, THANK YOU SO MUCH TO MY EDITOR K-SAMA! ☂" I REALLY APPRECIATE IT! ☂"

ALSO, TO EVERYONE WHO HAS READ MY AWKWARD MANGA, THANK YOU VERY MUCH TOO! ☂" I CONSIDER MYSELF BLESSED IF YOU GOT JUST A LITTLE ENTERTAINMENT FROM IT!

ARUTO SUZUKI

MANAGER IS NUMBER ONE. ☂"

居長

MANAGER

ARUTO SUZUKI

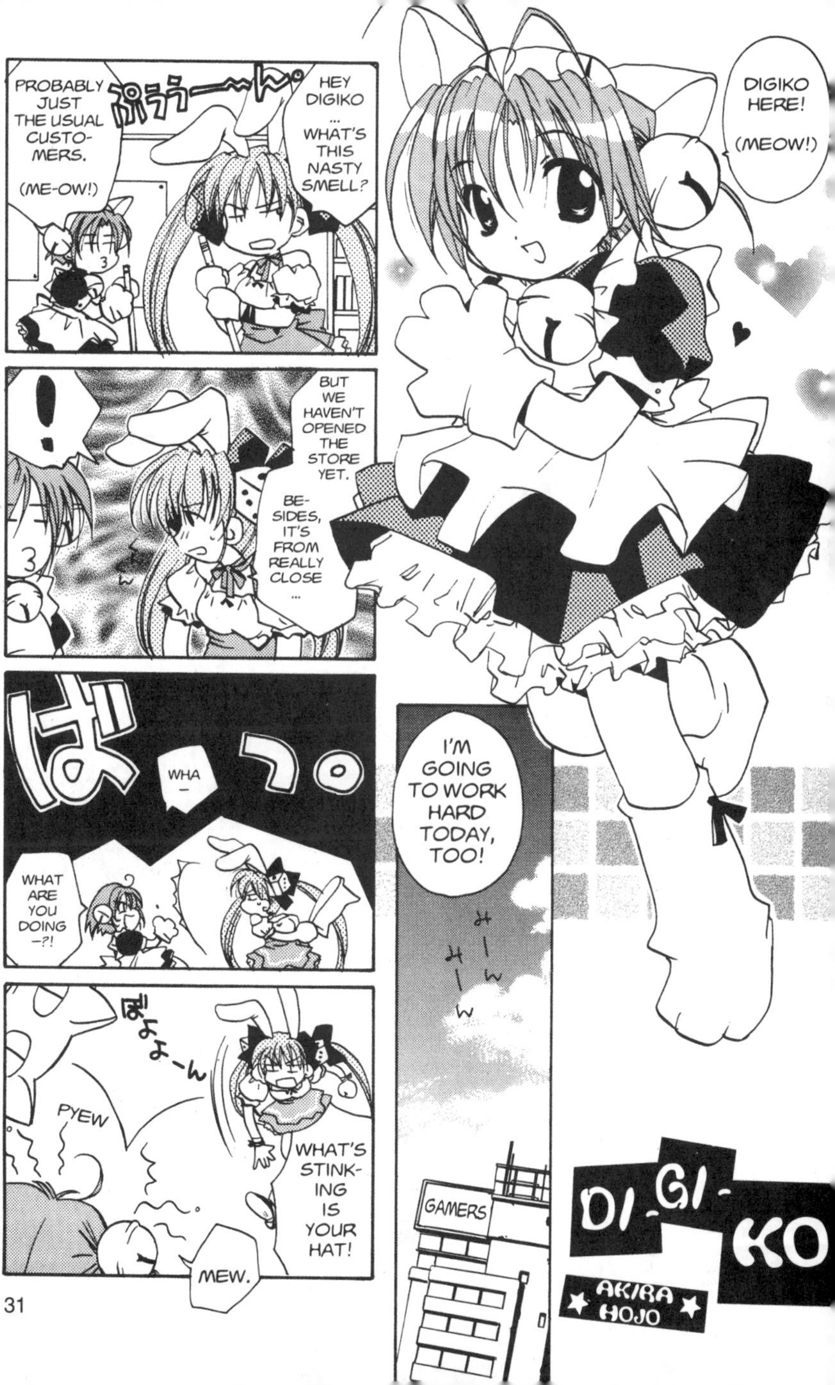
DIGIKO HERE! (MEOW!)
I'M GOING TO WORK HARD TODAY, TOO!
みーんみーん
GAMERS
DI GI KO
AKIRA HOJO
HEY DIGIKO ... WHAT'S THIS NASTY SMELL?
ぷううーーん。
PROBABLY JUST THE USUAL CUSTO-MERS.
(ME-OW!)
BUT WE HAVEN'T OPENED THE STORE YET.
BE-SIDES, IT'S FROM REALLY CLOSE ...
!
ばっ。
WHA —
WHAT ARE YOU DOING —?!
ぼよよーん
WHAT'S STINK-ING IS YOUR HAT!
PYEW
MEW.

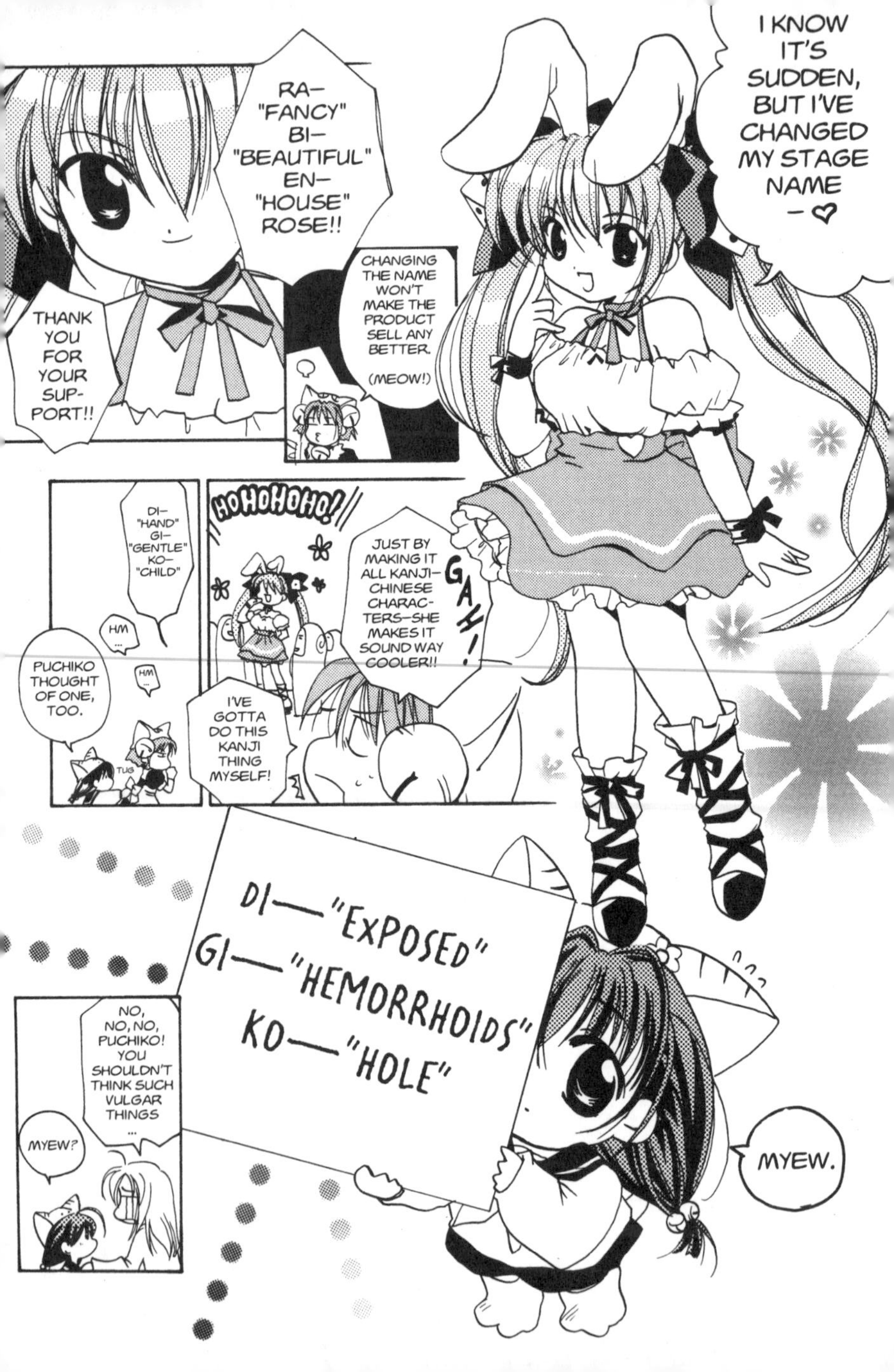
I KNOW IT'S SUDDEN, BUT I'VE CHANGED MY STAGE NAME –♡
RA— "FANCY" BI— "BEAUTIFUL" EN— "HOUSE" ROSE!!
THANK YOU FOR YOUR SUP-PORT!!
CHANGING THE NAME WON'T MAKE THE PRODUCT SELL ANY BETTER.
(MEOW!)
HOHOHOHOHO!
JUST BY MAKING IT ALL KANJI—CHINESE CHARAC-TERS—SHE MAKES IT SOUND WAY COOLER!!
GAH!
I'VE GOTTA DO THIS KANJI THING MYSELF!
DI— "HAND" GI— "GENTLE" KO— "CHILD"
HM ...
HM ...
PUCHIKO THOUGHT OF ONE, TOO.
TUG
DI—"EXPOSED"
GI—"HEMORRHOIDS"
KO—"HOLE"
MYEW.
NO, NO, NO, PUCHIKO! YOU SHOULDN'T THINK SUCH VULGAR THINGS ...
MYEW?

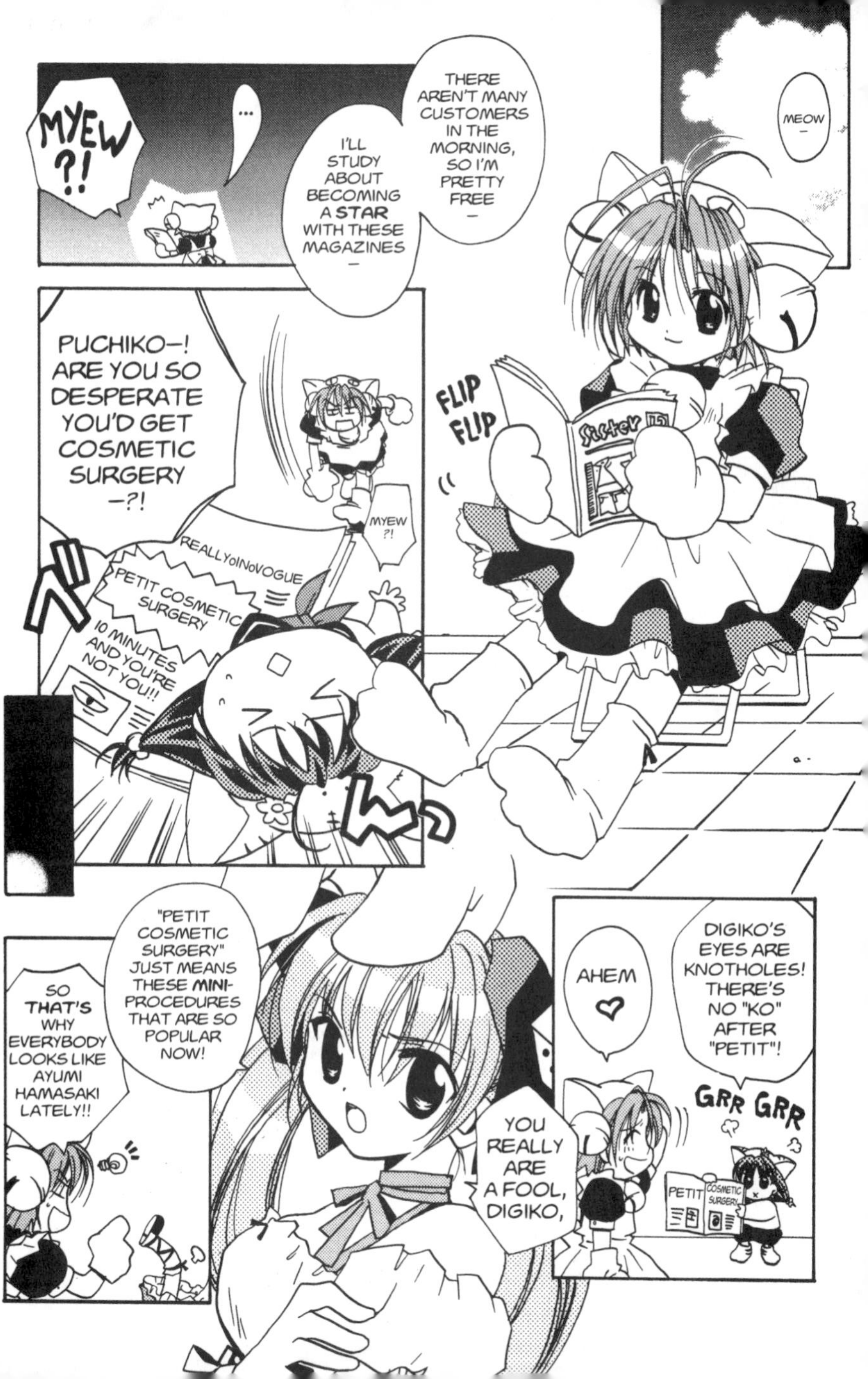
MEOW —
THERE AREN'T MANY CUSTOMERS IN THE MORNING, SO I'M PRETTY FREE —
I'LL STUDY ABOUT BECOMING A **STAR** WITH THESE MAGAZINES —
FLIP FLIP
...
MYEW ?!
PUCHIKO—! ARE YOU SO DESPERATE YOU'D GET COSMETIC SURGERY —?!
MYEW ?!
REALLYoINoVOGUE
PETIT COSMETIC SURGERY
10 MINUTES AND YOU'RE NOT YOU!!
DIGIKO'S EYES ARE KNOTHOLES! THERE'S NO "KO" AFTER "PETIT"!
AHEM ♡
GRR GRR
PETIT
COSMETIC SURGERY
YOU REALLY ARE A FOOL, DIGIKO,
"PETIT COSMETIC SURGERY" JUST MEANS THESE **MINI-**PROCEDURES THAT ARE SO POPULAR NOW!
SO **THAT'S** WHY EVERYBODY LOOKS LIKE AYUMI HAMASAKI LATELY!!

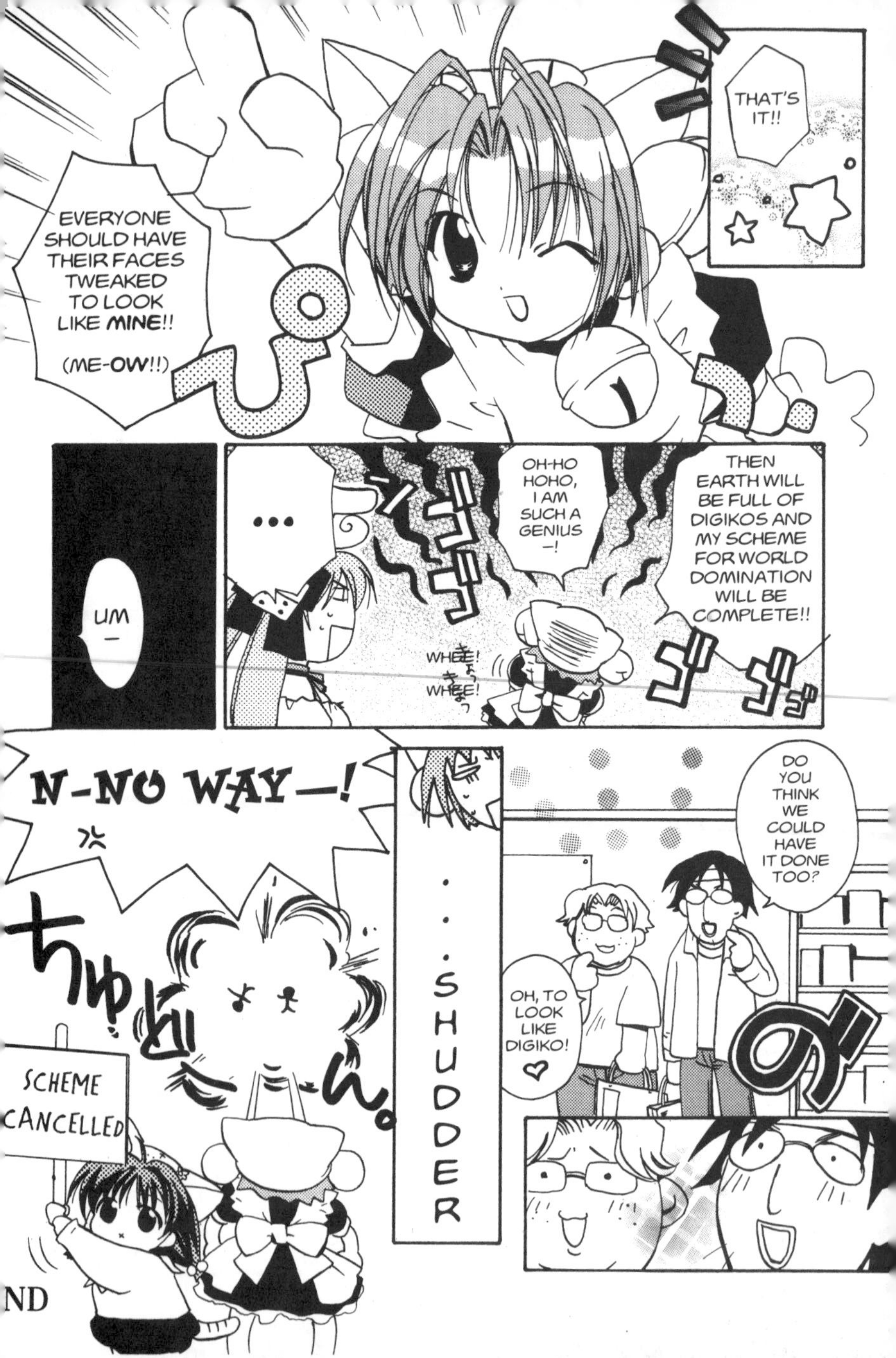

THAT'S IT!!
EVERYONE SHOULD HAVE THEIR FACES TWEAKED TO LOOK LIKE **MINE**!!
(ME-**OW**!!)
OH-HO HOHO, I AM SUCH A GENIUS—!
THEN EARTH WILL BE FULL OF DIGIKOS AND MY SCHEME FOR WORLD DOMINATION WILL BE COMPLETE!!
WHEE! WHEE!
...
UM—
DO YOU THINK WE COULD HAVE IT DONE TOO?
OH, TO LOOK LIKE DIGIKO! ♡
...SHUDDER
N-NO WAY—!
SCHEME CANCELLED

ND

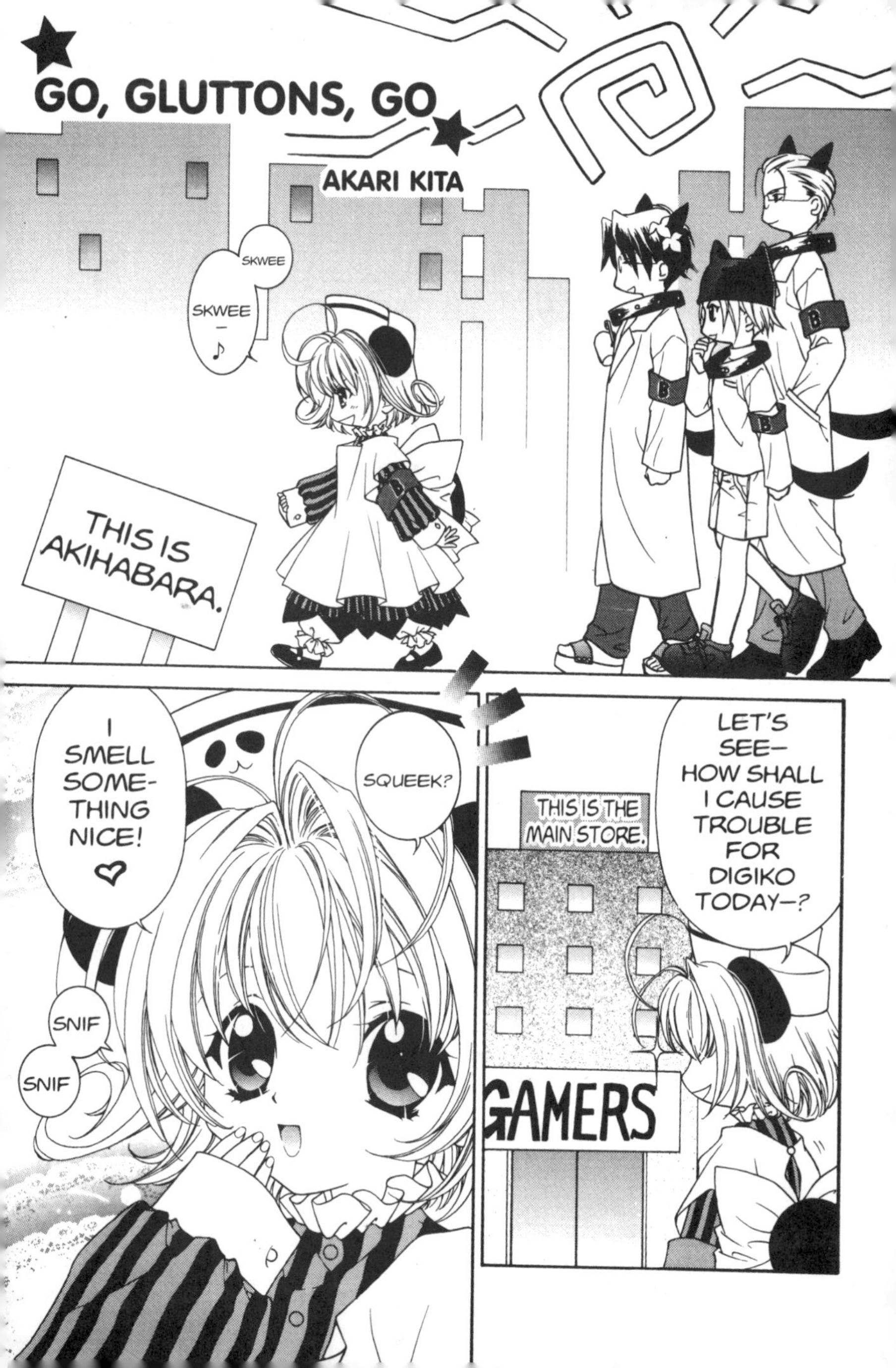
GO, GLUTTONS, GO
AKARI KITA
SKWEE
SKWEE—♪
THIS IS AKIHABARA.
LET'S SEE— HOW SHALL I CAUSE TROUBLE FOR DIGIKO TODAY—?
THIS IS THE MAIN STORE.
GAMERS
SQUEEK?
I SMELL SOMETHING NICE! ♡
SNIF
SNIF

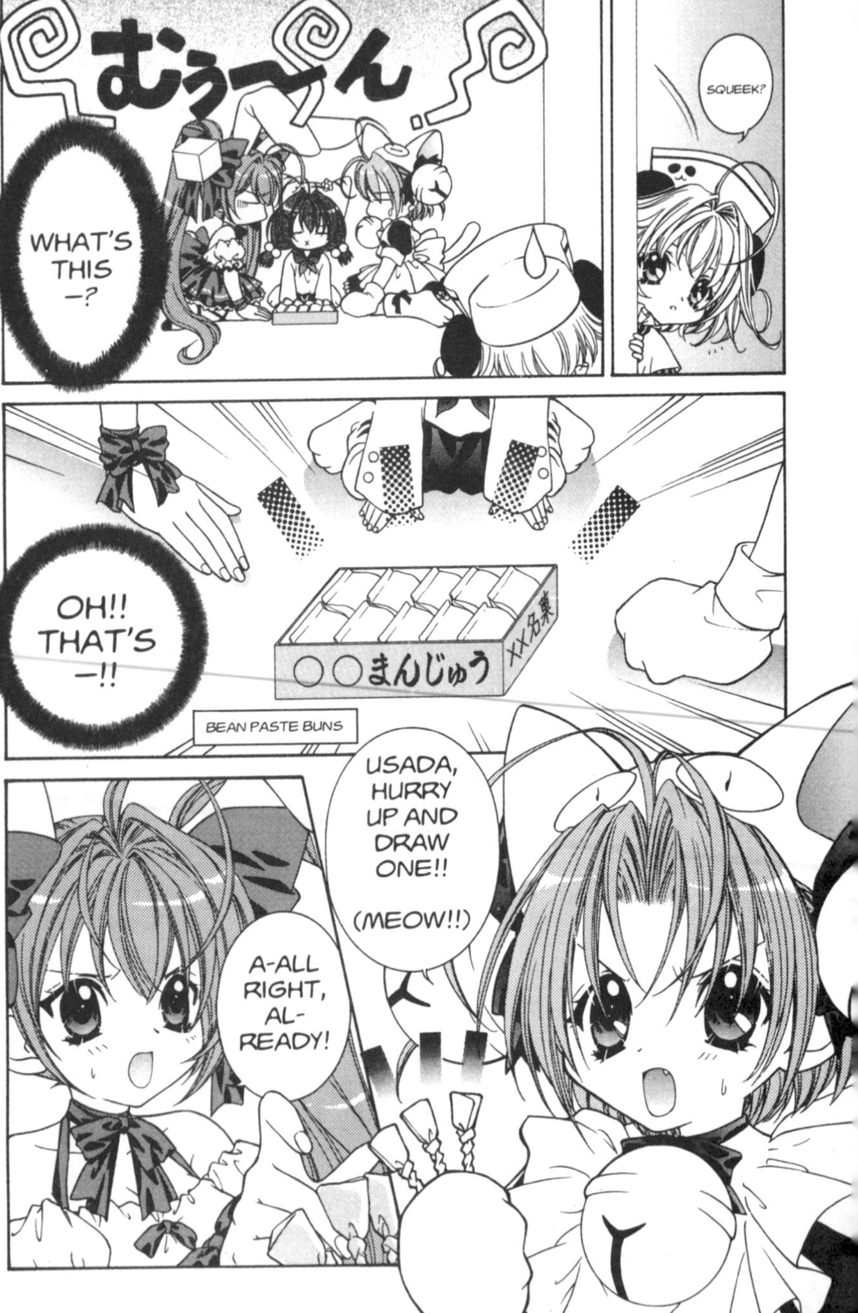

SQUEEK?
むぅ～ん。
WHAT'S THIS —?
OH!! THAT'S —!!
XX名菓
○○まんじゅう
BEAN PASTE BUNS
USADA, HURRY UP AND DRAW ONE!! (MEOW!!)
A-ALL RIGHT, AL-READY!

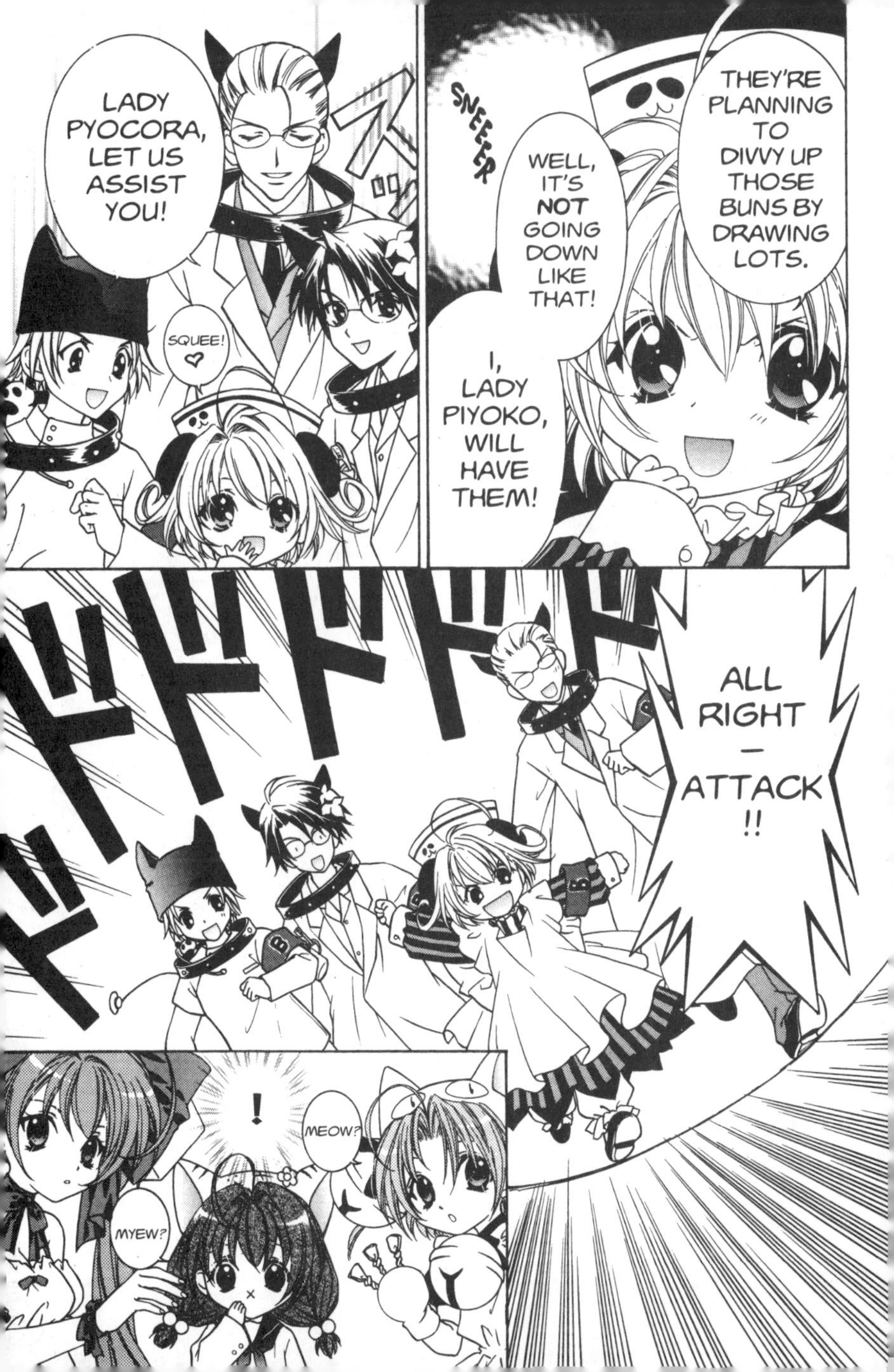

THEY'RE PLANNING TO DIVVY UP THOSE BUNS BY DRAWING LOTS.
SNEEEER
WELL, IT'S **NOT** GOING DOWN LIKE THAT!
I, LADY PIYOKO, WILL HAVE THEM!
LADY PYOCORA, LET US ASSIST YOU!
SQUEE! ♡
ALL RIGHT — ATTACK !!
MEOW?
!
MYEW?

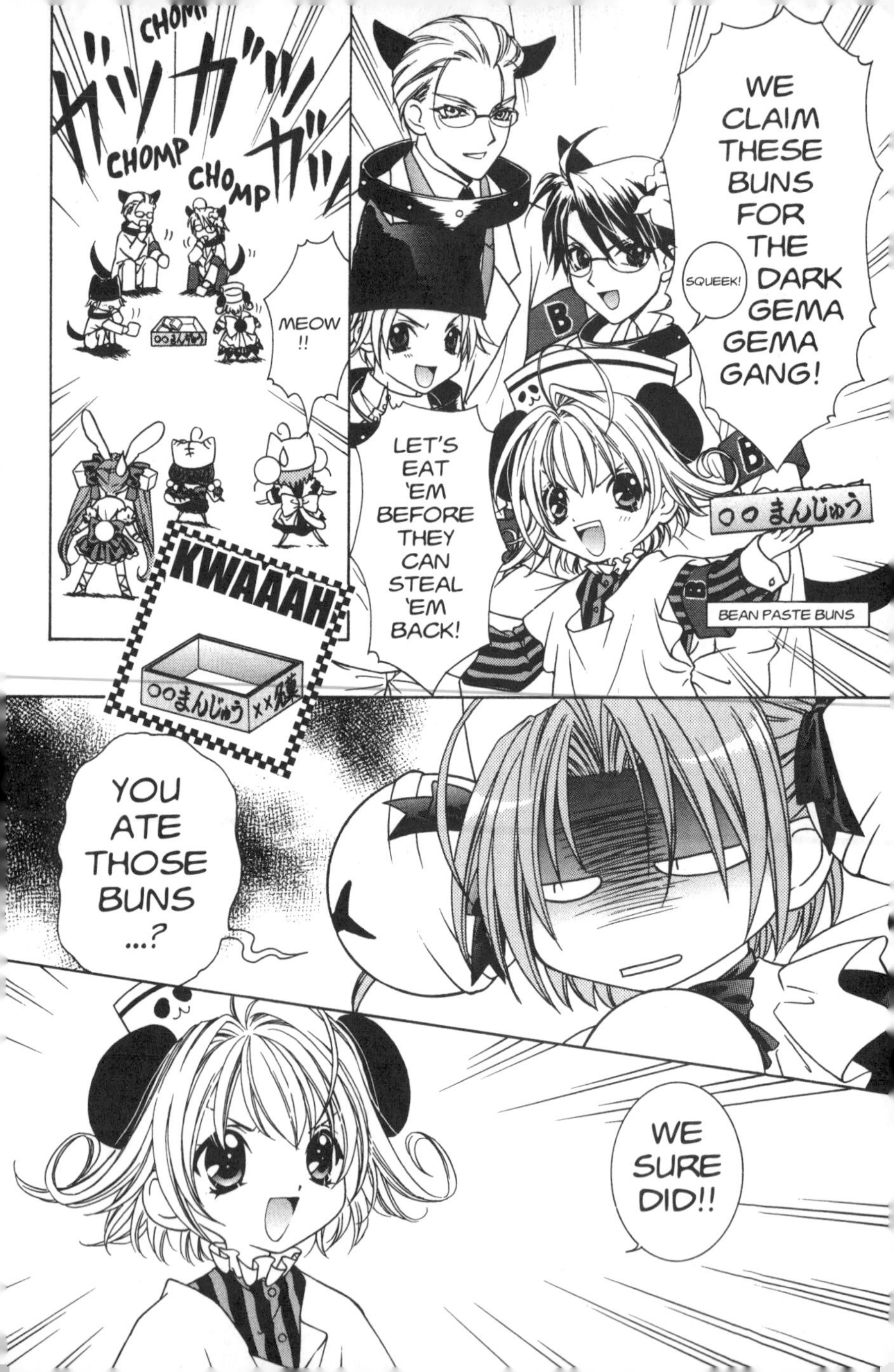
WE CLAIM THESE BUNS FOR THE DARK GEMA GEMA GANG!
SQUEEK!
LET'S EAT 'EM BEFORE THEY CAN STEAL 'EM BACK!
○○ まんじゅう
BEAN PASTE BUNS
CHOMP
ガツガツ
CHOMP
CHOMP
MEOW !!
KWAAAH
○○まんじゅう
YOU ATE THOSE BUNS ...?
WE SURE DID!!

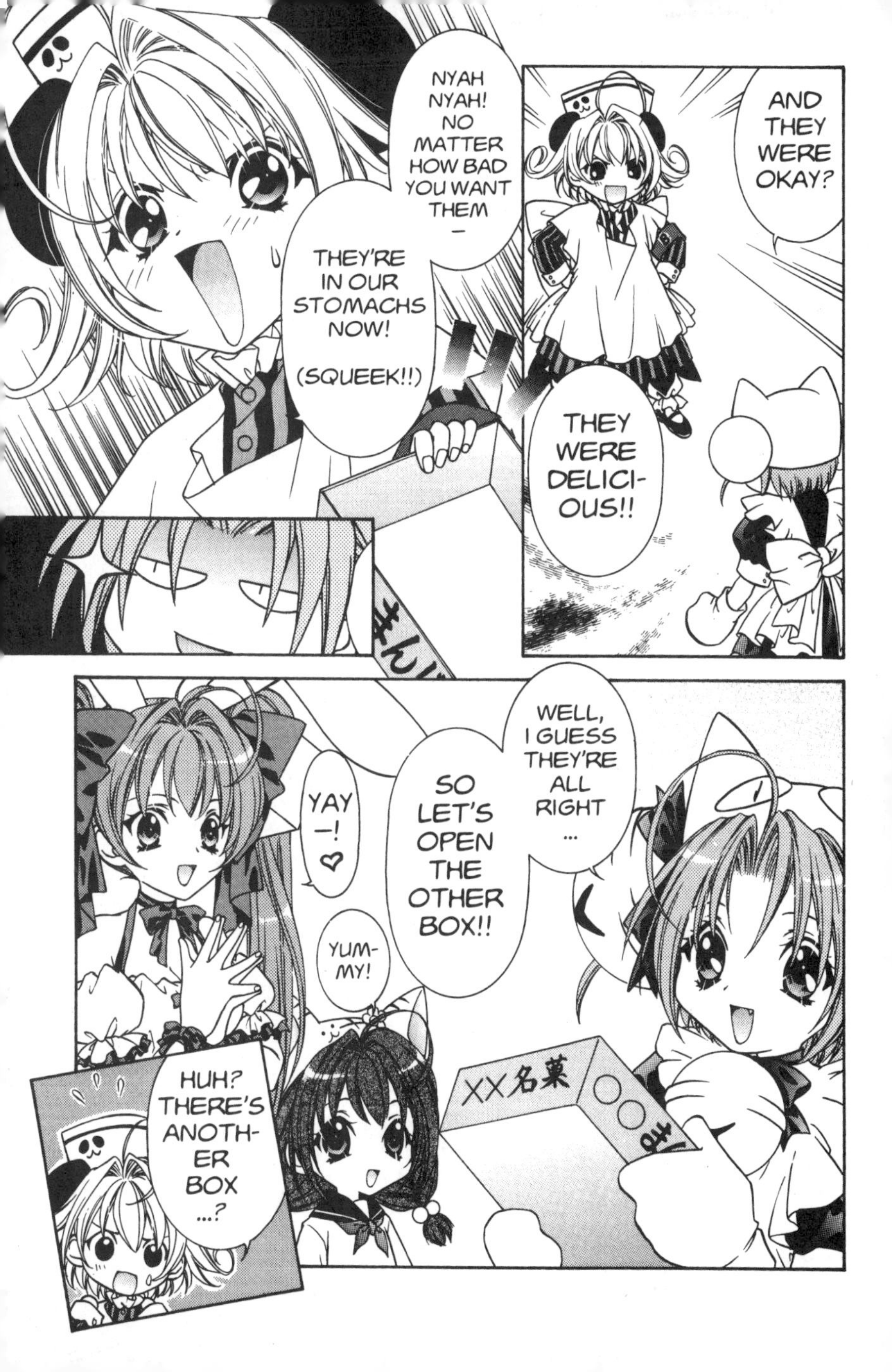
AND THEY WERE OKAY?
THEY WERE DELICIOUS!!
NYAH NYAH! NO MATTER HOW BAD YOU WANT THEM —
THEY'RE IN OUR STOMACHS NOW!
(SQUEEK!!)
WELL, I GUESS THEY'RE ALL RIGHT ...
SO LET'S OPEN THE OTHER BOX!!
YAY —! ♡
YUM-MY!
XX名菓
HUH? THERE'S ANOTH-ER BOX ...?

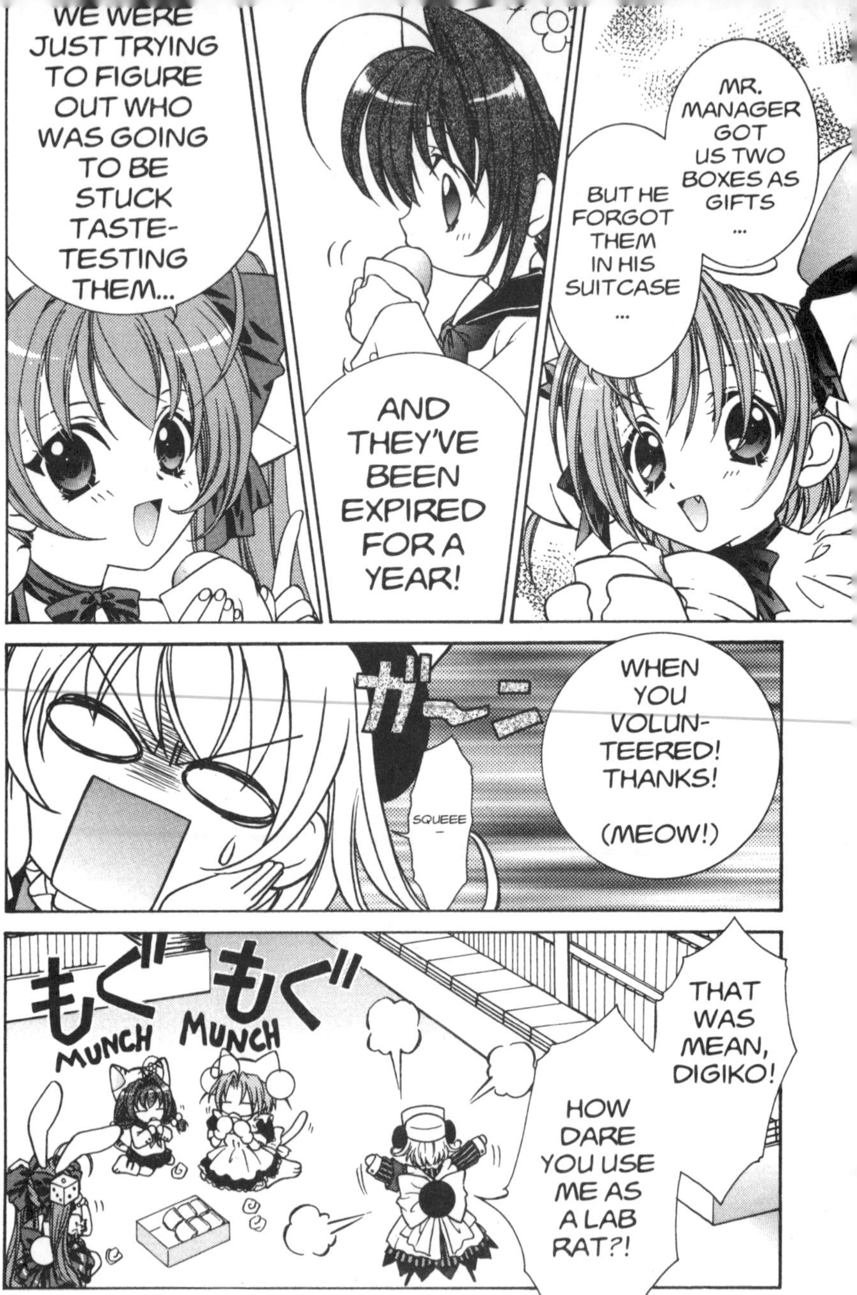
MR. MANAGER GOT US TWO BOXES AS GIFTS ...
BUT HE FORGOT THEM IN HIS SUITCASE ...
AND THEY'VE BEEN EXPIRED FOR A YEAR!
WE WERE JUST TRYING TO FIGURE OUT WHO WAS GOING TO BE STUCK TASTE-TESTING THEM...
WHEN YOU VOLUNTEERED! THANKS!
(MEOW!)
ガーン
SQUEEE—
THAT WAS MEAN, DIGIKO!
HOW DARE YOU USE ME AS A LAB RAT?!
もぐ もぐ
MUNCH MUNCH

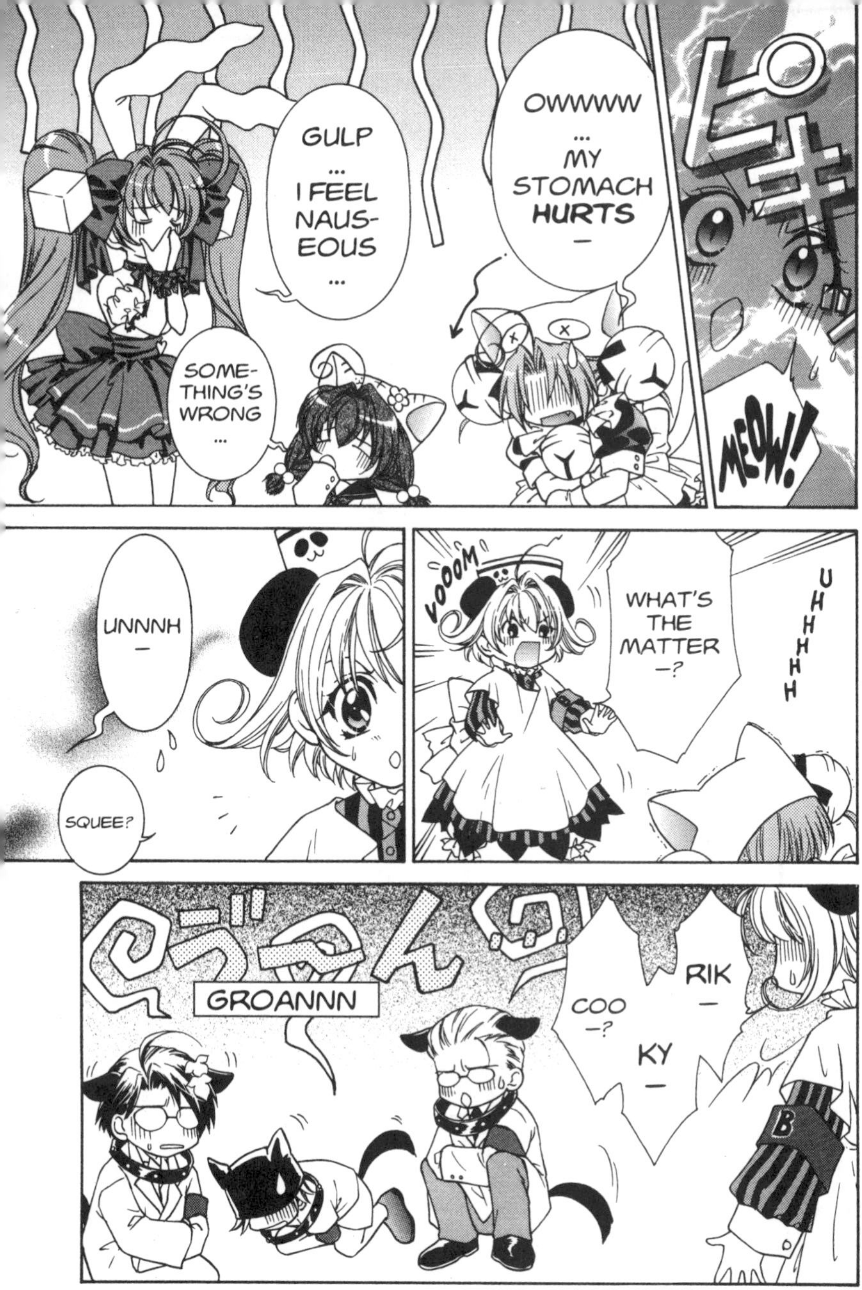
MEOW!
OWWWW ... MY STOMACH HURTS —
GULP ... I FEEL NAUS-EOUS ...
SOME-THING'S WRONG ...
UHHHHHH
WHAT'S THE MATTER —?
VOOOM
UNNNH —
SQUEE?
RIK — KY —
COO —?
GROANNN

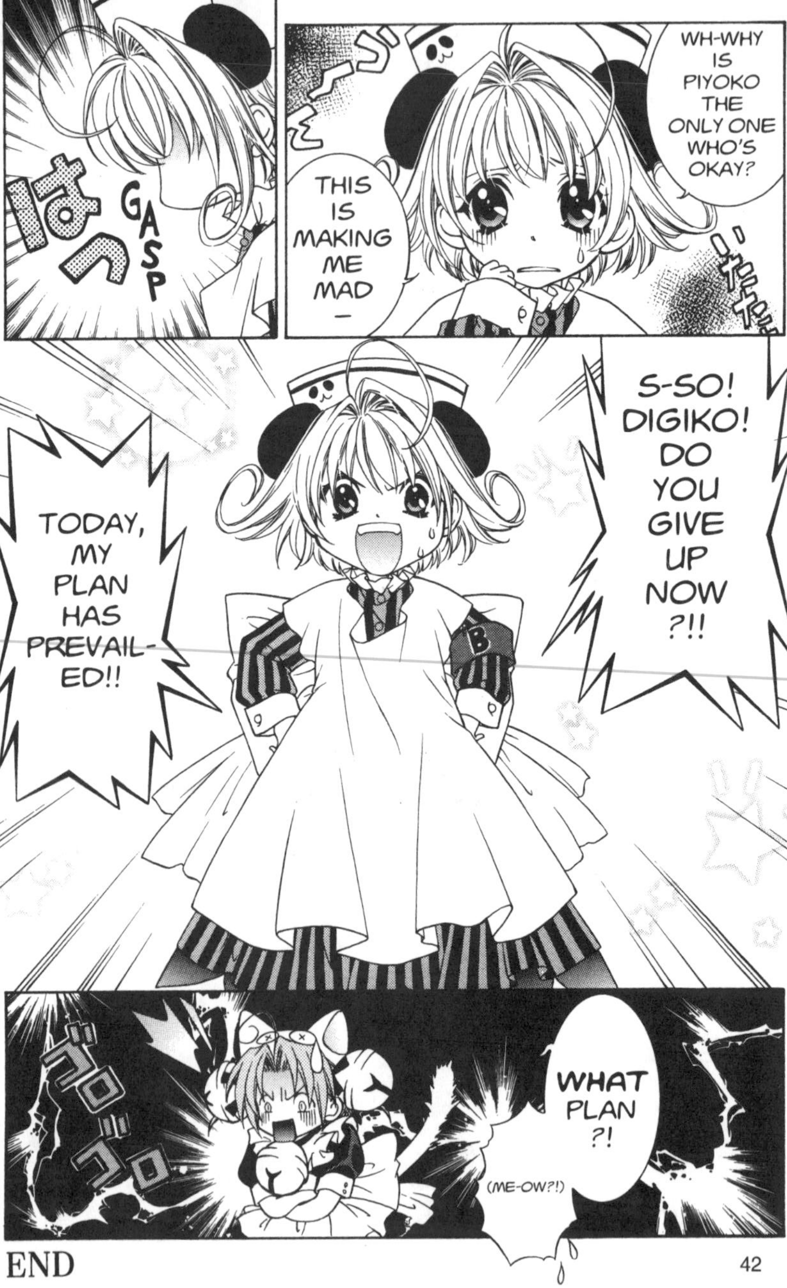
WH-WHY IS PIYOKO THE ONLY ONE WHO'S OKAY?
THIS IS MAKING ME MAD —
はっ
GASP
S-SO! DIGIKO! DO YOU GIVE UP NOW?!!
TODAY, MY PLAN HAS PREVAIL-ED!!
ゴロゴロ
WHAT PLAN?!
(ME-OW?!)

END

A WORD ABOUT "DI-GI-CHARAT"!

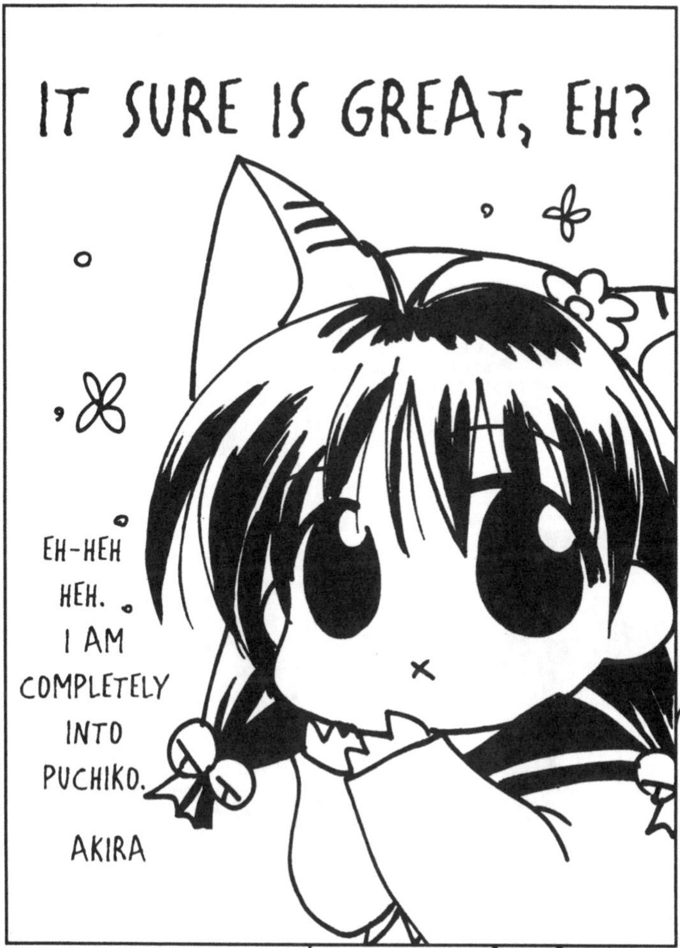
IT SURE IS GREAT, EH?
EH-HEH HEH. I AM COMPLETELY INTO PUCHIKO.
AKIRA

AKIRA HOJO

A WORD ABOUT "DI-GI-CHARAT"!

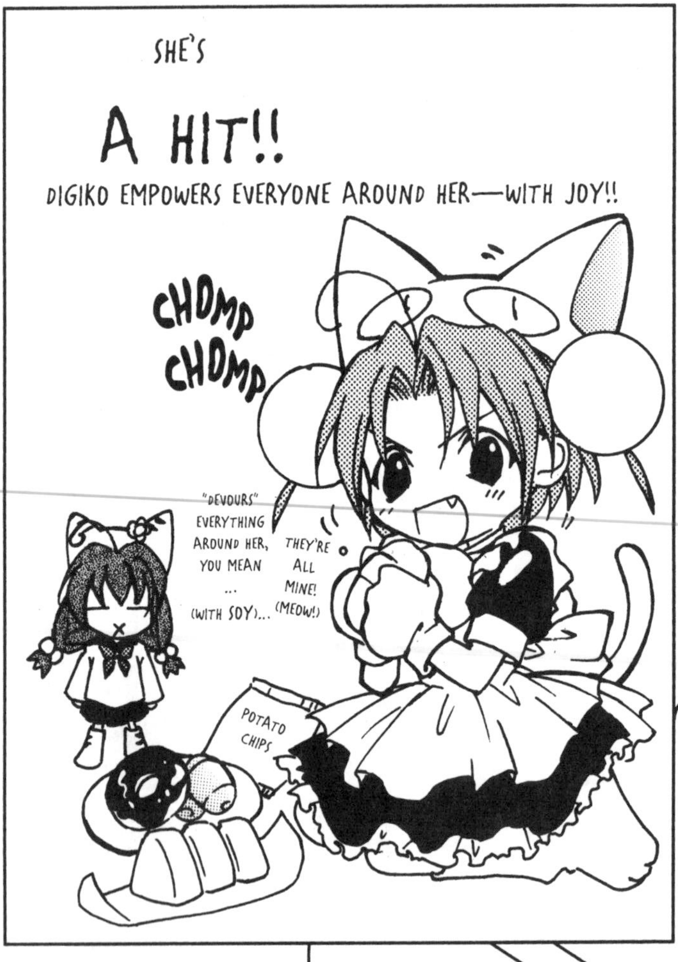
SHE'S
A HIT!!
DIGIKO EMPOWERS EVERYONE AROUND HER—WITH JOY!!
CHOMP CHOMP
THEY'RE ALL MINE! (MEOW!)
"DEVOURS" EVERYTHING AROUND HER, YOU MEAN ... (WITH SOY)...
POTATO CHIPS

AKARI KITA

WITH MOM

J-TA YAMADA

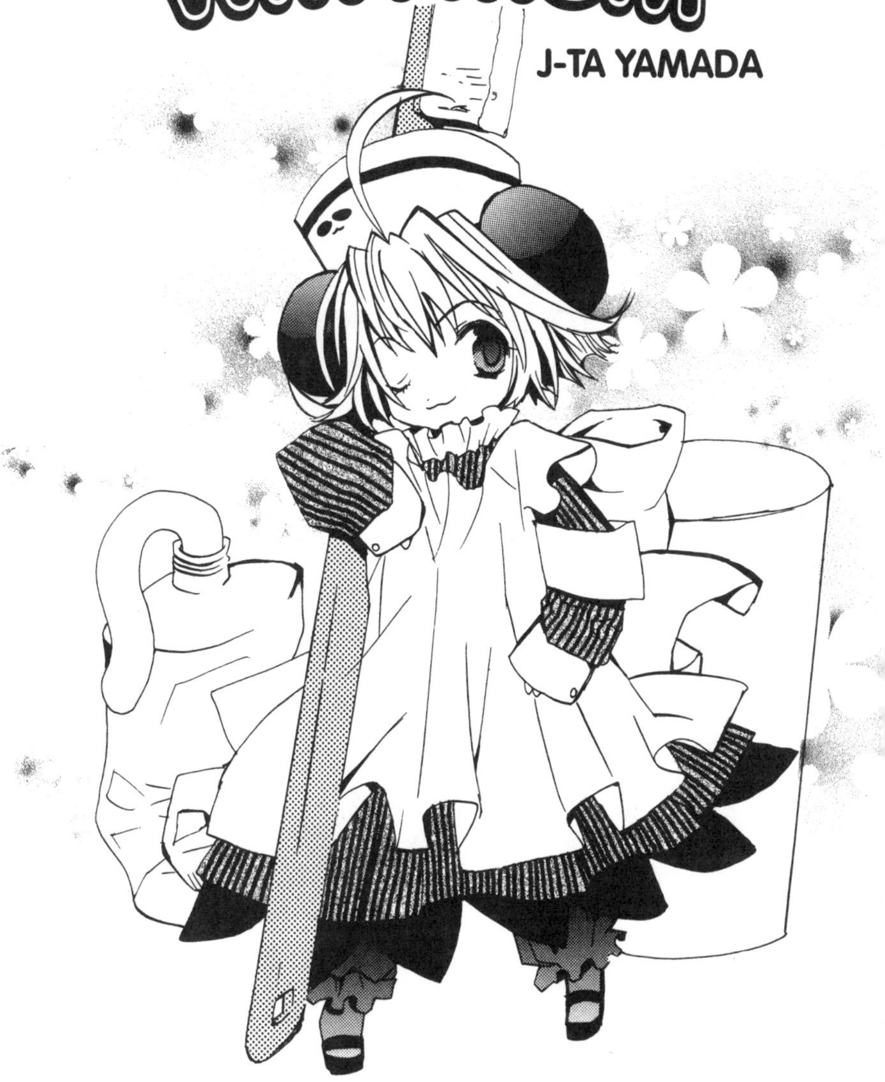

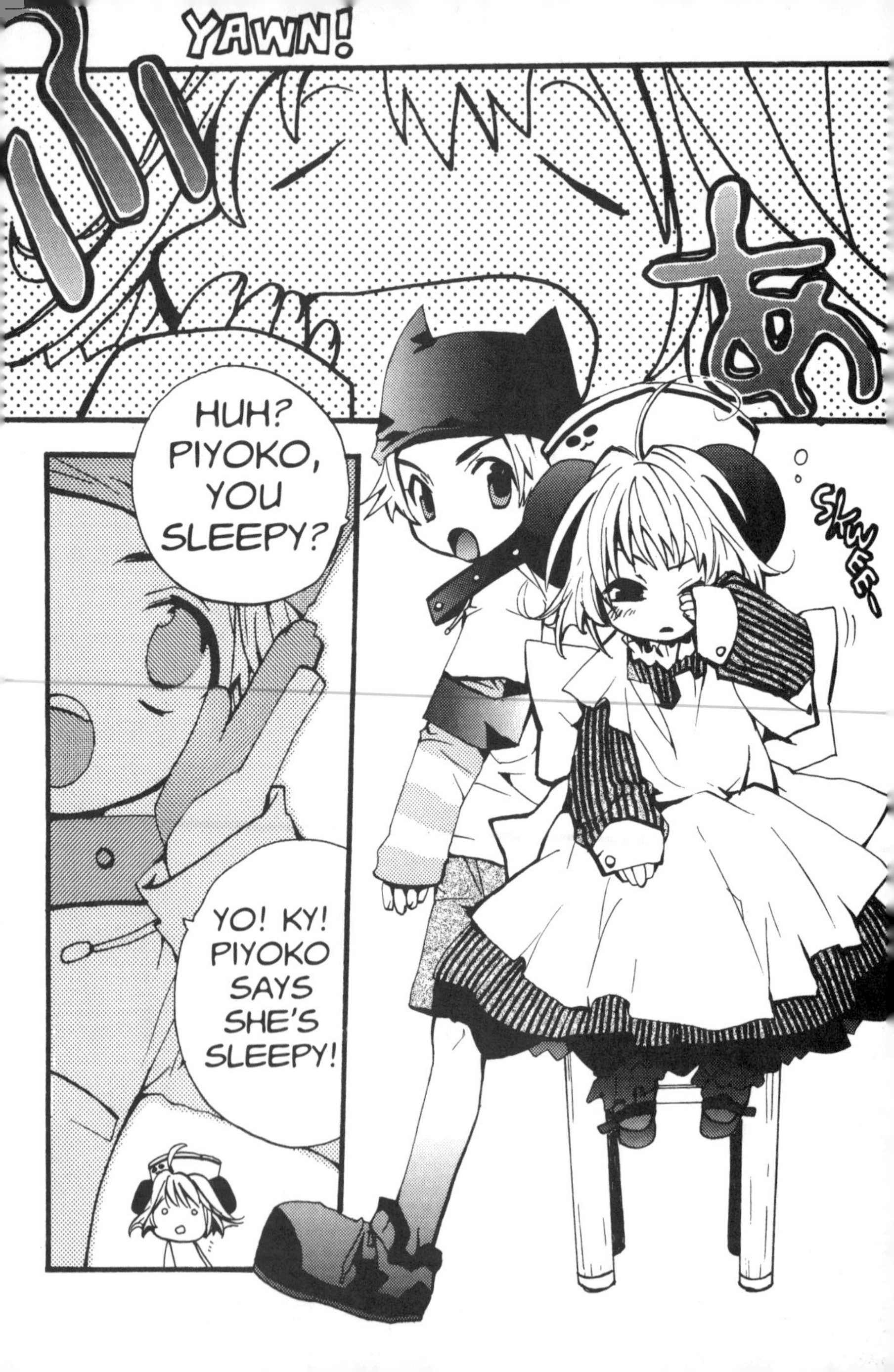

YAWN!
SKWEE-
HUH? PIYOKO, YOU SLEEPY?
YO! KY! PIYOKO SAYS SHE'S SLEEPY!

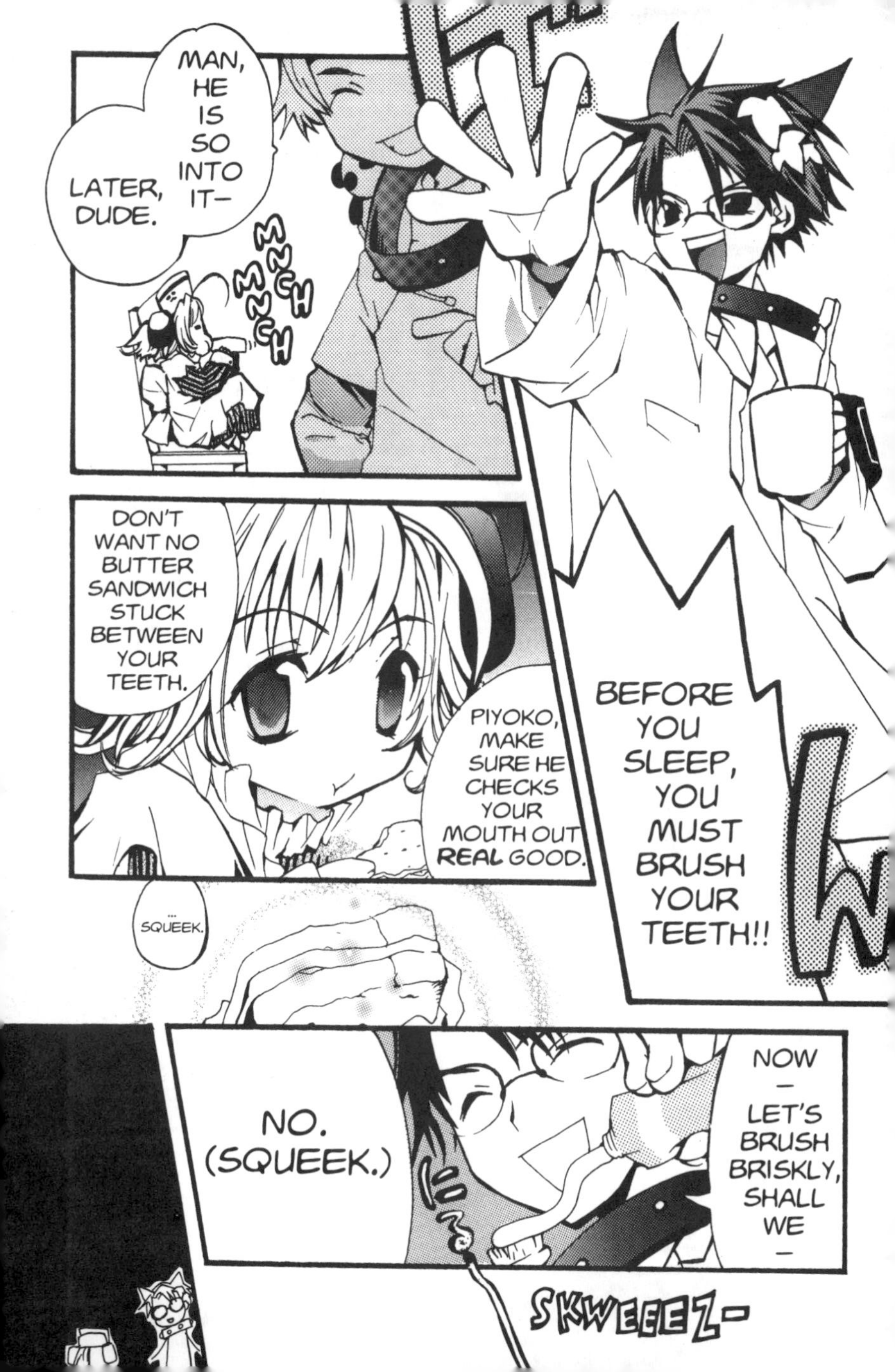
BEFORE YOU SLEEP, YOU MUST BRUSH YOUR TEETH!!
MAN, HE IS SO INTO IT—
LATER, DUDE.
MNCH MNCH MNCH
DON'T WANT NO BUTTER SANDWICH STUCK BETWEEN YOUR TEETH.
PIYOKO, MAKE SURE HE CHECKS YOUR MOUTH OUT **REAL** GOOD.
... SQUEEK.
NOW — LET'S BRUSH BRISKLY, SHALL WE —
NO. (SQUEEK.)
SKWEEEZ-

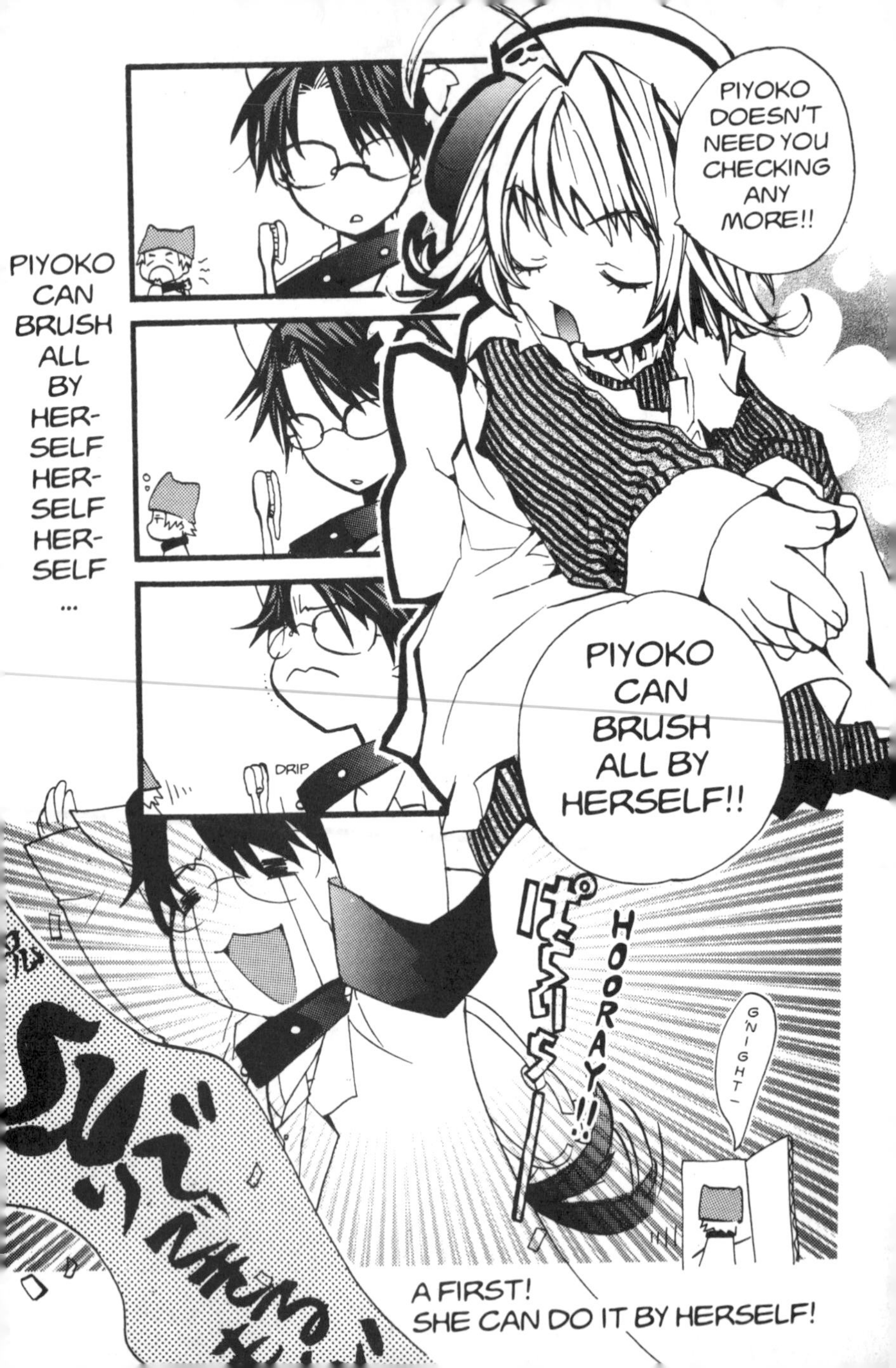
PIYOKO DOESN'T NEED YOU CHECKING ANY MORE!!
PIYOKO CAN BRUSH ALL BY HERSELF!!
PIYOKO CAN BRUSH ALL BY HER-SELF HER-SELF HER-SELF ...
DRIP
G'NIGHT
HOORAY!!
A FIRST! SHE CAN DO IT BY HERSELF!

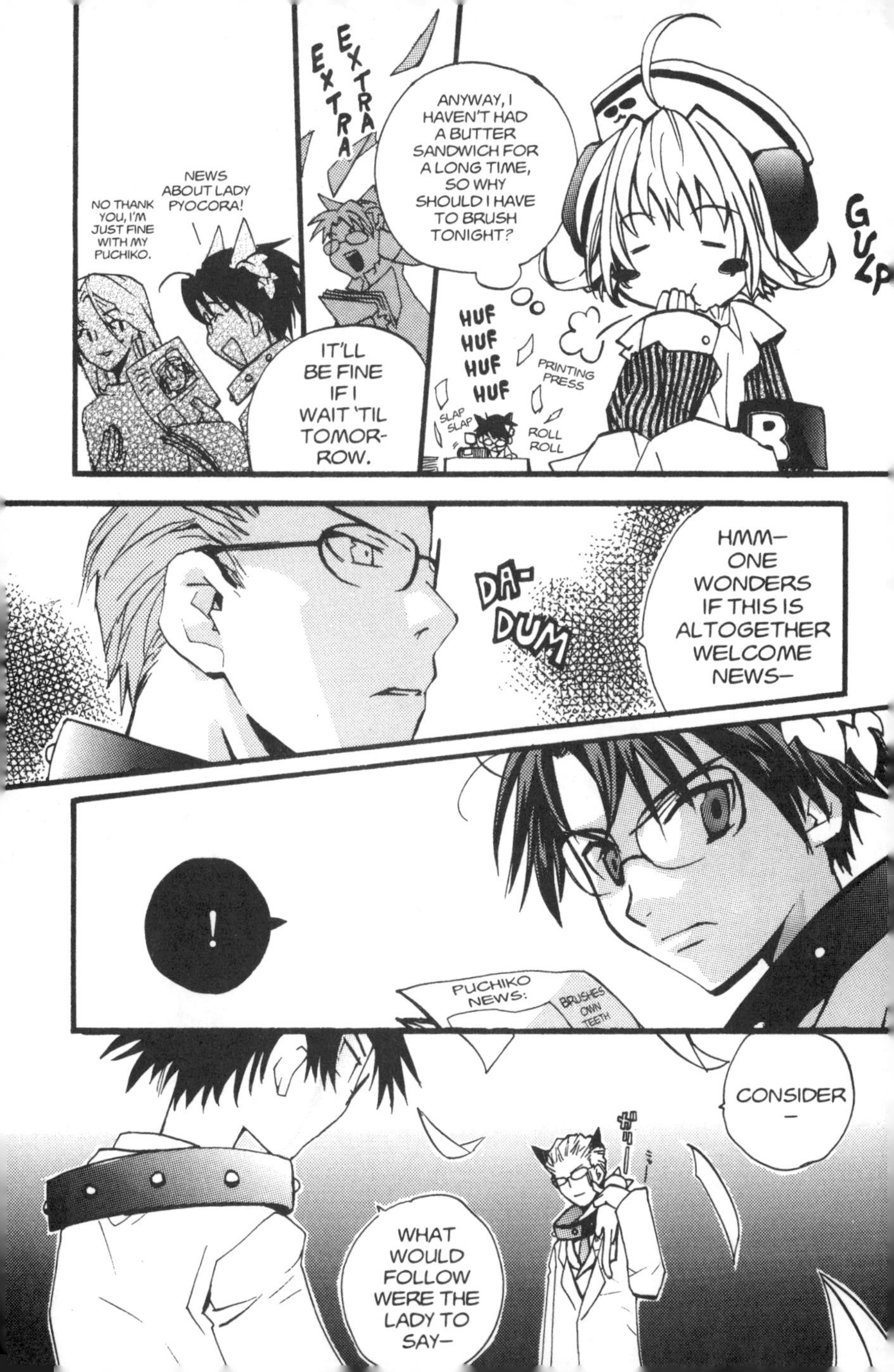
GULP
ANYWAY, I HAVEN'T HAD A BUTTER SANDWICH FOR A LONG TIME, SO WHY SHOULD I HAVE TO BRUSH TONIGHT?
HUF HUF HUF HUF
PRINTING PRESS
SLAP SLAP
ROLL ROLL
IT'LL BE FINE IF I WAIT 'TIL TOMORROW.
EXTRA EXTRA
NEWS ABOUT LADY PYOCORA!
NO THANK YOU, I'M JUST FINE WITH MY PUCHIKO.
HMM— ONE WONDERS IF THIS IS ALTOGETHER WELCOME NEWS—
DA-DUM
PUCHIKO NEWS:
BRUSHES OWN TEETH
!
CONSIDER —
WHAT WOULD FOLLOW WERE THE LADY TO SAY—

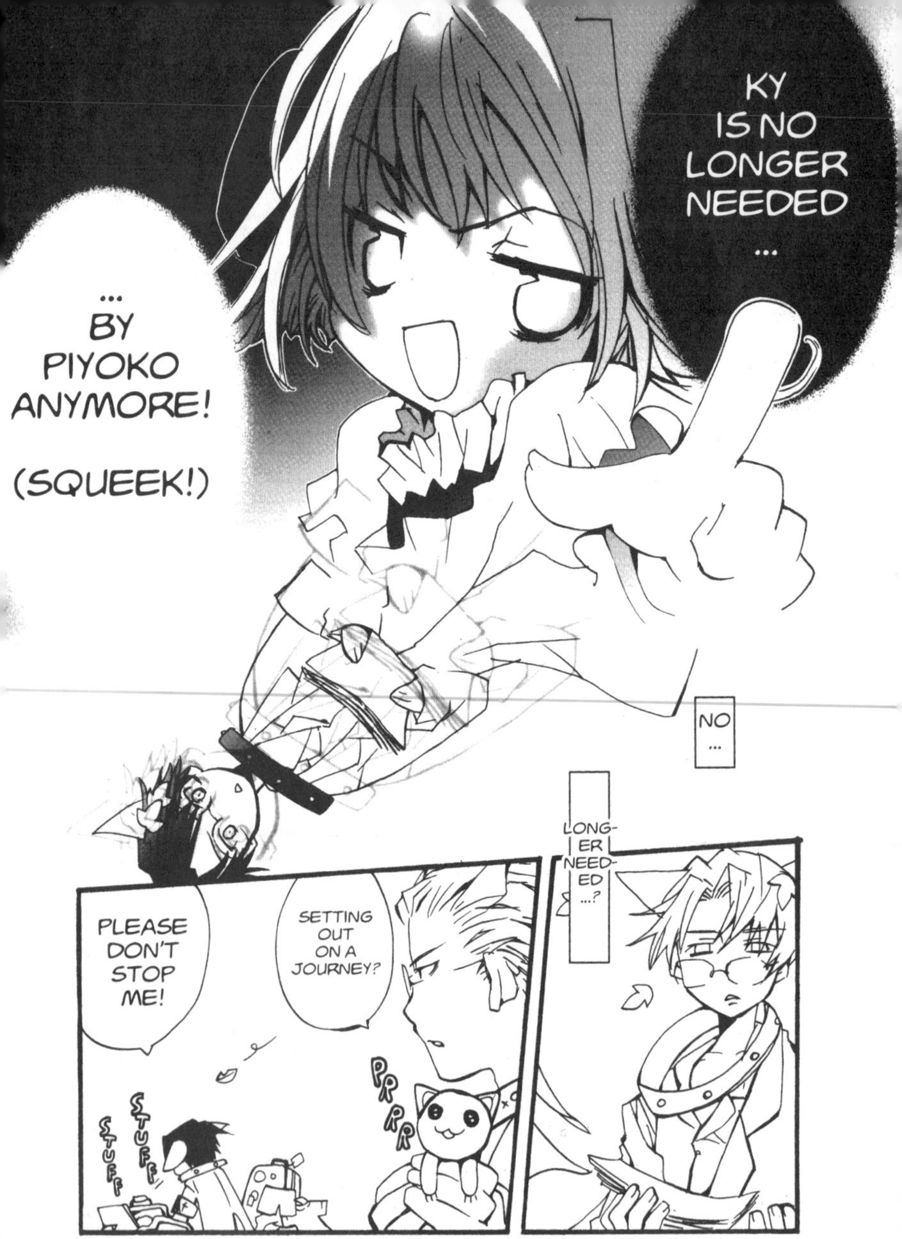

KY IS NO LONGER NEEDED ...
... BY PIYOKO ANYMORE!
(SQUEEK!)
NO ...
LONG-ER NEED-ED ...?
SETTING OUT ON A JOURNEY?
PLEASE DON'T STOP ME!
PRRR
STUFF STUFF

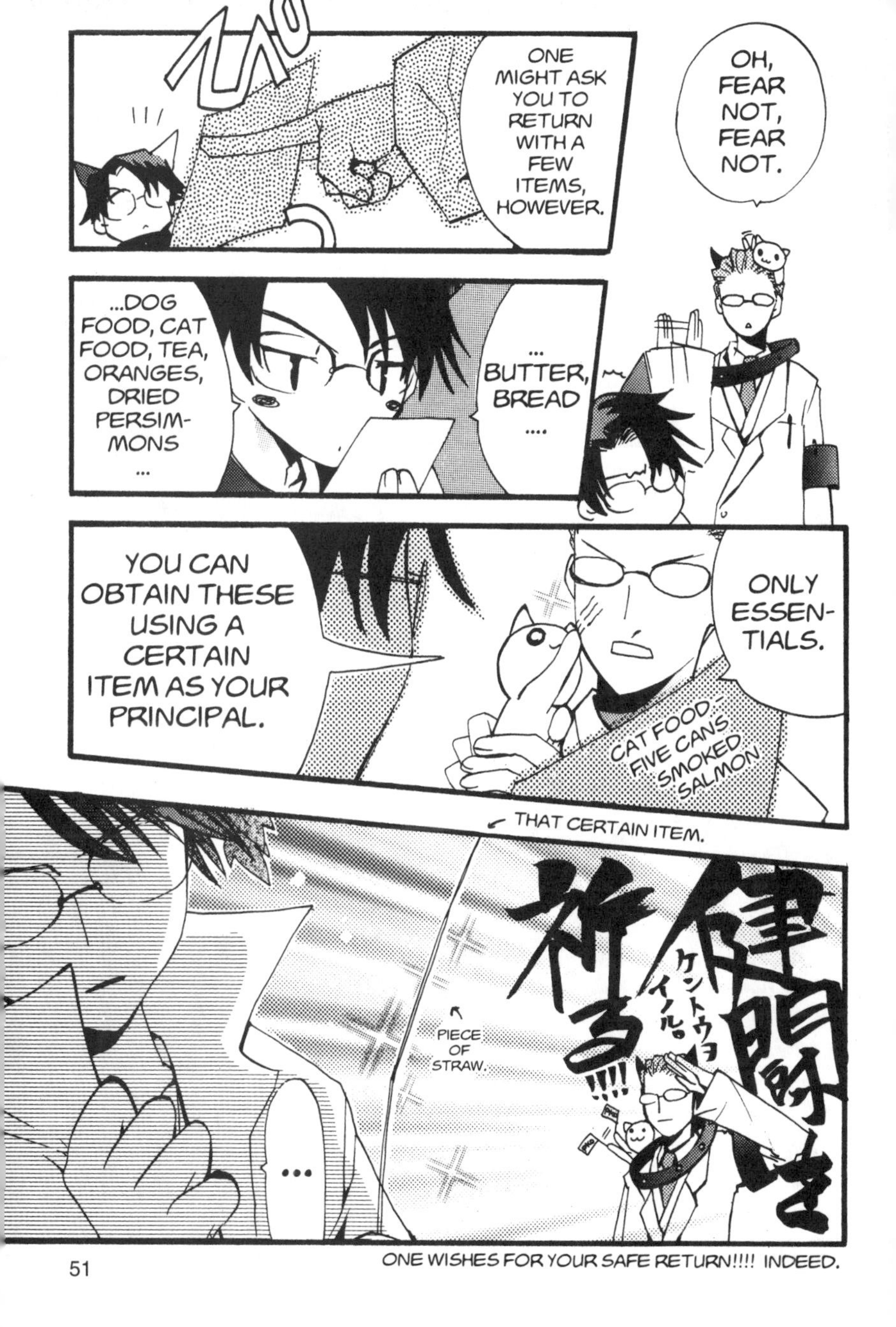
OH, FEAR NOT, FEAR NOT.
ONE MIGHT ASK YOU TO RETURN WITH A FEW ITEMS, HOWEVER.
... BUTTER, BREAD ....
...DOG FOOD, CAT FOOD, TEA, ORANGES, DRIED PERSIM-MONS ...
ONLY ESSEN-TIALS.
YOU CAN OBTAIN THESE USING A CERTAIN ITEM AS YOUR PRINCIPAL.
CAT FOOD - FIVE CANS SMOKED SALMON
THAT CERTAIN ITEM.
健闘を祈る!!!!
ケントウヲイノル。
PIECE OF STRAW.
...

ONE WISHES FOR YOUR SAFE RETURN!!!! INDEED.

—SEVERAL WEEKS LATER—

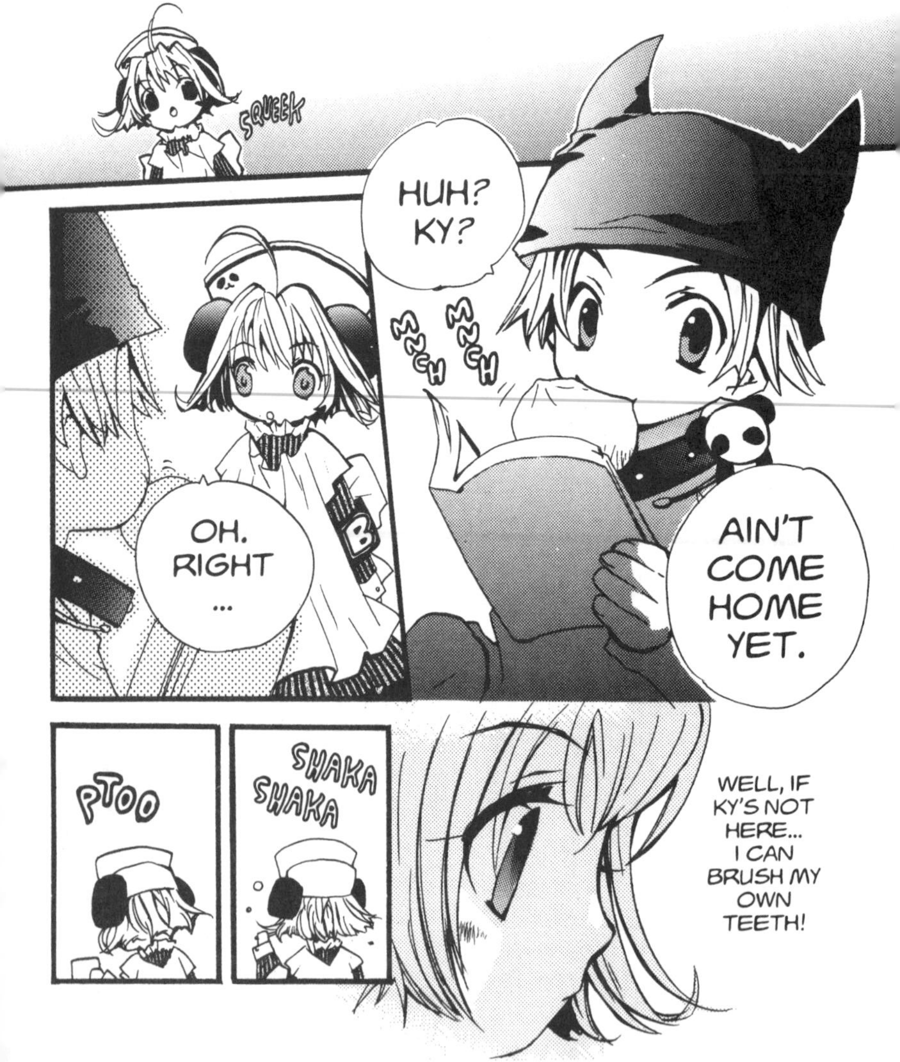
SQUEEK
HUH? KY?
MNCH MNCH
AIN'T COME HOME YET.
OH. RIGHT ...
WELL, IF KY'S NOT HERE... I CAN BRUSH MY OWN TEETH!
SHAKA SHAKA
PTOO

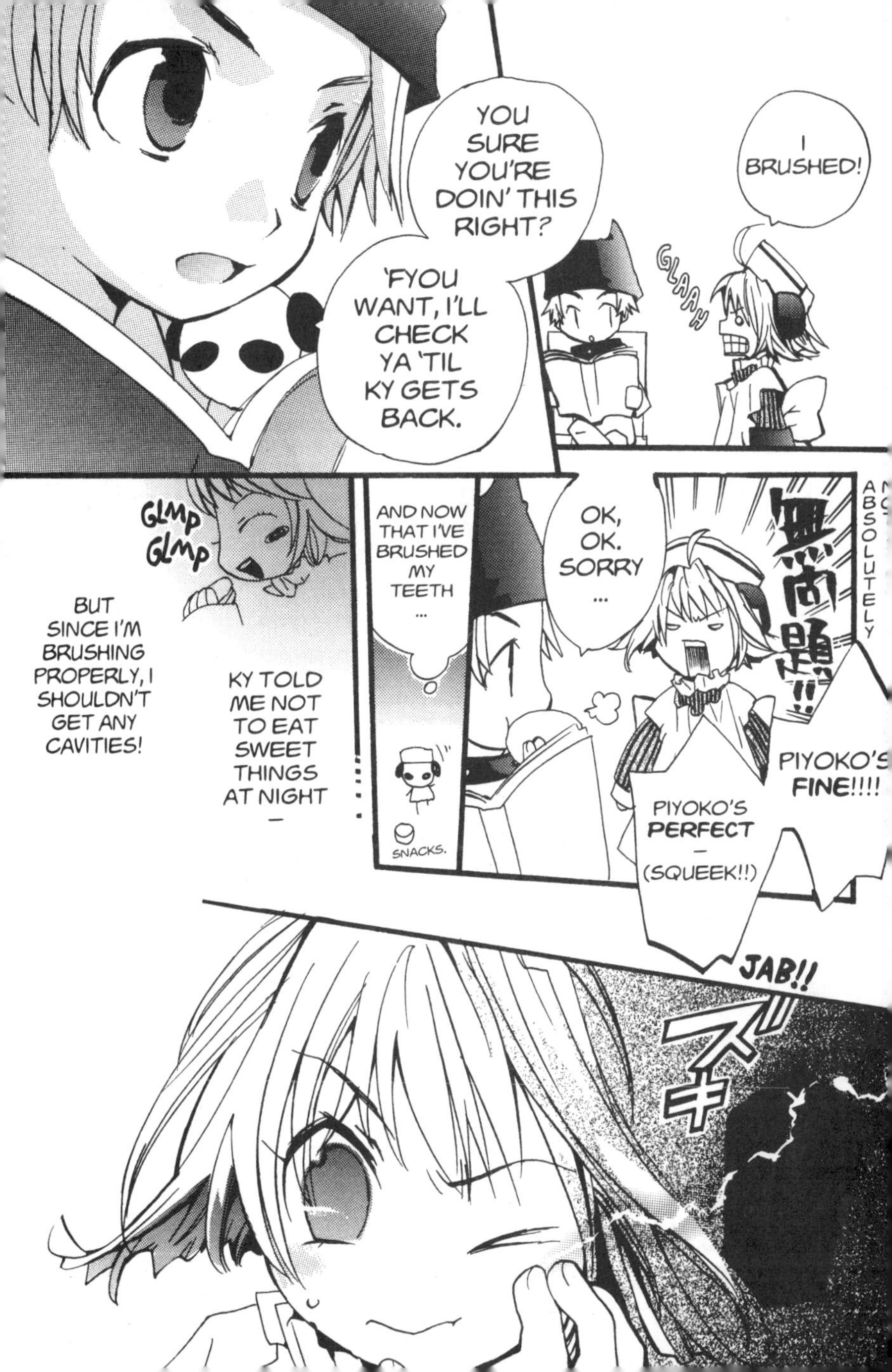

I BRUSHED!
GLAAAH
YOU SURE YOU'RE DOIN' THIS RIGHT?
'FYOU WANT, I'LL CHECK YA 'TIL KY GETS BACK.
ABSOLUTELY
無問題!!
PIYOKO'S **FINE**!!!!
PIYOKO'S **PERFECT** — (SQUEEK!!)
OK, OK. SORRY ...
AND NOW THAT I'VE BRUSHED MY TEETH ...
SNACKS.
GLMP GLMP
KY TOLD ME NOT TO EAT SWEET THINGS AT NIGHT —
BUT SINCE I'M BRUSHING PROPERLY, I SHOULDN'T GET ANY CAVITIES!
JAB!!
ズキ

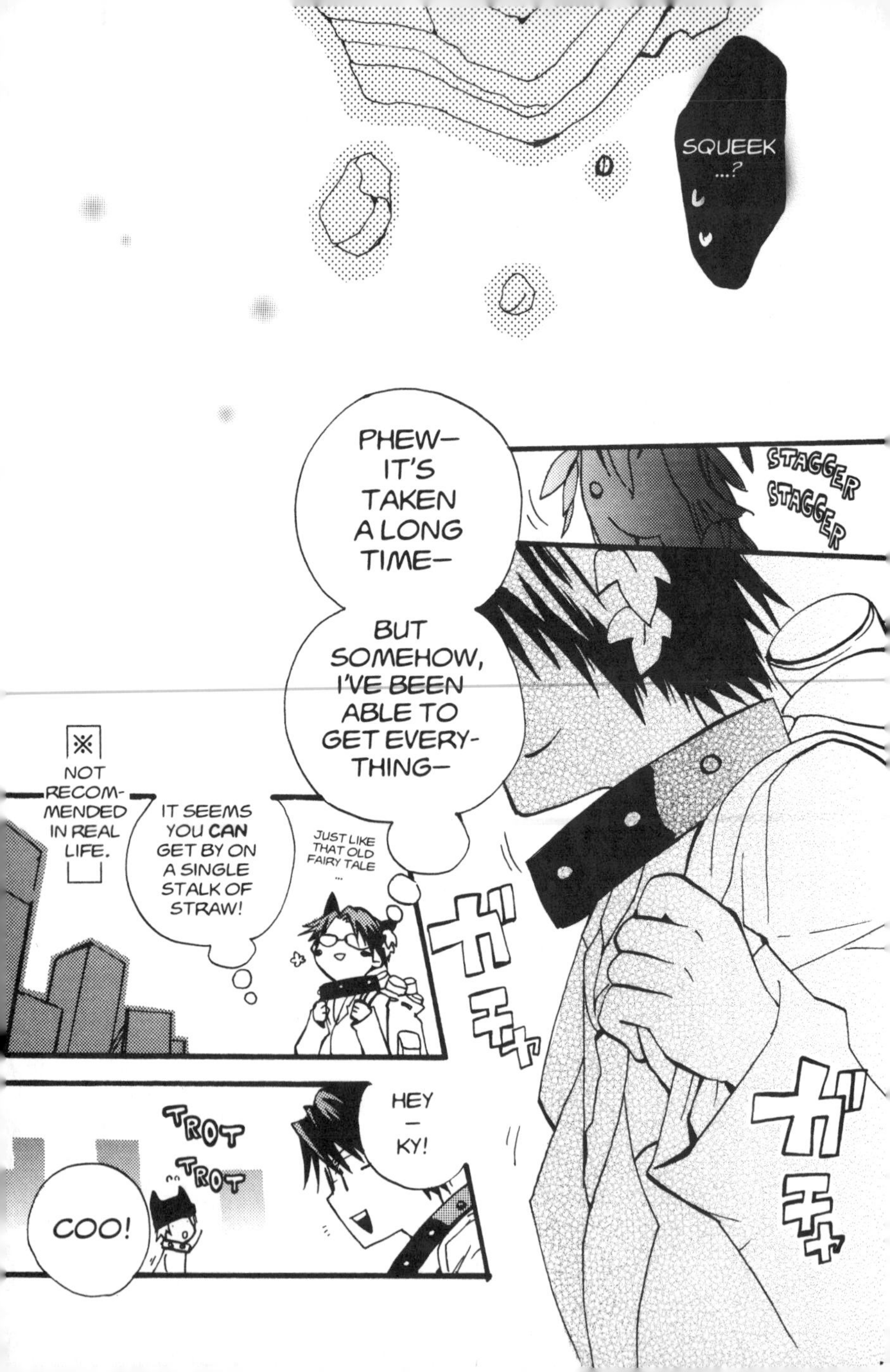
SQUEEK ...?
STAGGER STAGGER
PHEW— IT'S TAKEN A LONG TIME—
BUT SOMEHOW, I'VE BEEN ABLE TO GET EVERY-THING—
ガチャ
ガチャ
JUST LIKE THAT OLD FAIRY TALE ...
IT SEEMS YOU CAN GET BY ON A SINGLE STALK OF STRAW!
※ NOT RECOM-MENDED IN REAL LIFE.
HEY—KY!
TROT TROT
COO!

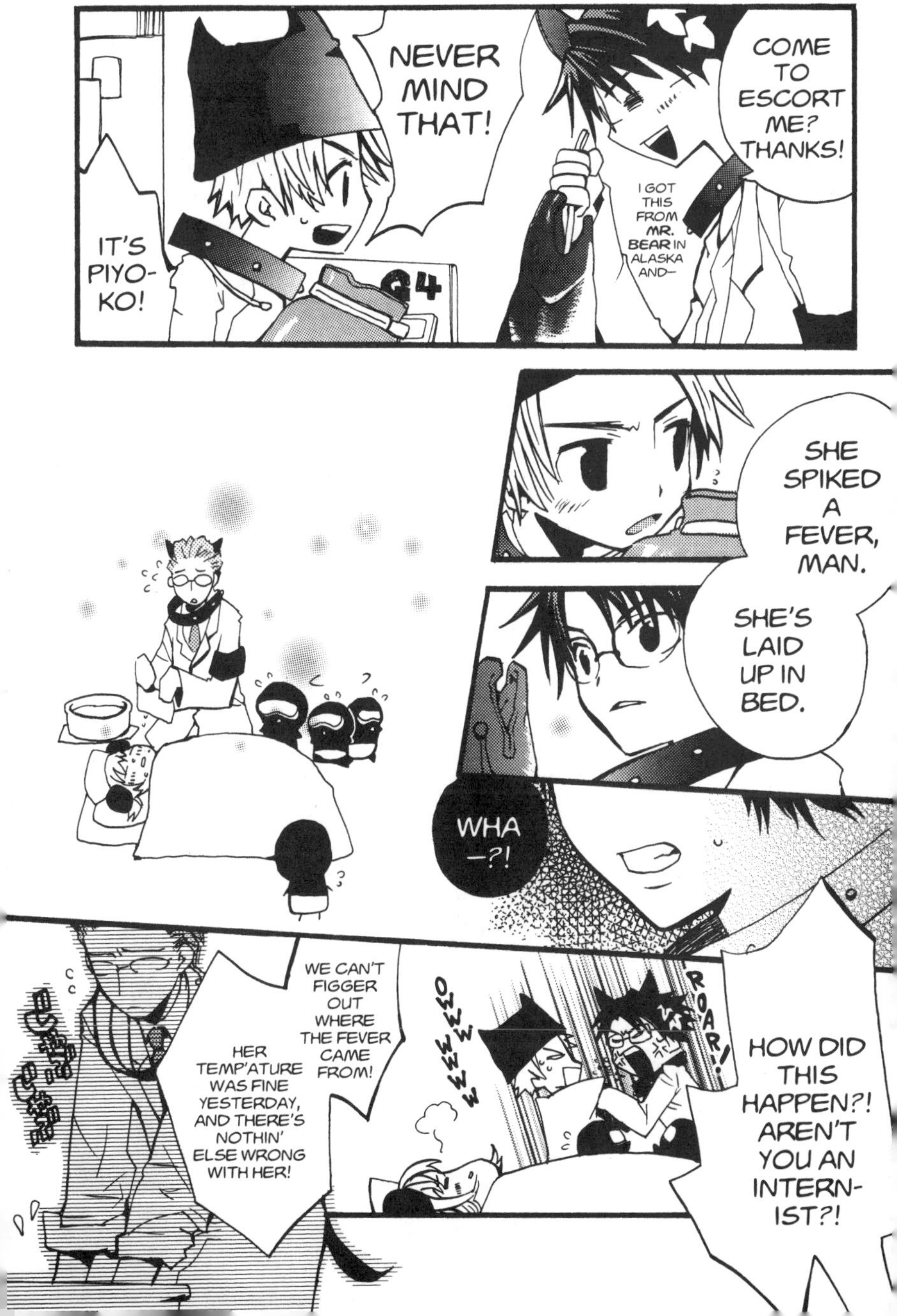
COME TO ESCORT ME? THANKS!
I GOT THIS FROM MR. BEAR IN ALASKA AND—
NEVER MIND THAT!
IT'S PIYO-KO!
SHE SPIKED A FEVER, MAN.
SHE'S LAID UP IN BED.
WHA—?!
HOW DID THIS HAPPEN?! AREN'T YOU AN INTERN-IST?!
ROAR!
OWWWWWWW
WE CAN'T FIGGER OUT WHERE THE FEVER CAME FROM!
HER TEMP'ATURE WAS FINE YESTERDAY, AND THERE'S NOTHIN' ELSE WRONG WITH HER!

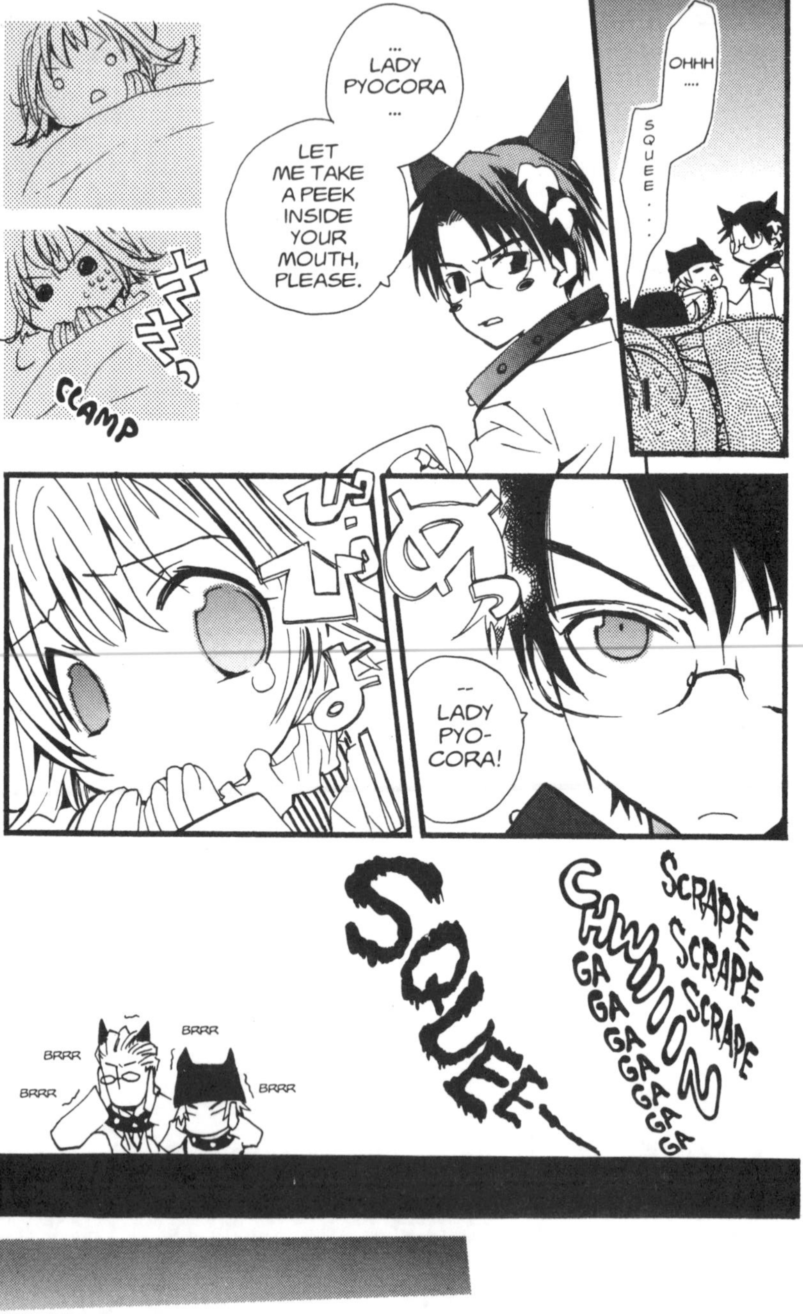
OHHH ....
SQUEE . . .
... LADY PYOCORA ...
LET ME TAKE A PEEK INSIDE YOUR MOUTH, PLEASE.
CLAMP
-- LADY PYO-CORA!
SCRAPE SCRAPE SCRAPE SCRAPE
CHWOOON
GA GA GA GA GA GA GA GA
SQUEE
BRRR
BRRR
BRRR
BRRR

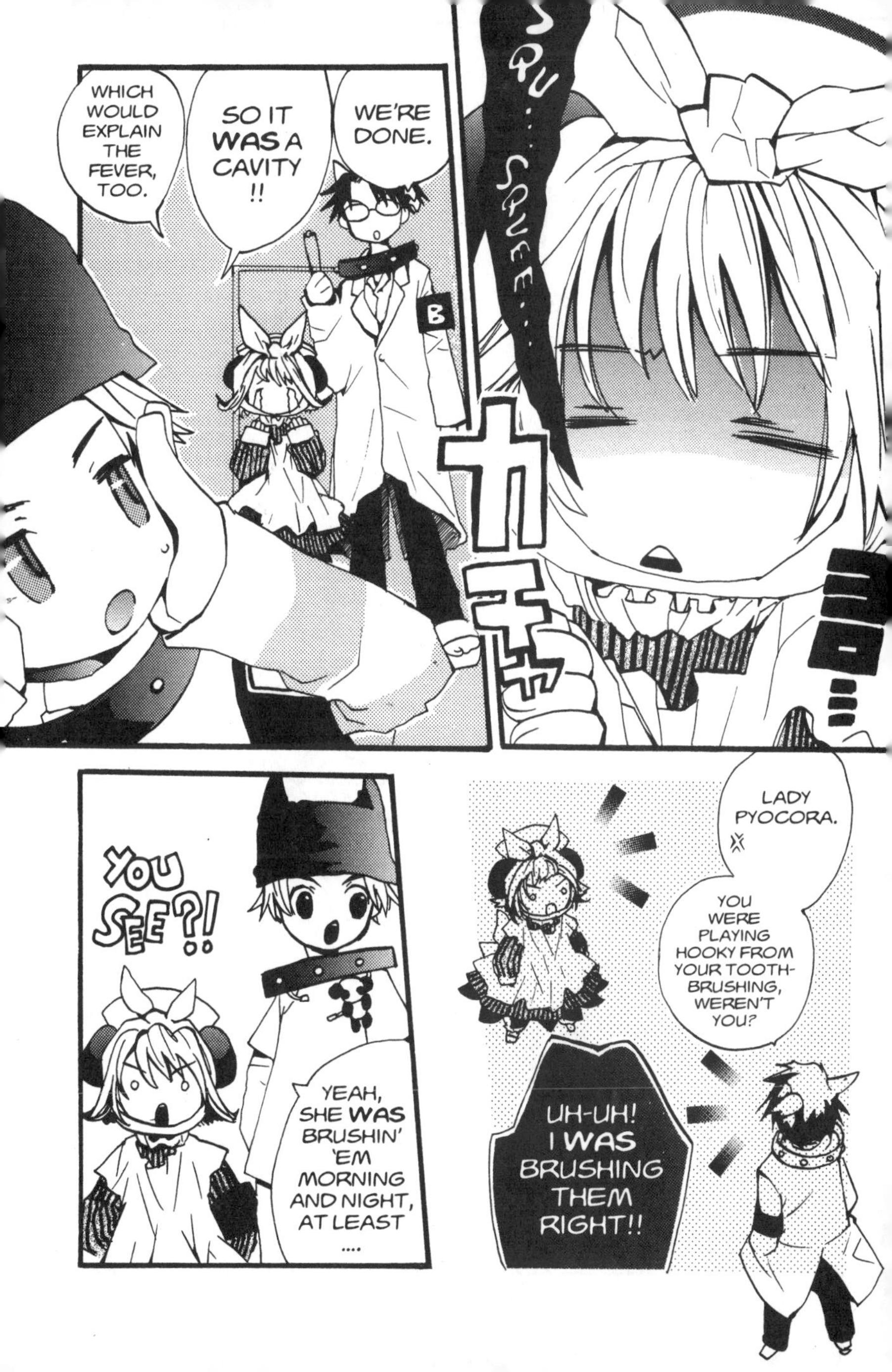
SQU... SQUEE...
カチャ
WE'RE DONE.
SO IT WAS A CAVITY!!
WHICH WOULD EXPLAIN THE FEVER, TOO.
LADY PYOCORA.
YOU WERE PLAYING HOOKY FROM YOUR TOOTH-BRUSHING, WEREN'T YOU?
UH-UH! I WAS BRUSHING THEM RIGHT!!
YOU SEE?!
YEAH, SHE WAS BRUSHIN' 'EM MORNING AND NIGHT, AT LEAST ....

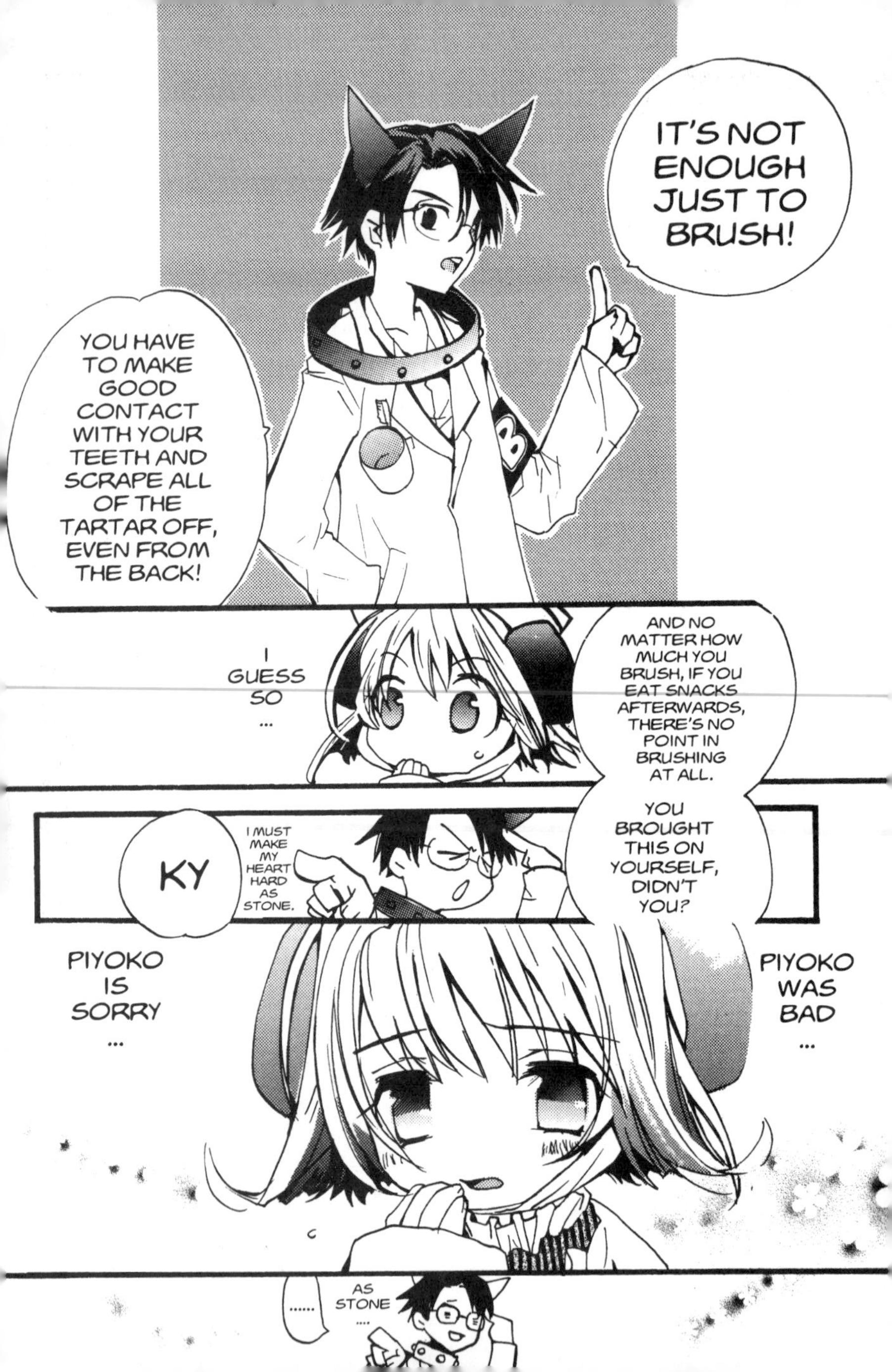
IT'S NOT ENOUGH JUST TO BRUSH!
YOU HAVE TO MAKE GOOD CONTACT WITH YOUR TEETH AND SCRAPE ALL OF THE TARTAR OFF, EVEN FROM THE BACK!
AND NO MATTER HOW MUCH YOU BRUSH, IF YOU EAT SNACKS AFTERWARDS, THERE'S NO POINT IN BRUSHING AT ALL.
I GUESS SO ...
YOU BROUGHT THIS ON YOURSELF, DIDN'T YOU?
I MUST MAKE MY HEART HARD AS STONE.
KY
PIYOKO WAS BAD ...
PIYOKO IS SORRY ...
AS STONE ....
......

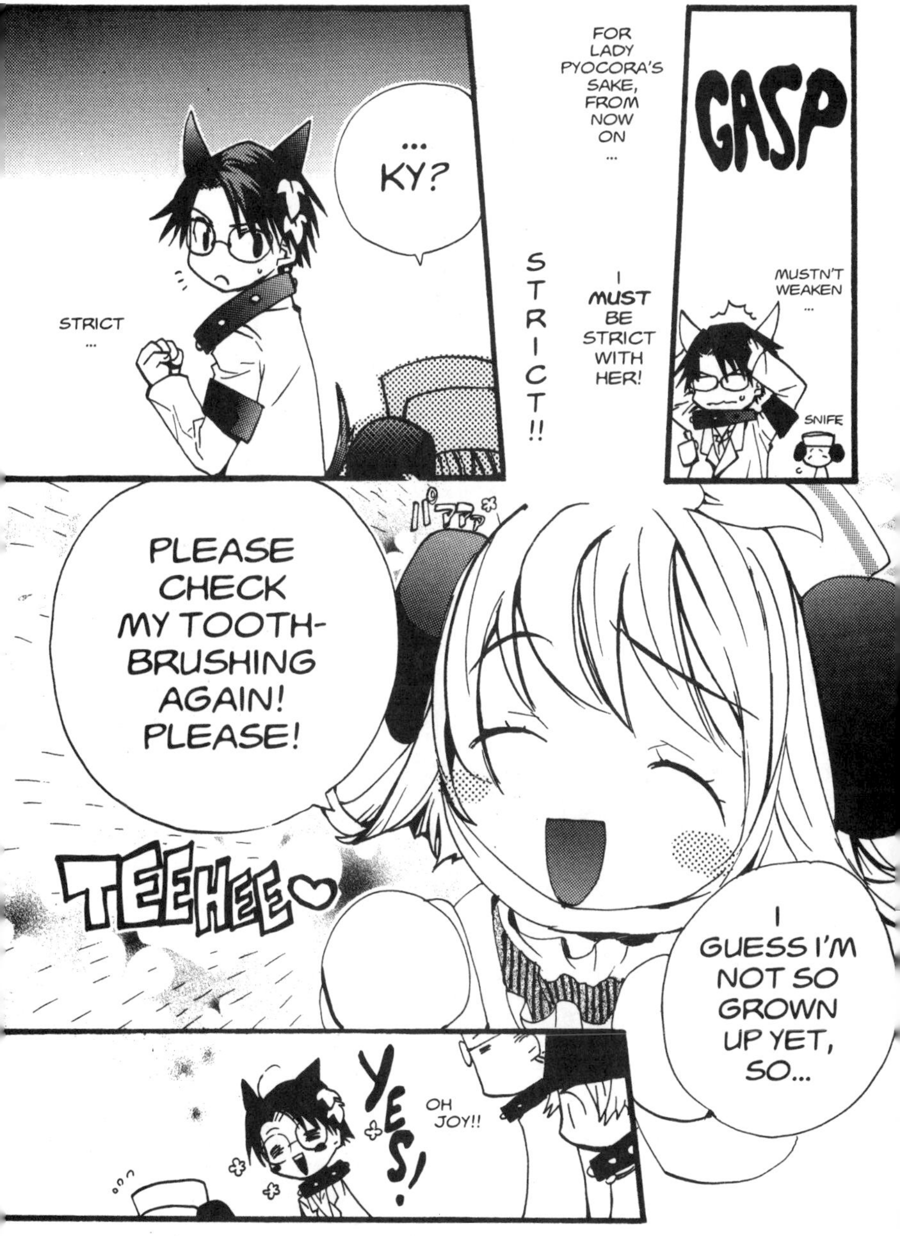
GASP
MUSTN'T WEAKEN ...
SNIFE
FOR LADY PYOCORA'S SAKE, FROM NOW ON ...
I MUST BE STRICT WITH HER!
STRICT!!
... KY?
STRICT ...
I GUESS I'M NOT SO GROWN UP YET, SO...
PLEASE CHECK MY TOOTH-BRUSHING AGAIN! PLEASE!
TEEHEE
YES!
OH JOY!!

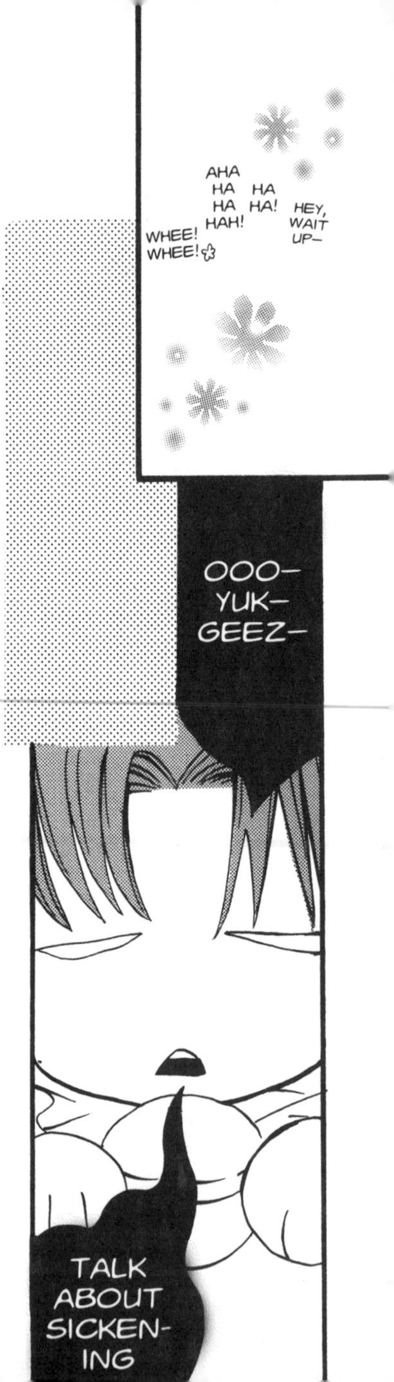
AHA HA HA HAH!
HA HA!
HEY, WAIT UP–
WHEE! WHEE!
OOO-YUK-GEEZ–
TALK ABOUT SICKEN-ING

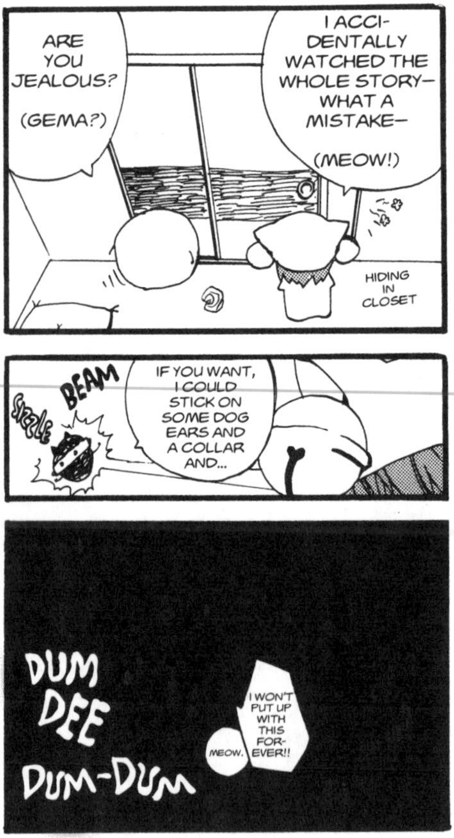
I ACCI-DENTALLY WATCHED THE WHOLE STORY–WHAT A MISTAKE–
(MEOW!)
ARE YOU JEALOUS?
(GEMA?)
HIDING IN CLOSET
IF YOU WANT, I COULD STICK ON SOME DOG EARS AND A COLLAR AND...
BEAM
SIZZLE
DUM DEE DUM-DUM
I WON'T PUT UP WITH THIS FOR-EVER!!
MEOW.

END

A WORD ABOUT "DI-GI-CHARAT"!

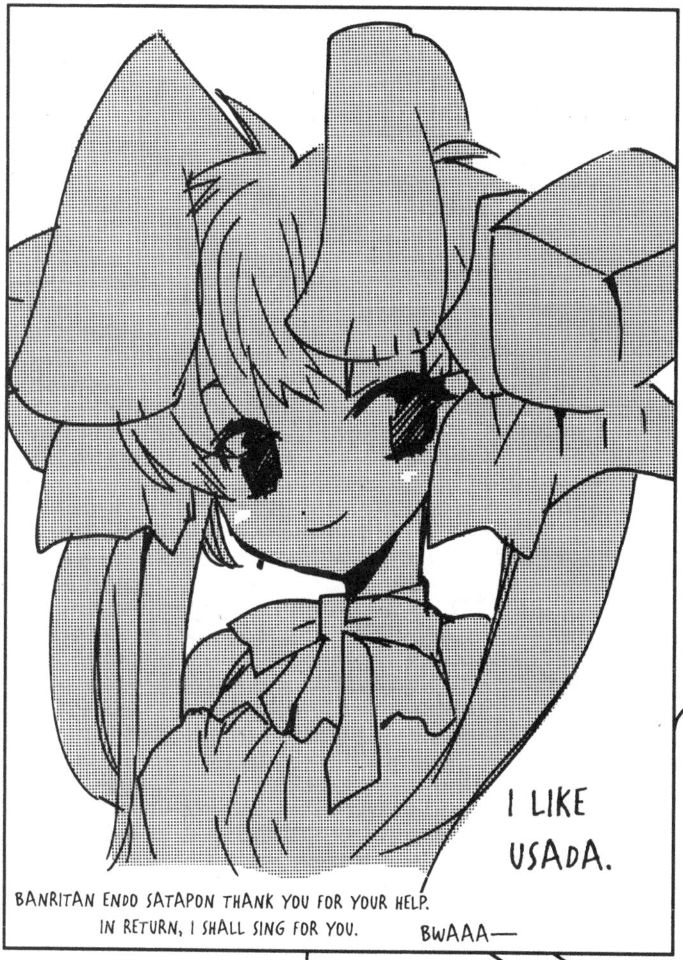
I LIKE USADA.
BANRITAN ENDO SATAPON THANK YOU FOR YOUR HELP.
IN RETURN, I SHALL SING FOR YOU.
BWAAA—

J-TA YAMADA

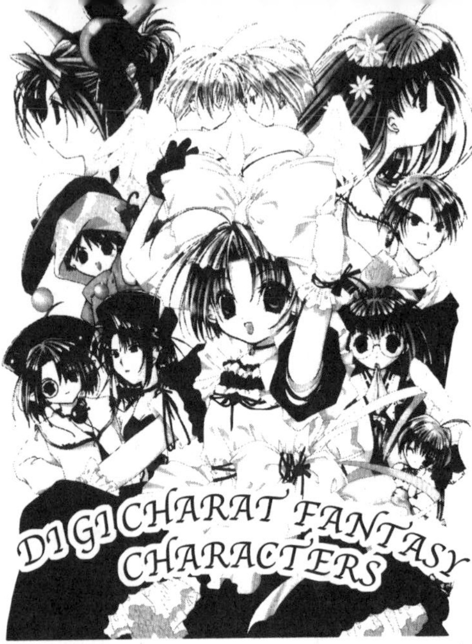
DIGICHARAT FANTASY
CHARACTERS

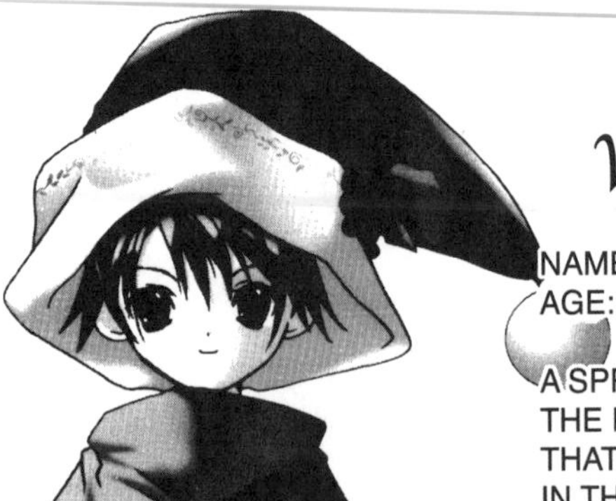

WENDY

NAME: WENDY
AGE: 15

A SPRITE WHO LIVES IN THE FOREST. IT'S SAID THAT SHE WAS ABANDONED IN THE WOODS AS AN INFANT, BUT SHE FORGES ON WITH HER INNATE CHEERFULNESS. BECAUSE SHE GREW UP AMONG BOYS, SHE IS OFTEN CALLED BOYISH...BUT HER FEELINGS ARE QUITE KIND AND GENTLE.

LUNE

NAME: LUNE
AGE: 13

ESCAPED FROM AN ORPHANAGE
WITH HIS TWIN LITTLE
BROTHER LUNA. SINCE THEN,
THEY'VE BEEN LIVING
TOGETHER OUTSIDE TOWN.
THE TWO MAKE THEIR LIVING
WITH THE HANDMADE
ACCESSORIES LUNE SELLS AT
THE MARKETPLACE. AN
ALTRUISTIC, DEPENDABLE
FELLOW. WHEN HE LIFTS HIS
HANDS HIGH, HE CAN MANIPULATE
FLAMES AND THE WIND.

LUNA

NAME: LUNA
AGE: 13

LUNE'S TWIN LITTLE BROTHER.
THE FACT THAT HE HAD WINGS BUT
WAS TOO WEAK TO FLY USED TO
GIVE HIM HIM AN INFERIORITY
COMPLEX. LATER, THANKS TO
PUCHIKO'S SPECIAL TRAINING, HE
LEARNED HOW TO FLY.
HIS OVER-DEPENDENCE ON LUNE
IRRITATES HIM. WHEN HE LIFTS
HIS HAND HIGH, HE CAN HEAL
INJURIES.

CECILE

NAME: CECILE
AGE: 15

THE LADY-LIKE DAUGHTER OF
THE NOBLE GLASSE CLAN.
GENTLE AND QUIET, SHE HAS A
SLIGHTLY FORGETFUL NATURE
AS WELL. BECAUSE OF A PAST
TRAUMA, SHE IS SO TERRIFIED
OF CATS THAT EVEN CAT-EARED
HATS FRIGHTEN HER. DESPITE
HER FRAGILE EXTERIOR, SHE
ACTUALLY POSSESSES CONSIDER-
ABLE SORCEROUS POWERS.

KAYIN

NAME: KAYIN
AGE: 19

CECILE'S OLDER BROTHER AND
A KNIGHT-IN-TRAINING. DESPITE
BEING AN APPRENTICE, HE IS
ALREADY ACCOMPLISHED IN THE
USE OF THE SWORD. HE IS
AWFULLY FOND OF HIS LITTLE
SISTER CECILE. CHASING AFTER
THE WANDERING CECILE HAS
BECOME PART OF HIS DAILY ROUTINE.
AFTER HE MET USADA HE
INSTANTLY BECAME A HUGE FAN.

CARRERA

NAME: CARRERA
AGE: 19

A MAD SCIENTIST WHO IS
PLOTTING WORLD CONQUEST
VIA ALCHEMY. HER SPECIALTY
IS CREATING MYSTERIOUS DRUGS
WITH ASTOUNDING EFFECTS. BUT
SINCE THEY ALSO HAVE HARMFUL
SIDE EFFECTS, SHE HAS TO USE
THEM CAREFULLY. ALTHOUGH SHE
DOES RESPECT HER FATHER GREG,
SHE HAS TROUBLE BEING HONEST
ABOUT HER FEELINGS—
AND SO SHE'S CONSTANTLY
FIGHTING WITH HIM.

GREG

NAME: GREG

CARRERA'S FATHER AND ANOTHER
SCIENTIST. WORLD CONQUEST IS
HIS LIFE'S WORK TOO, AND HE
DILIGENTLY CARRIES ON HIS EXPER-
IMENTS DAY AND NIGHT. HE HAS A
BOLD PERSONALITY, AND ISN'T ONE
TO WORRY ABOUT TRIVIAL DETAILS.
PERHAPS BECAUSE OF THAT,
CALCULATIONS ARE HIS BIG WEAK
SPOT. ALTHOUGH HE'S ALWAYS
FIGHTING WITH HER, IN TRUTH HE
TREASURES HIS DAUGHTER
CARRERA.

HINAGIKU

NAME: HINAGIKU
AGE: 14

A KIND, CHEERFUL PRIESTESS.
SHE IS GOOD AT COOKING, AND
HAS A STRONG MATERNAL
INSTINCT. 8 YEARS AGO, SHE
LOST HER MOTHER IN THE
BATTLE AGAINST THE DEMON
JYASHIN, SO NOW SHE LIVES WITH
HER FATHER. ALTHOUGH SHE IS
PRESENTLY TRAINING HARD
DILIGENTLY AS PRIESTESS TO THE
"DEMON-BREAKING" CLAN, SHE
DOESN'T HAVE MUCH CONFIDENCE
IN HER OWN ABILITIES.

HINAGIKU'S FATHER

HINAGIKU'S FATHER, EMPLOYED
AS HEAD PRIEST OF THE SHRINE.
THE CHIEF OF THE CLAN, WHO
CAN WIELD THE SWORD OF
EXORCISM. HE IMPOSES HARSH
LESSONS ON HIS ONLY DAUGHTER
HINAGIKU SO THAT SHE TOO WILL
LEARN TO HANDLE THE SWORD.

ERIKA

NAME: ERIKA
AGE: 22

THE VILLAGE SHERIFF'S
DEPUTY, ASSIGNED SEVERAL
YEARS AGO. HAS A STRONG,
MATERNAL DESIRE TO CARE
FOR PEOPLE, AND IS WELL
LOVED BY THE VILLAGERS.
HER SPECIALTY IS THE LASSO—
AND SHE'S A PRETTY HEAVY
DRINKER. EVEN NOW, SHE
STILL CAN'T FORGIVE HER
ELDER SISTER, WHO
ABANDONED HER FAMILY AND
LEFT THE VILLAGE 10 YEARS
AGO.

RIN

NAME: RIN
AGE: 14

THE LAST LIVING DESCENDANT
OF THE "MAGIC-SEALING CLAN,"
WHO LIVES ALL BY HERSELF IN
THE FOREST THAT HOLDS
JYASHIN'S SHRINE. BECAUSE
OF THE HORNS ON HER HEAD,
THE VILLAGERS THINK SHE IS
ONE OF JYASHIN'S SERVANTS.
EVEN SO, SHE WATCHES OVER
THE VILLAGERS FROM AFAR
WITH HER SAD AND LONELY EYES.

JYASHIN

SINCE TIME IMMEMORIAL HE HAS BEEN FEARED AS THE DEVIL. THE NEGATIVE EMOTIONS OF MORTALS ARE HIS FOODSTUFF. FOR AGES HE WAS SEALED AWAY. BUT THEN HE USED DIGIKO'S POWERFUL ENERGY TO BREAK FREE AND LIVE AGAIN.

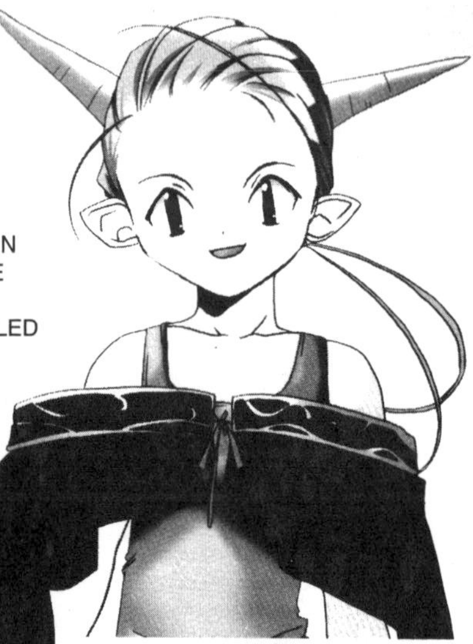

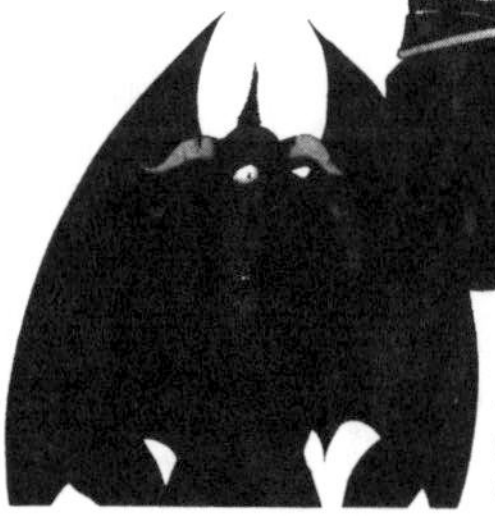

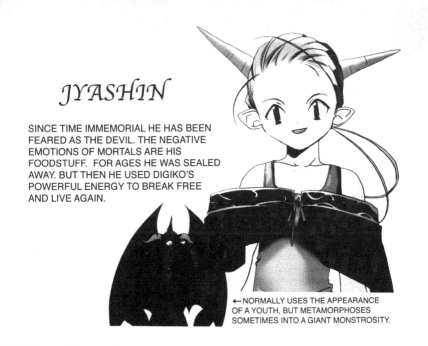

← NORMALLY USES THE APPEARANCE OF A YOUTH, BUT METAMORPHOSES SOMETIMES INTO A GIANT MONSTROSITY.

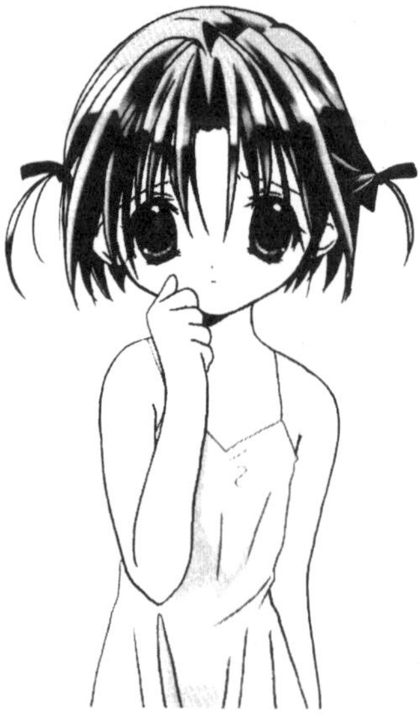

DI GI CHARAT?

DIGIKO, WHOSE MEMORY HAS BEEN SEALED BY JYASHIN. INSTEAD OF OUR USUAL SCHEMING DIGIKO, HERE SHE'S FRAGILE AND VULNERABLE AND IN NEED OF PROTECTION. SHE IS MODEST AND KIND, BUT ALWAYS LOOKS SOMEHOW LONELY AND UNEASY.

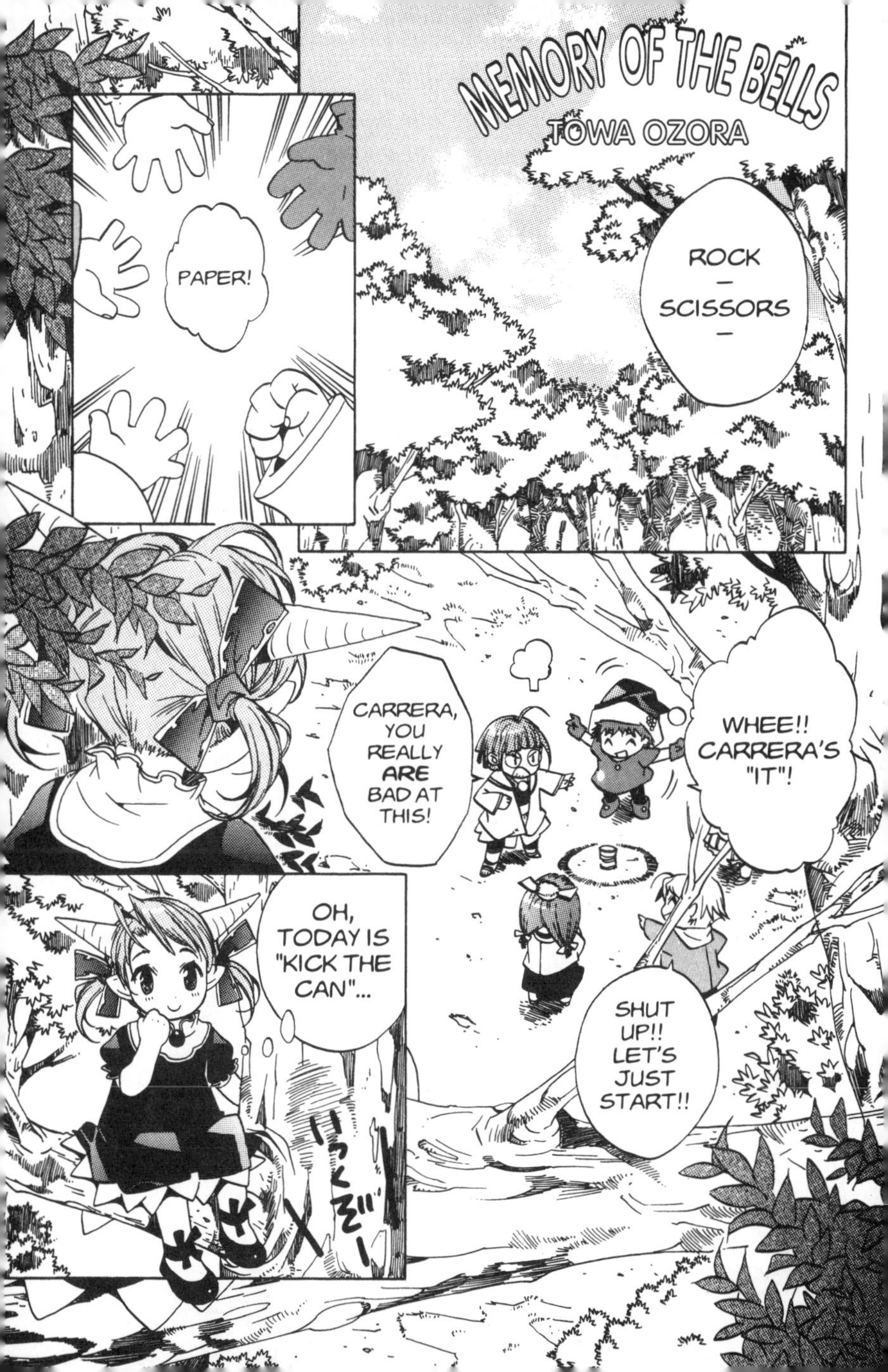
MEMORY OF THE BELLS
TOWA OZORA
ROCK — SCISSORS —
PAPER!
WHEE!! CARRERA'S "IT"!
CARRERA, YOU REALLY **ARE** BAD AT THIS!
SHUT UP!! LET'S JUST START!!
OH, TODAY IS "KICK THE CAN"...

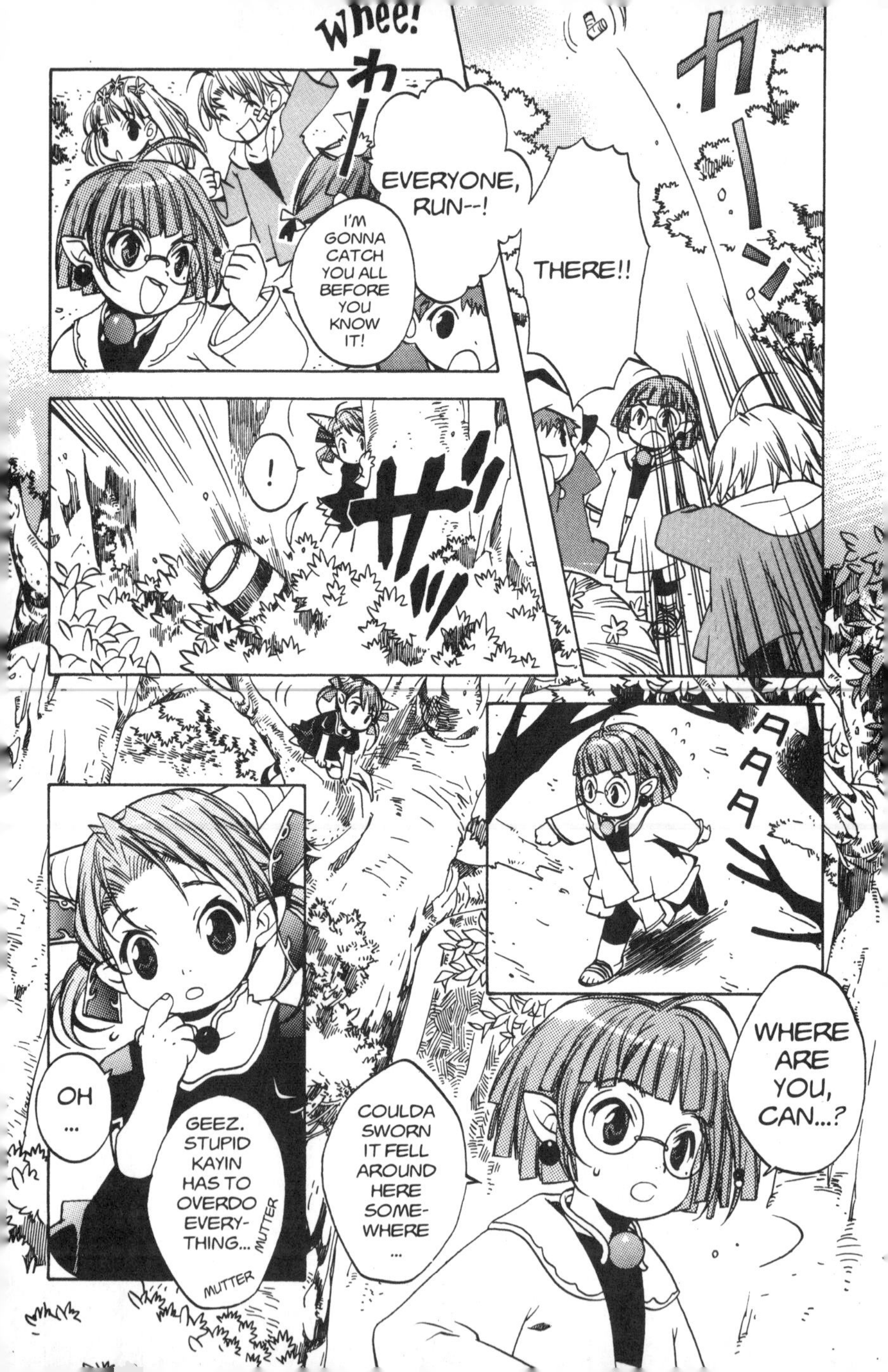

カーン
THERE!!
whee!
わー
EVERYONE, RUN--!
I'M GONNA CATCH YOU ALL BEFORE YOU KNOW IT!
!
ザッ
WHERE ARE YOU, CAN...?
COULDA SWORN IT FELL AROUND HERE SOME-WHERE ...
OH ...
GEEZ. STUPID KAYIN HAS TO OVERDO EVERY-THING...
MUTTER
MUTTER

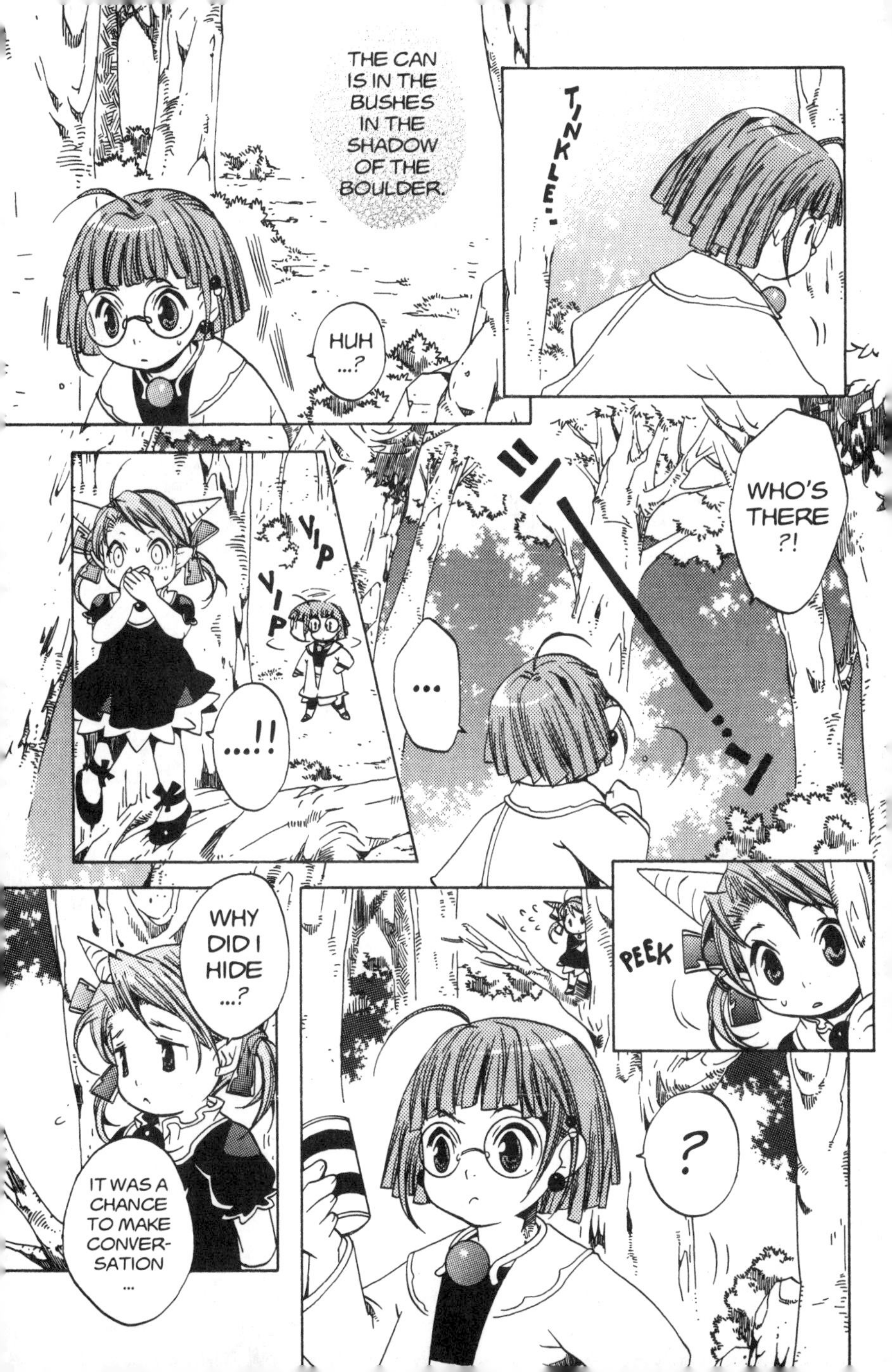
TINKLE!!
THE CAN IS IN THE BUSHES IN THE SHADOW OF THE BOULDER.
HUH ...?
WHO'S THERE ?!
...
VIP VIP
...!!
PEEK
?
WHY DID I HIDE ...?
IT WAS A CHANCE TO MAKE CONVERSATION ...

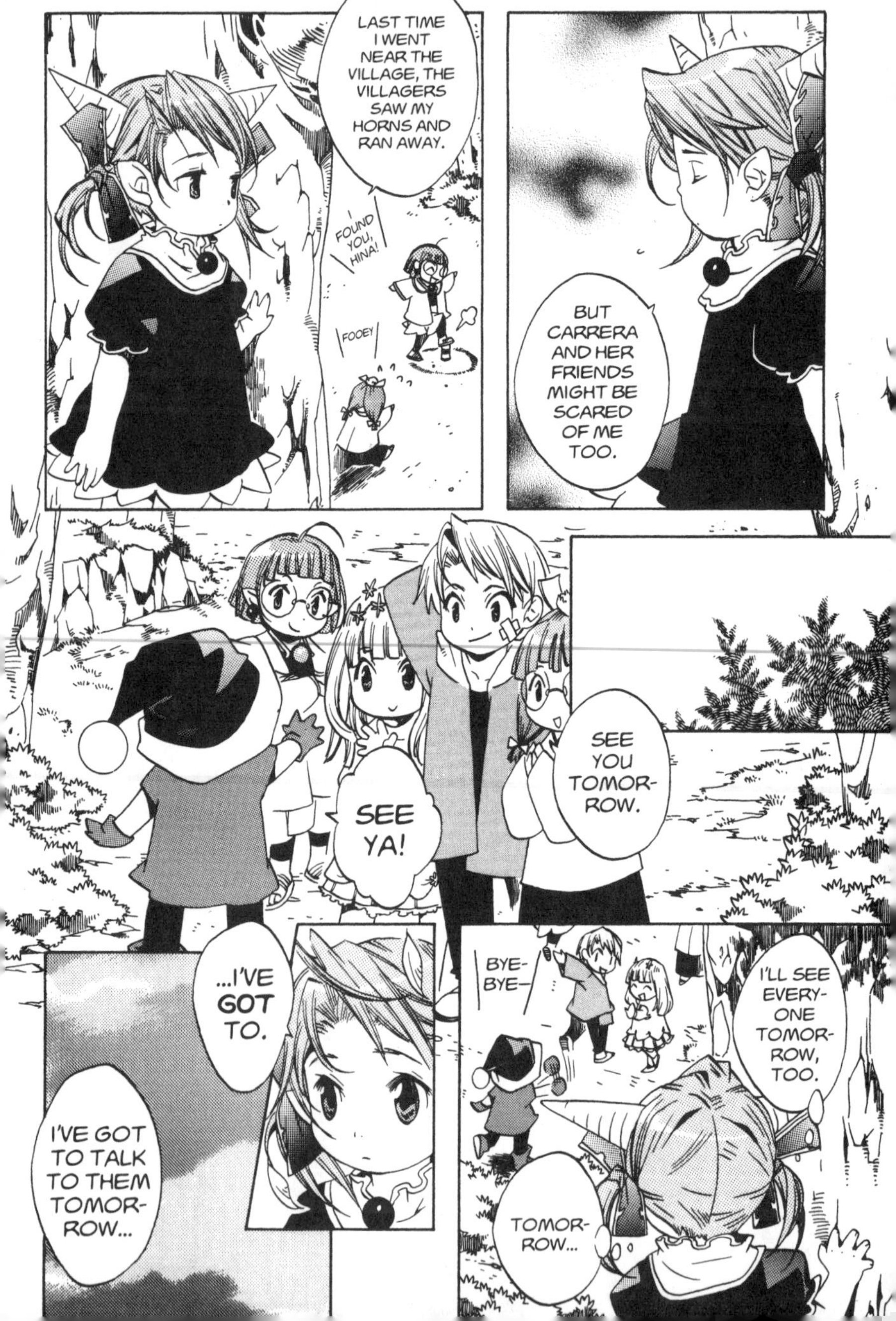
BUT CARRERA AND HER FRIENDS MIGHT BE SCARED OF ME TOO.
LAST TIME I WENT NEAR THE VILLAGE, THE VILLAGERS SAW MY HORNS AND RAN AWAY.
I FOUND YOU, HINA!
FOOEY
SEE YOU TOMORROW.
SEE YA!
I'LL SEE EVERYONE TOMORROW, TOO.
BYE-BYE—
TOMORROW...
...I'VE GOT TO.
I'VE GOT TO TALK TO THEM TOMORROW...

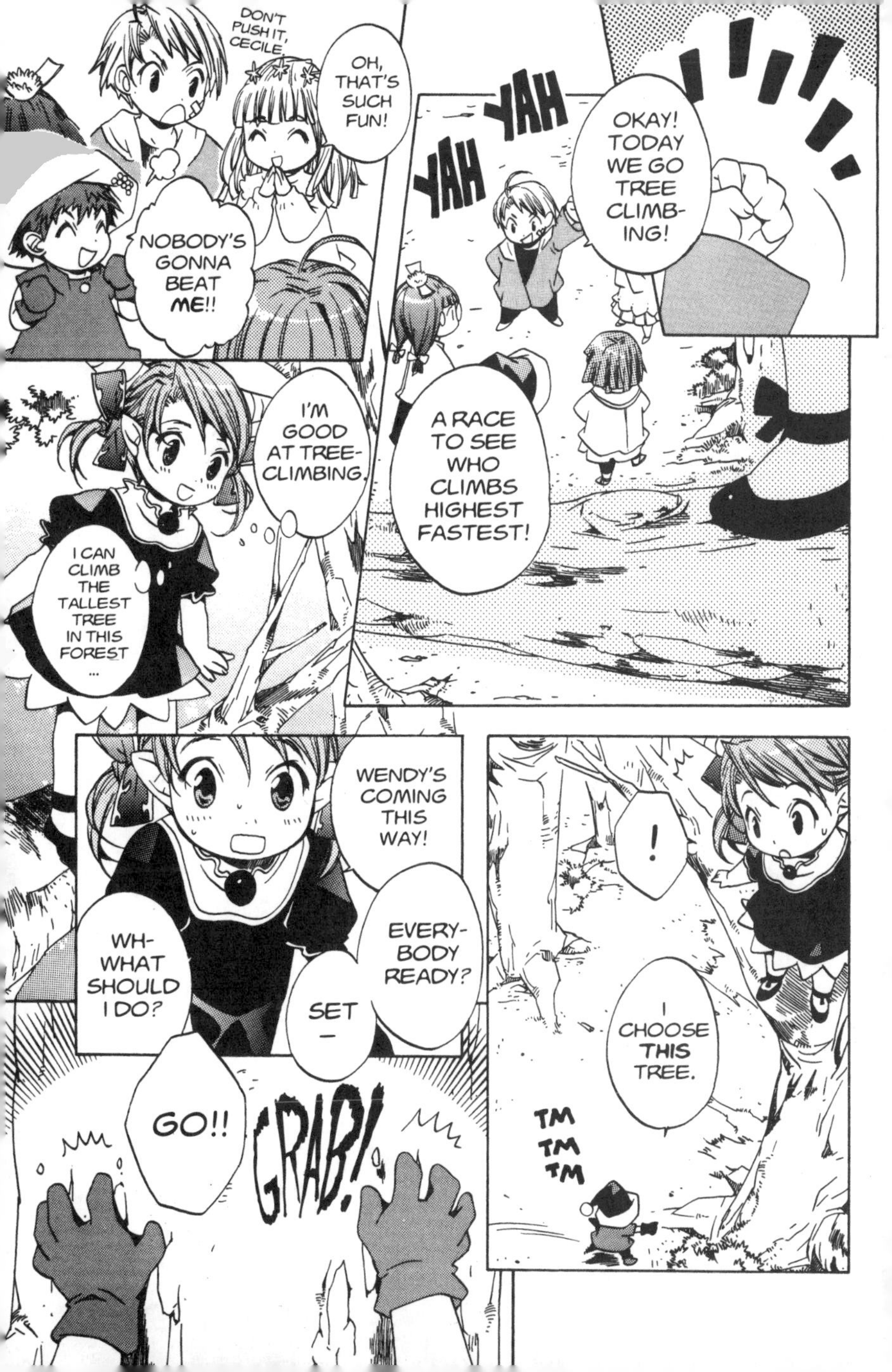

OKAY! TODAY WE GO TREE CLIMBING!
YAH
YAH
OH, THAT'S SUCH FUN!
DON'T PUSH IT, CECILE.
NOBODY'S GONNA BEAT ME!!
A RACE TO SEE WHO CLIMBS HIGHEST FASTEST!
I'M GOOD AT TREE-CLIMBING.
I CAN CLIMB THE TALLEST TREE IN THIS FOREST ...
!
I CHOOSE THIS TREE.
TM TM TM
WENDY'S COMING THIS WAY!
WH- WHAT SHOULD I DO?
EVERY-BODY READY?
SET —
GO!!
GRAB!

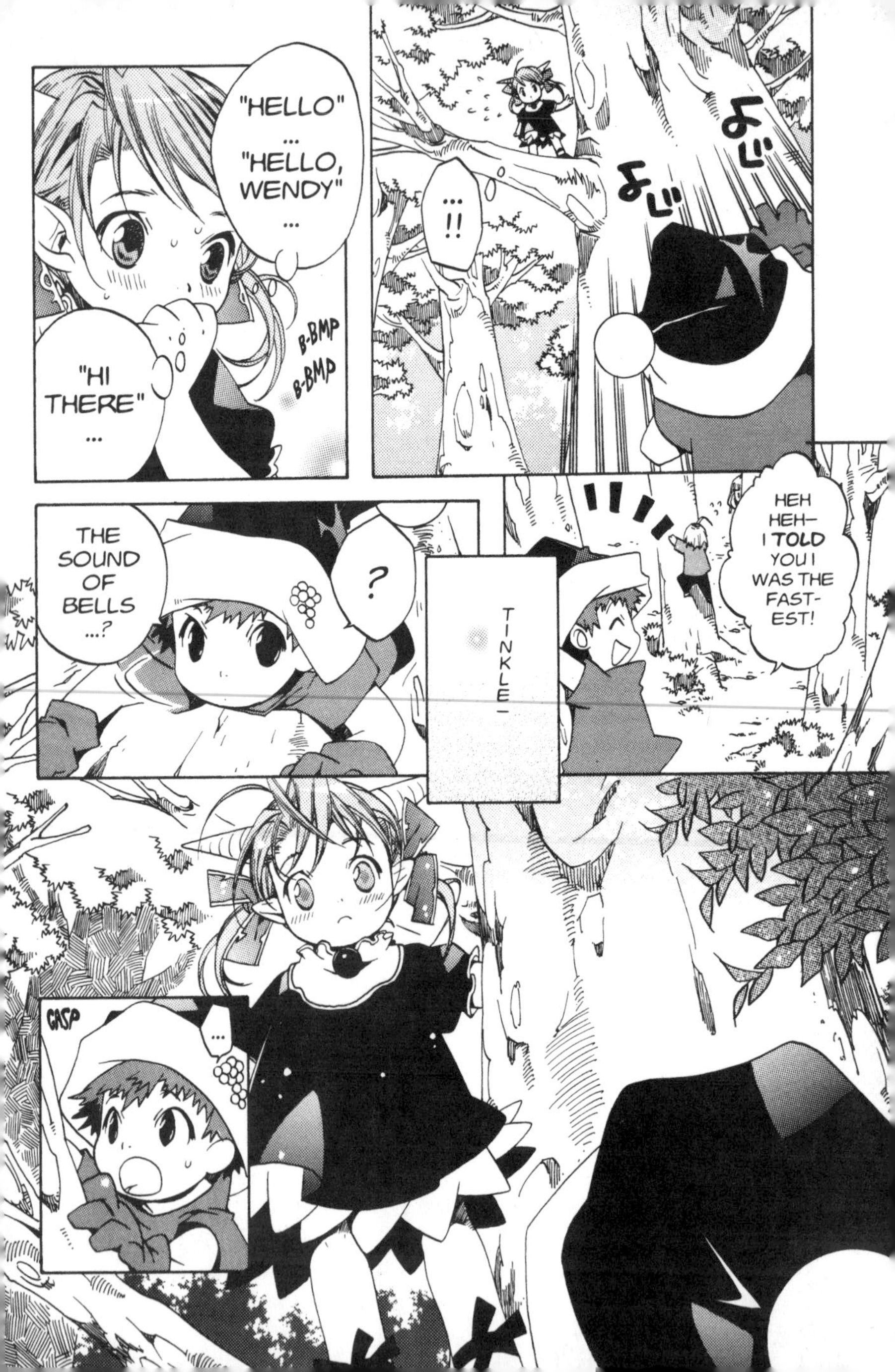
よじ
よじ
...!!
"HELLO" ... "HELLO, WENDY" ...
B-BMP B-BMP
"HI THERE" ...
HEH HEH— I TOLD YOU I WAS THE FAST-EST!
TINKLE—
?
THE SOUND OF BELLS ...?
GASP
...

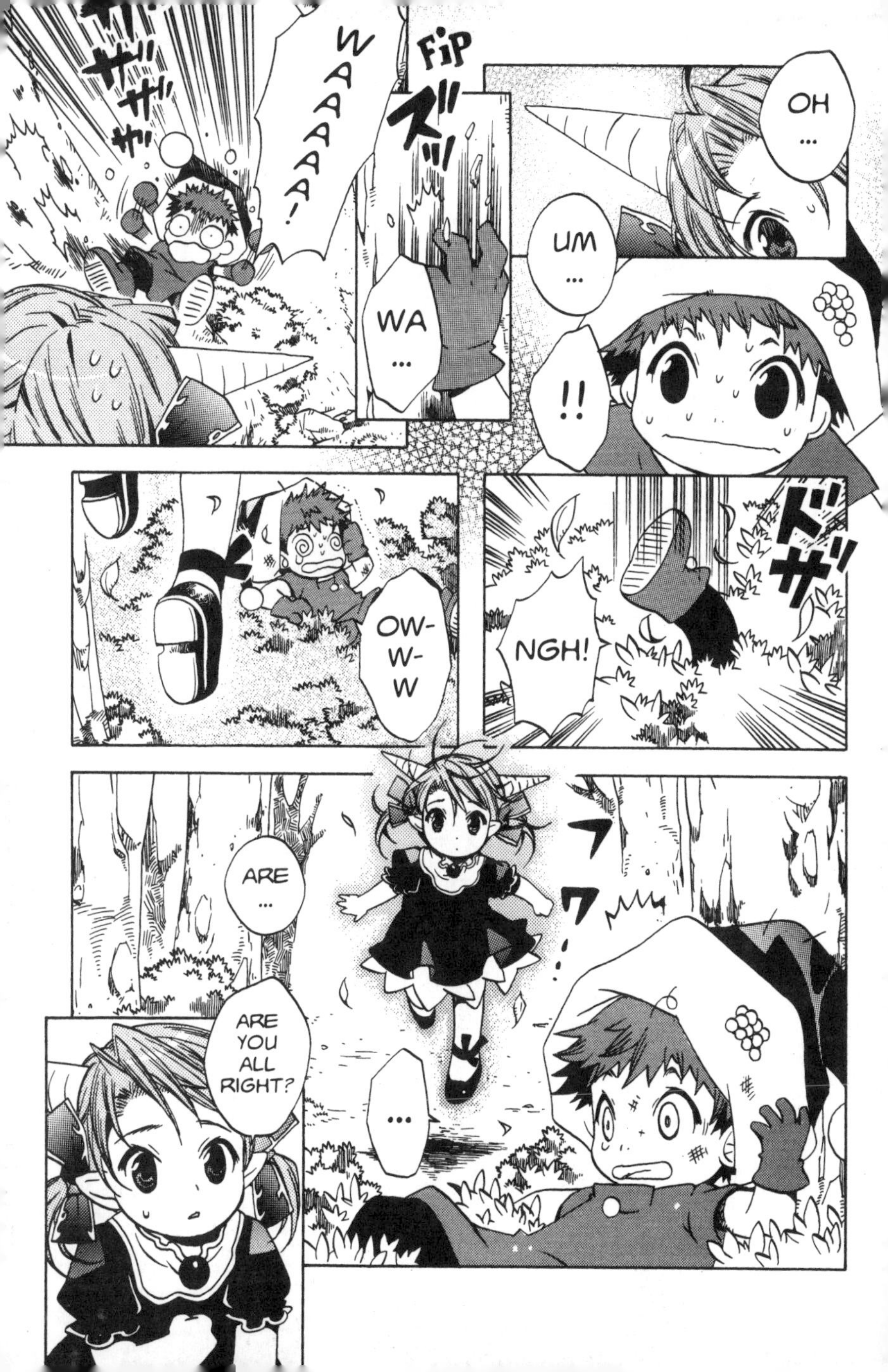
OH ...
UM ...
!!
FiP
ズッ
WA ...
WAAAAAAA!
NGH!
OW-W-W
ARE ...
...
ARE YOU ALL RIGHT?

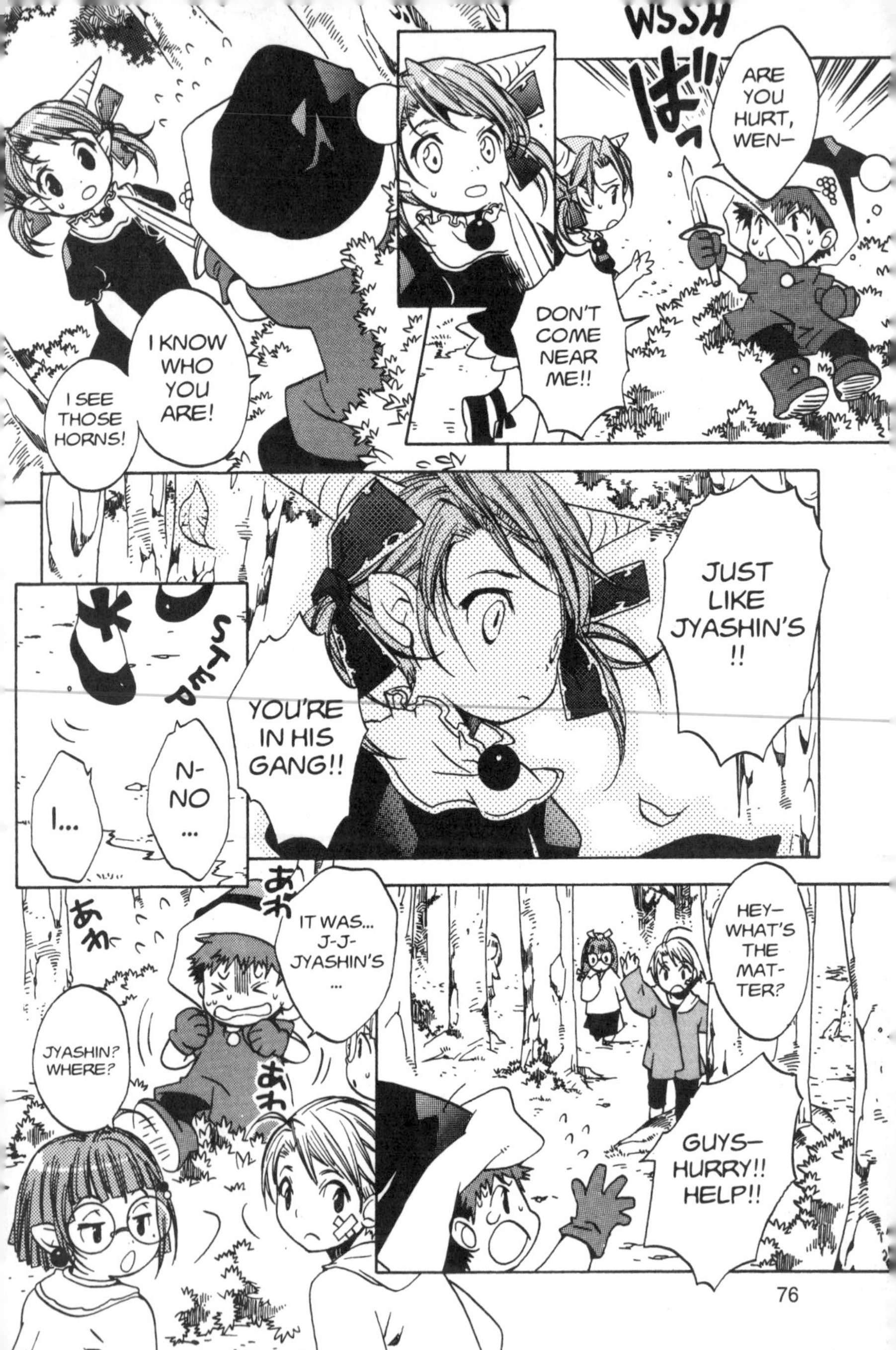
WSSH
ばッ
ARE YOU HURT, WEN—
DON'T COME NEAR ME!!
I KNOW WHO YOU ARE!
I SEE THOSE HORNS!
JUST LIKE JYASHIN'S !!
YOU'RE IN HIS GANG!!
STEP
N-NO ...
I...
HEY— WHAT'S THE MATTER?
GUYS— HURRY!! HELP!!
あわ
IT WAS... J-J-JYASHIN'S ...
あわ
あわ
JYASHIN? WHERE?

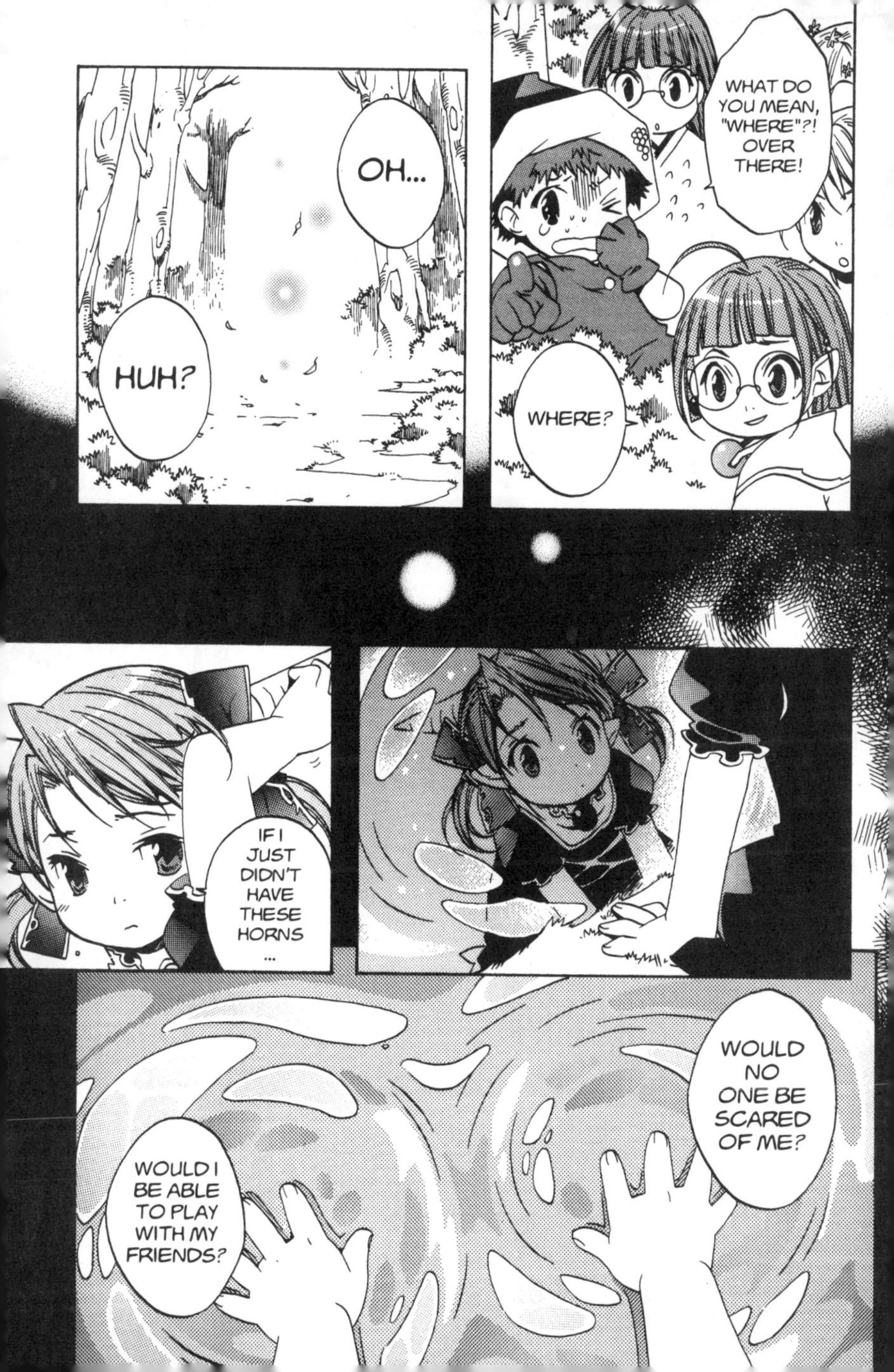
WHAT DO YOU MEAN, "WHERE"?! OVER THERE!
WHERE?
OH...
HUH?
IF I JUST DIDN'T HAVE THESE HORNS ...
WOULD NO ONE BE SCARED OF ME?
WOULD I BE ABLE TO PLAY WITH MY FRIENDS?

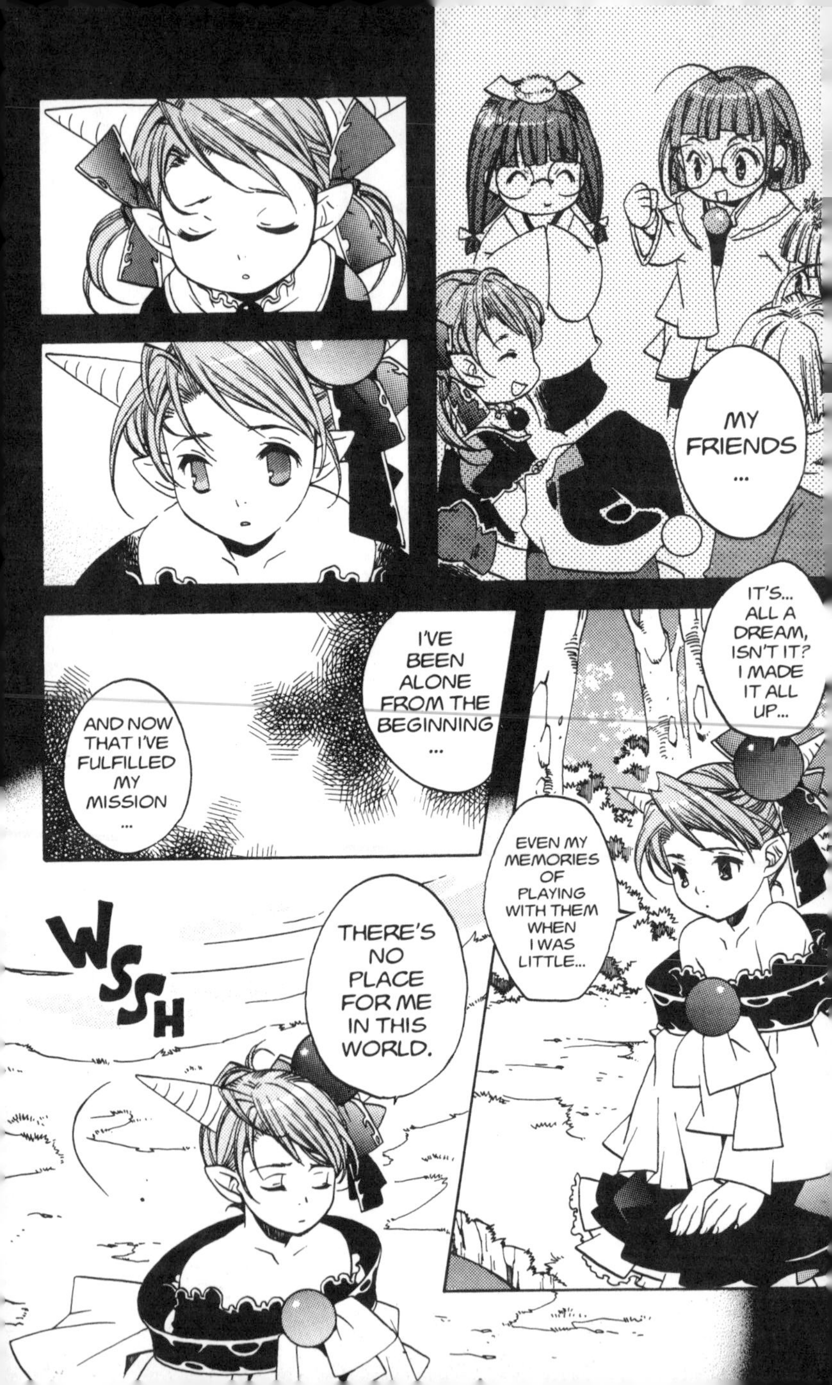
MY FRIENDS ...
IT'S... ALL A DREAM, ISN'T IT? I MADE IT ALL UP...
EVEN MY MEMORIES OF PLAYING WITH THEM WHEN I WAS LITTLE...
I'VE BEEN ALONE FROM THE BEGINNING ...
AND NOW THAT I'VE FULFILLED MY MISSION ...
THERE'S NO PLACE FOR ME IN THIS WORLD.
WSSH

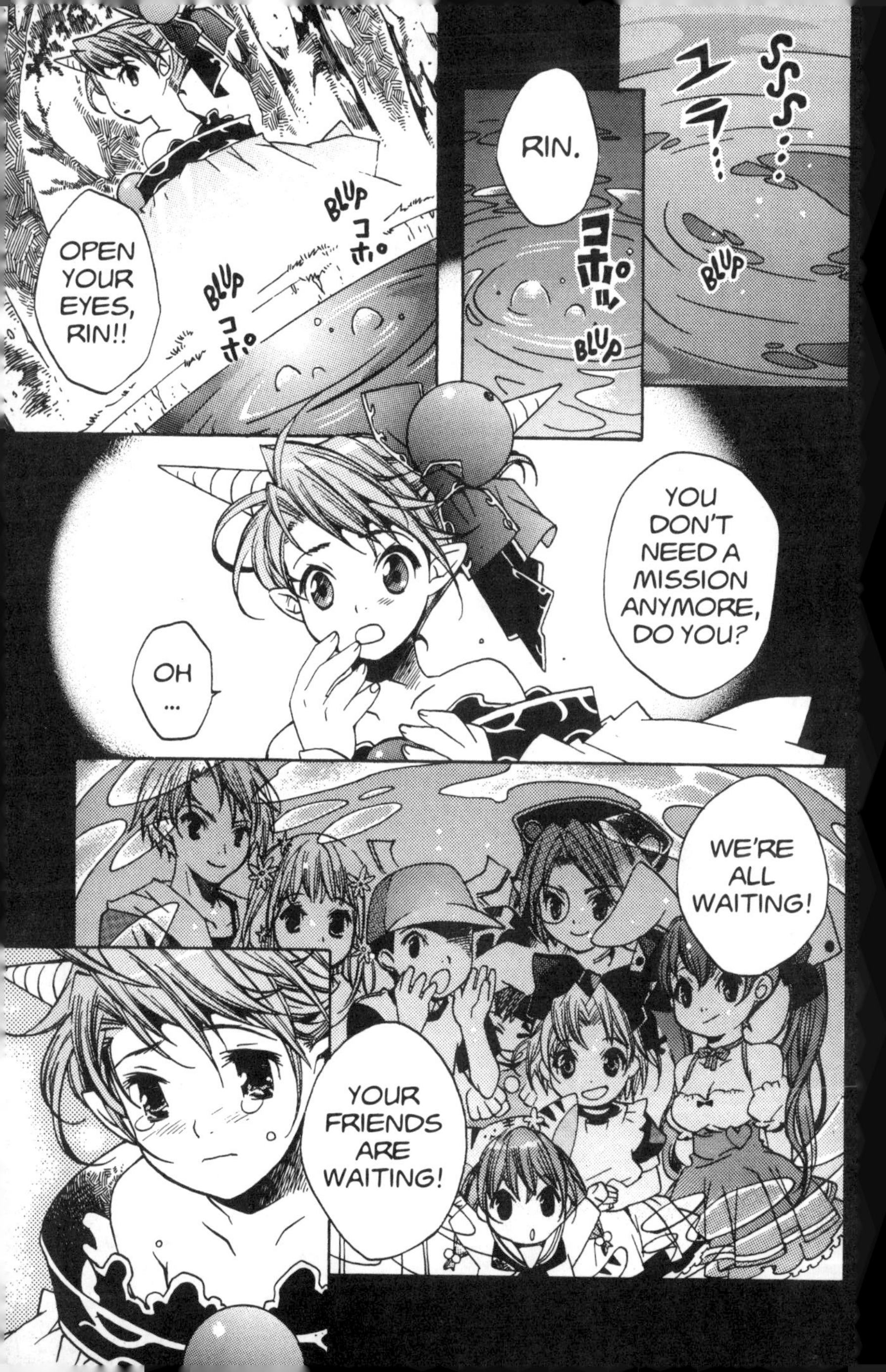
SSS...
ユラ...
RIN.
BLUP
コポッ
BLUP
OPEN YOUR EYES, RIN!!
BLUP
コポ
BLUP
コポ
YOU DON'T NEED A MISSION ANYMORE, DO YOU?
OH ...
WE'RE ALL WAITING!
YOUR FRIENDS ARE WAITING!

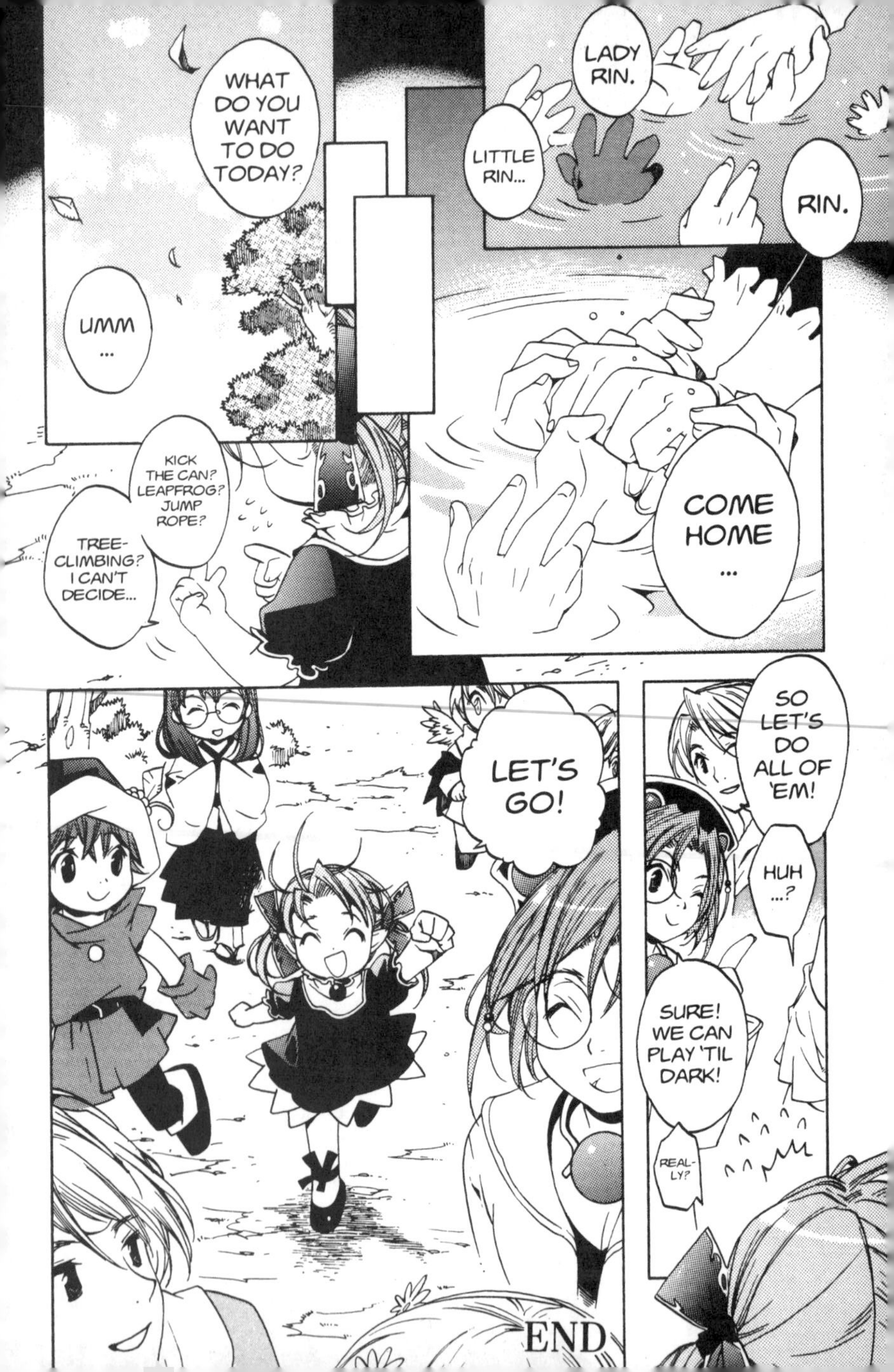
LADY RIN.
LITTLE RIN...
RIN.
COME HOME ...
WHAT DO YOU WANT TO DO TODAY?
UMM ...
KICK THE CAN? LEAPFROG? JUMP ROPE?
TREE-CLIMBING? I CAN'T DECIDE...
SO LET'S DO ALL OF 'EM!
HUH ...?
SURE! WE CAN PLAY 'TIL DARK!
REAL-LY?
LET'S GO!

END

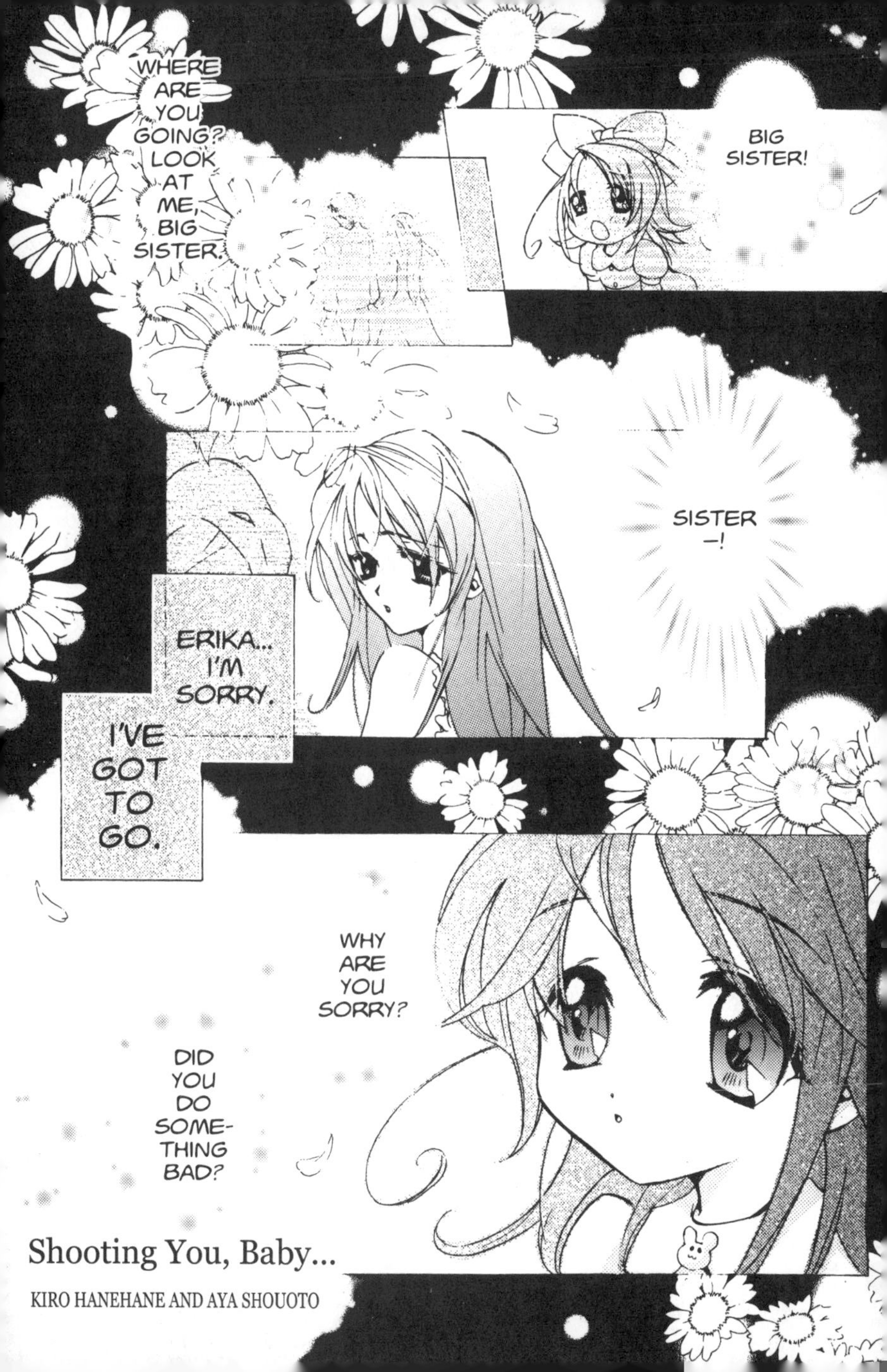
BIG SISTER!
WHERE ARE YOU GOING? LOOK AT ME, BIG SISTER.
SISTER —!
ERIKA... I'M SORRY.
I'VE GOT TO GO.
WHY ARE YOU SORRY?
DID YOU DO SOME-THING BAD?

Shooting You, Baby...

KIRO HANEHANE AND AYA SHOUOTO

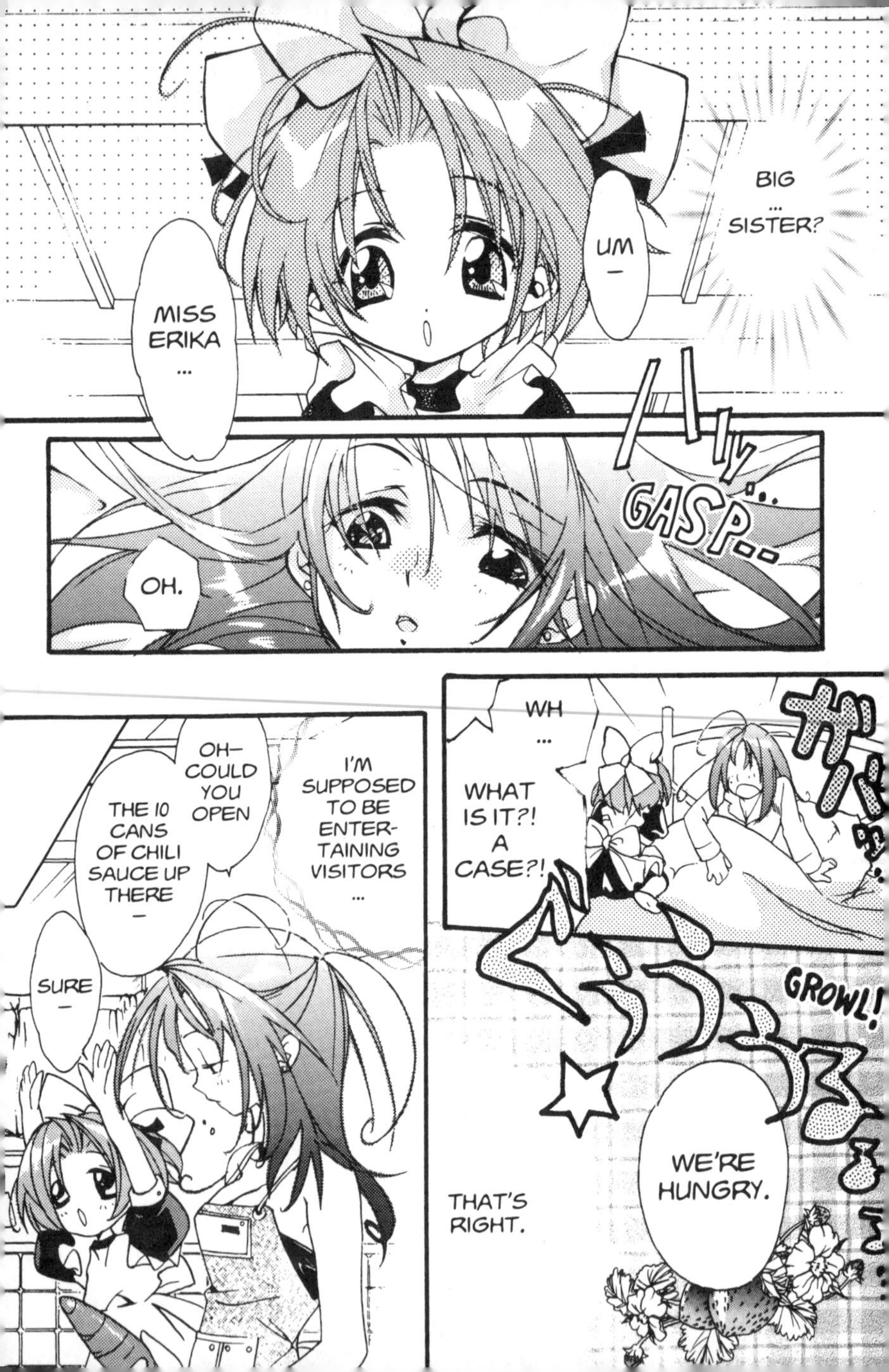
BIG ... SISTER?
UM —
MISS ERIKA ...
GASP...
OH.
WH ...
WHAT IS IT?! A CASE?!
GROWL!
WE'RE HUNGRY.
THAT'S RIGHT.
I'M SUPPOSED TO BE ENTER-TAINING VISITORS ...
OH— COULD YOU OPEN THE 10 CANS OF CHILI SAUCE UP THERE —
SURE —

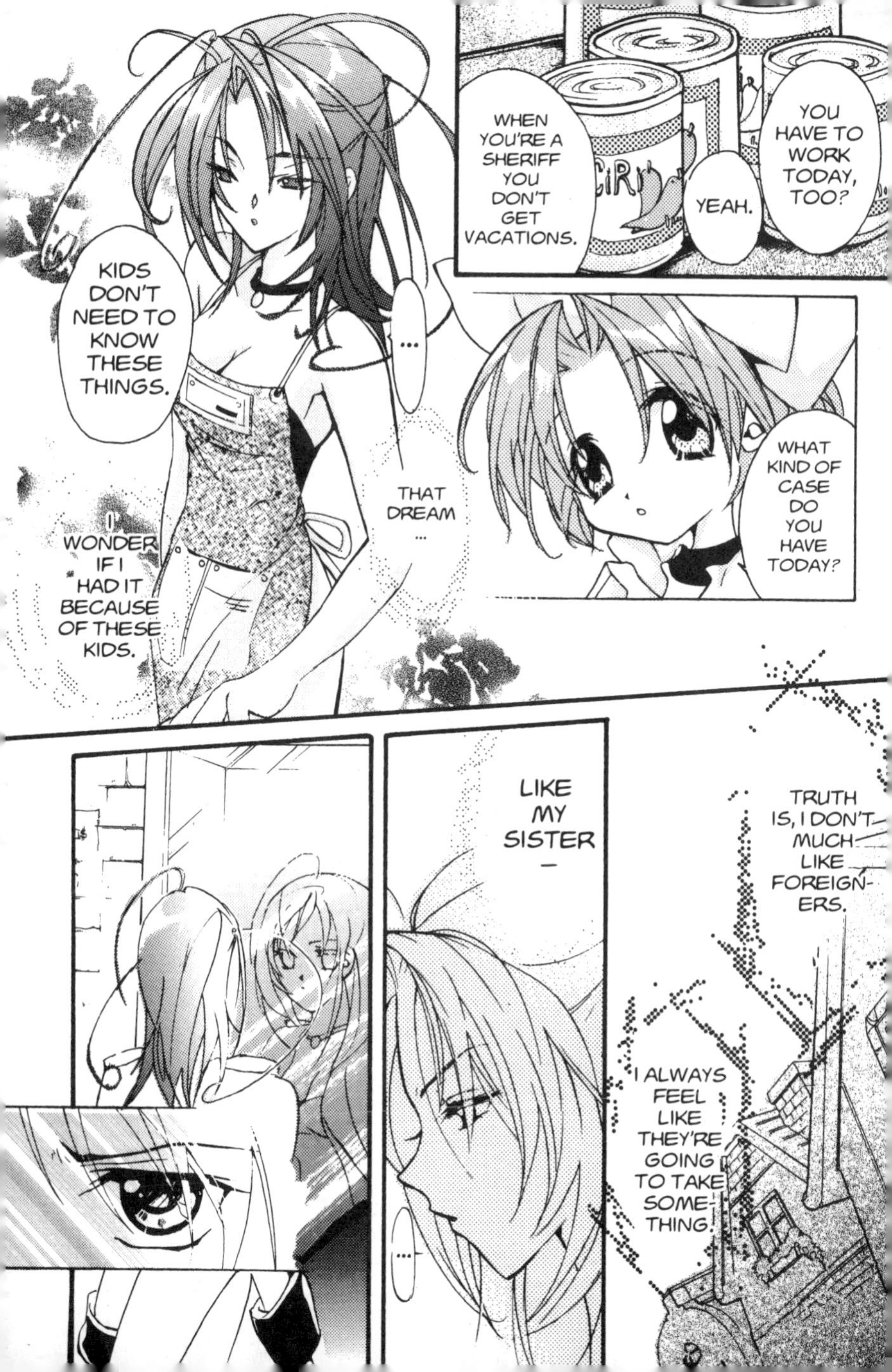
YOU HAVE TO WORK TODAY, TOO?
YEAH.
WHEN YOU'RE A SHERIFF YOU DON'T GET VACATIONS.
WHAT KIND OF CASE DO YOU HAVE TODAY?
...
KIDS DON'T NEED TO KNOW THESE THINGS.
THAT DREAM ...
I WONDER IF I HAD IT BECAUSE OF THESE KIDS.
TRUTH IS, I DON'T MUCH LIKE FOREIGNERS.
I ALWAYS FEEL LIKE THEY'RE GOING TO TAKE SOME-THING.
LIKE MY SISTER —
...

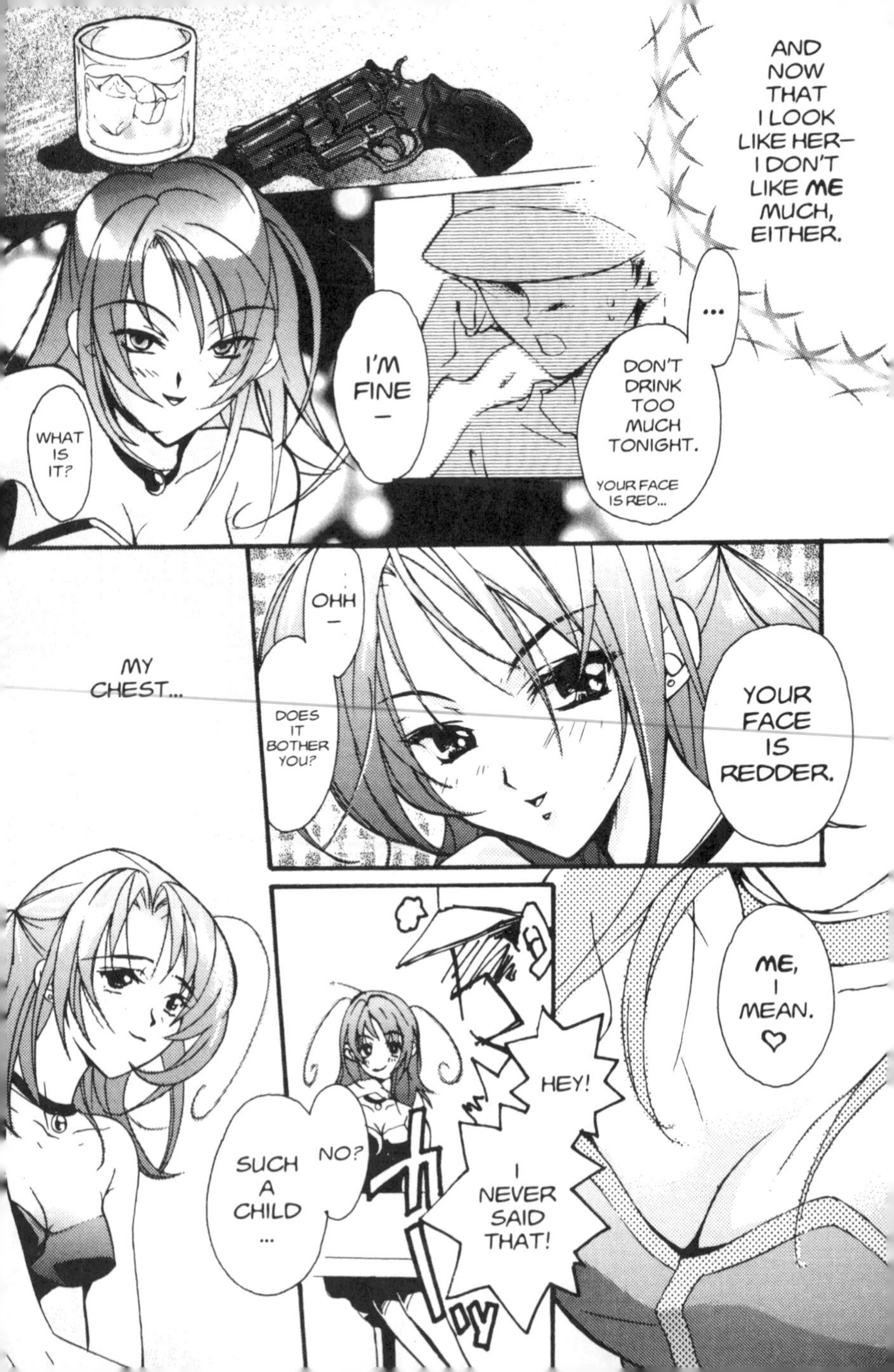
AND NOW THAT I LOOK LIKE HER— I DON'T LIKE ME MUCH, EITHER.
...
DON'T DRINK TOO MUCH TONIGHT.
YOUR FACE IS RED...
I'M FINE —
WHAT IS IT?
YOUR FACE IS REDDER.
OHH —
DOES IT BOTHER YOU?
MY CHEST...
ME, I MEAN. ♡
HEY!
I NEVER SAID THAT!
NO?
SUCH A CHILD ...

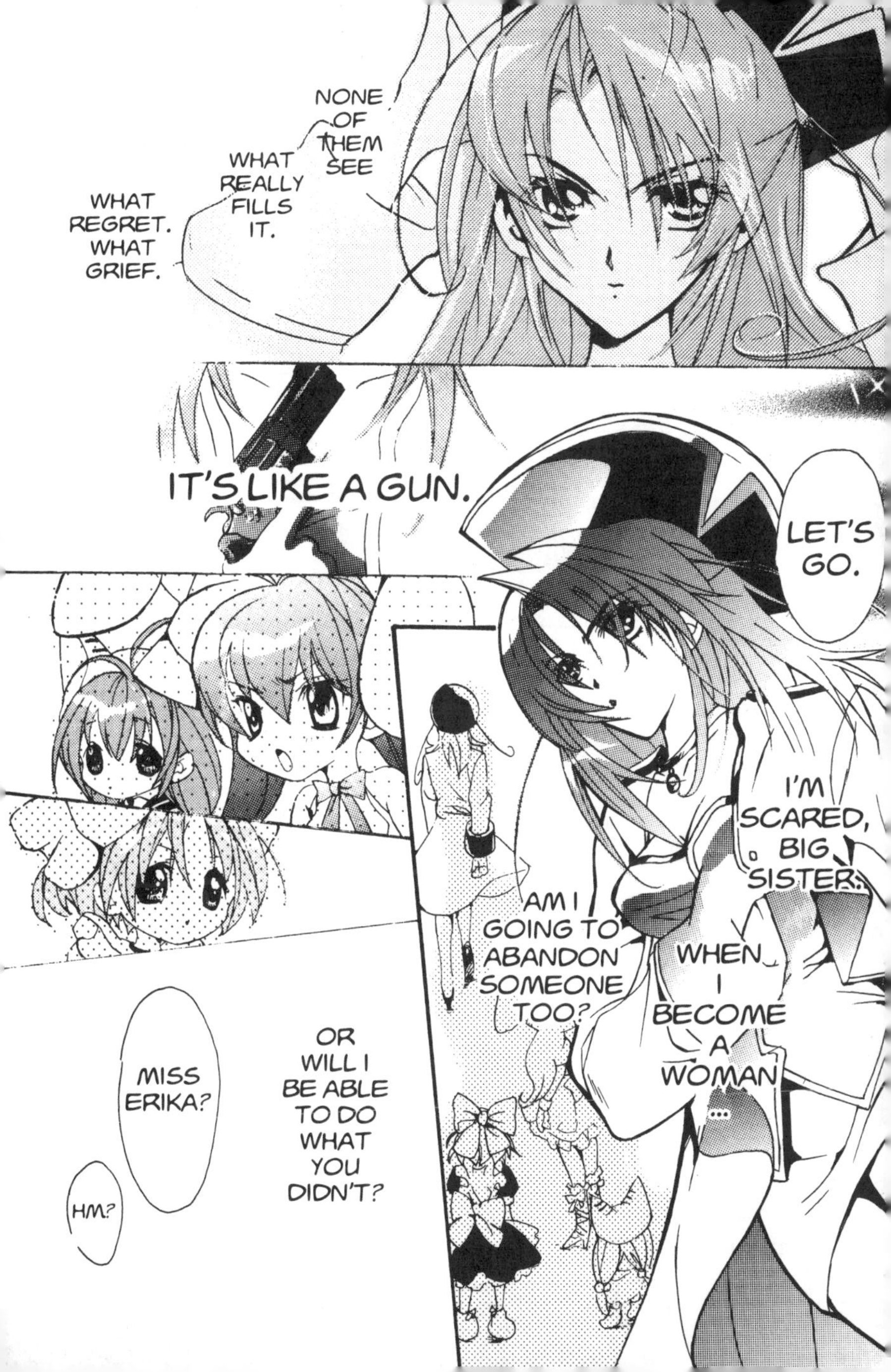
NONE OF THEM SEE
WHAT REALLY FILLS IT.
WHAT REGRET. WHAT GRIEF.
LET'S GO.
I'M SCARED, BIG SISTER.
WHEN I BECOME A WOMAN...
AM I GOING TO ABANDON SOMEONE TOO?
IT'S LIKE A GUN.
OR WILL I BE ABLE TO DO WHAT YOU DIDN'T?
MISS ERIKA?
HM?

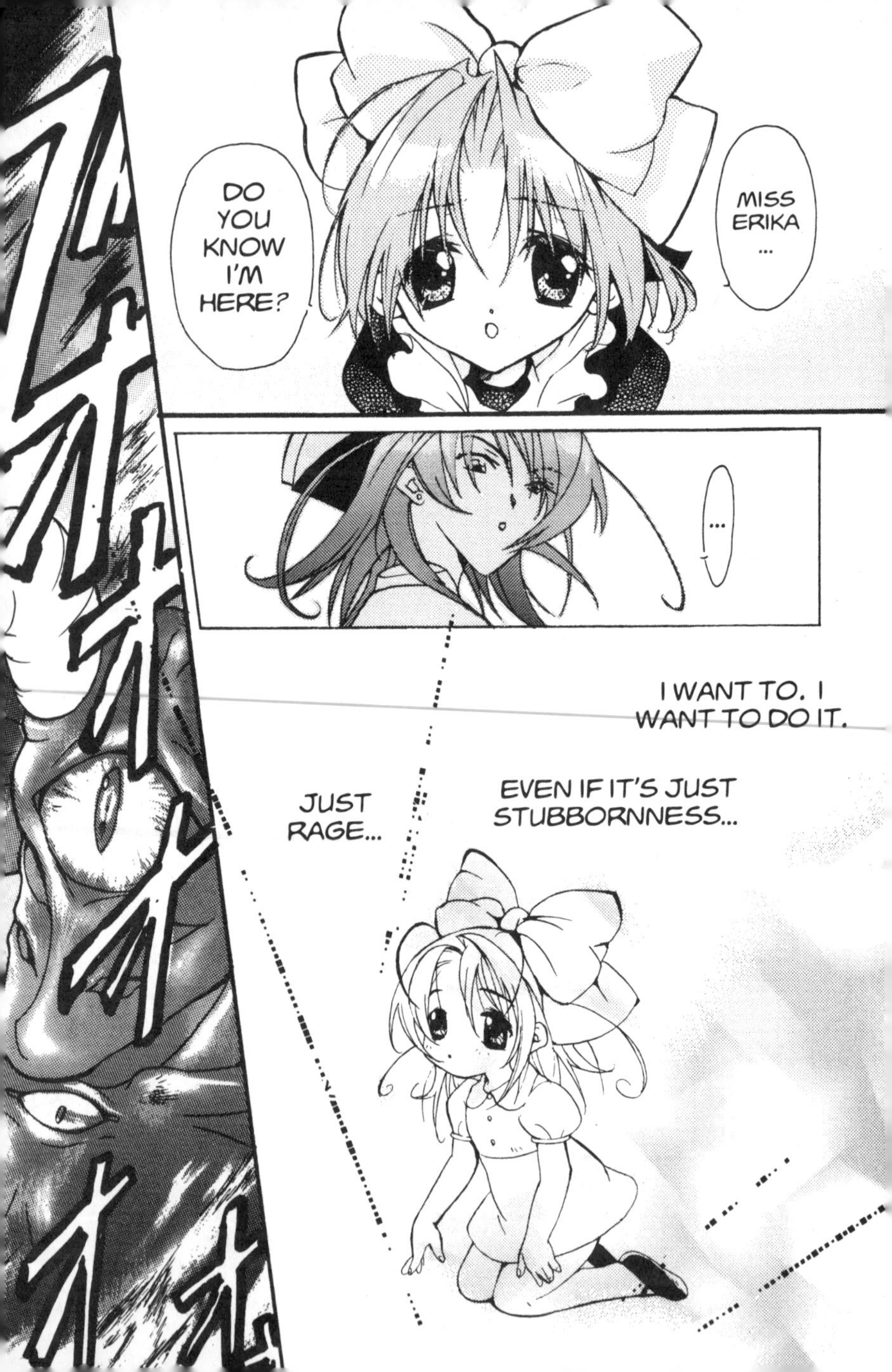
MISS ERIKA ...
DO YOU KNOW I'M HERE?
...
I WANT TO. I WANT TO DO IT.
EVEN IF IT'S JUST STUBBORNNESS...
JUST RAGE...

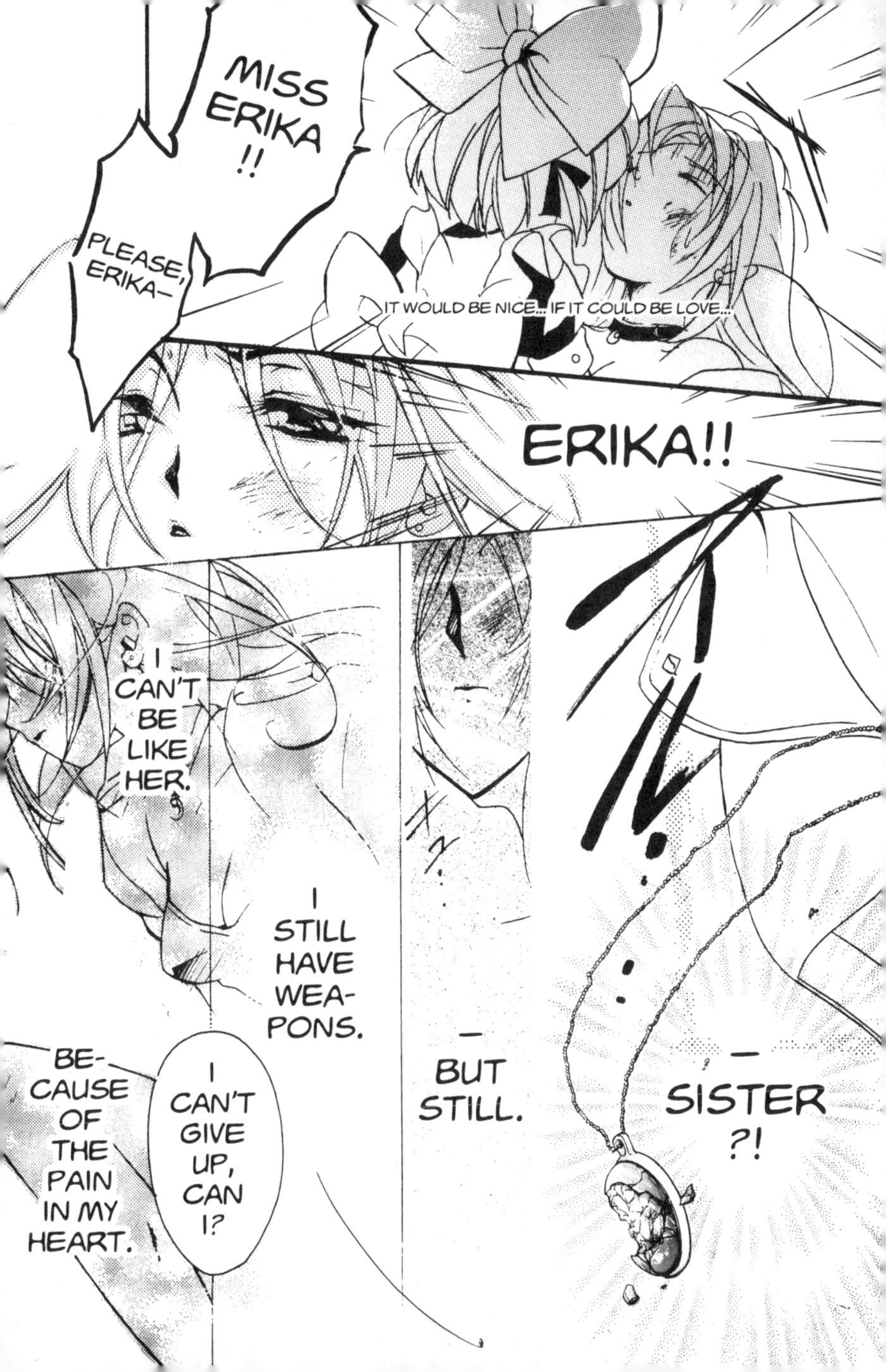
MISS ERIKA!!
PLEASE, ERIKA—
IT WOULD BE NICE... IF IT COULD BE LOVE...
ERIKA!!
—SISTER?!
—BUT STILL.
I STILL HAVE WEAPONS.
I CAN'T BE LIKE HER.
I CAN'T GIVE UP, CAN I?
BECAUSE OF THE PAIN IN MY HEART.

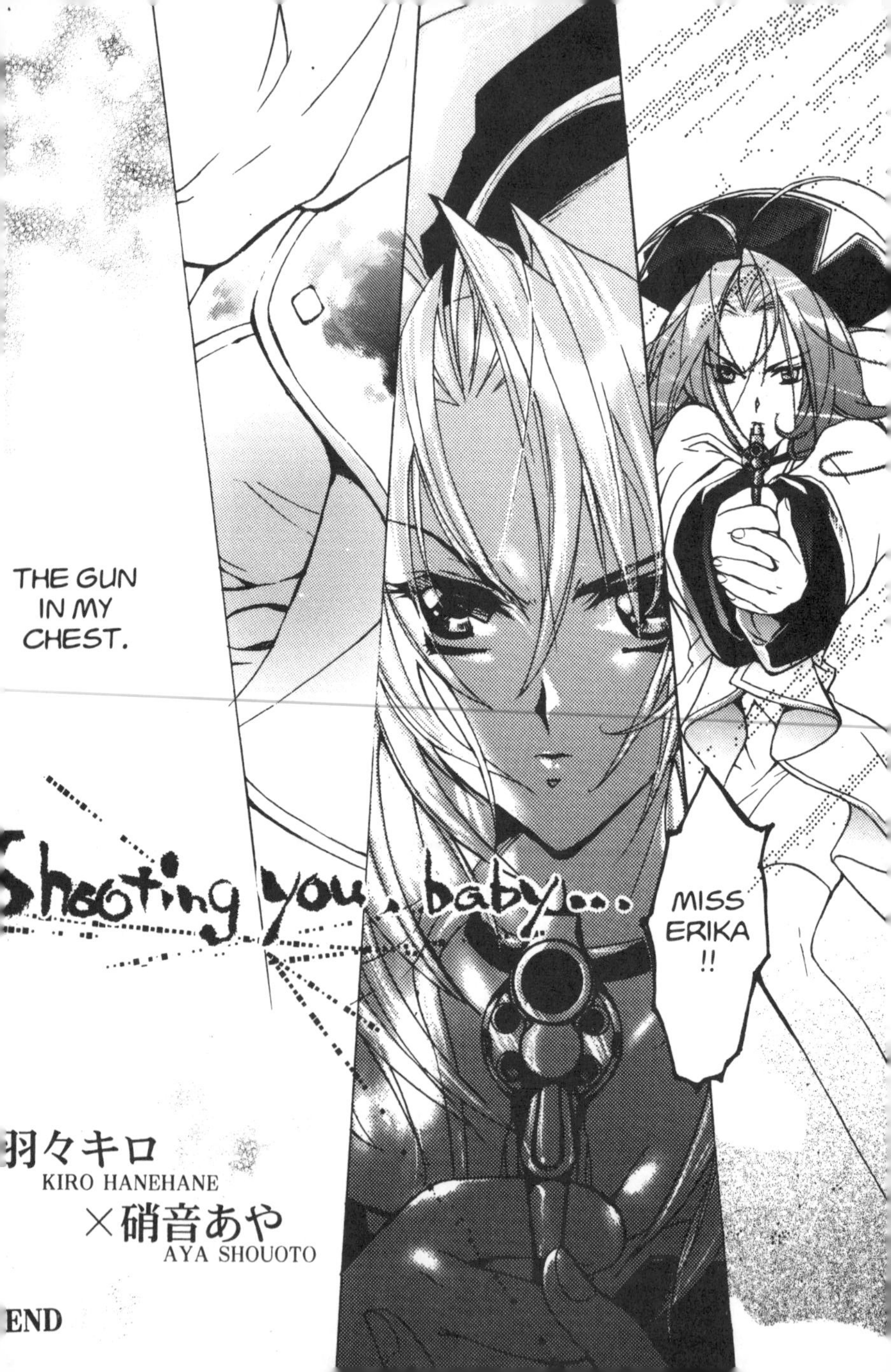
MISS ERIKA !!
THE GUN IN MY CHEST.
Shooting you...baby...
羽々キロ
KIRO HANEHANE
×硝音あや
AYA SHOUOTO
END

A WORD ABOUT "DI-GI-CHARAT"!

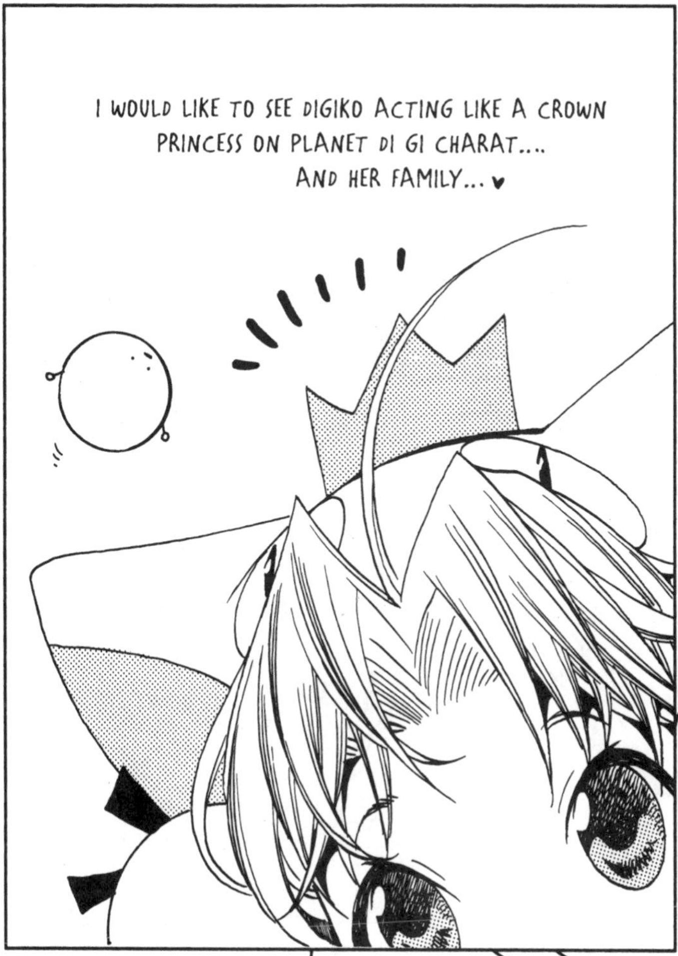
I WOULD LIKE TO SEE DIGIKO ACTING LIKE A CROWN PRINCESS ON PLANET DI GI CHARAT....
AND HER FAMILY...♥

TOWA OZORA

A WORD ABOUT "DI-GI-CHARAT"!

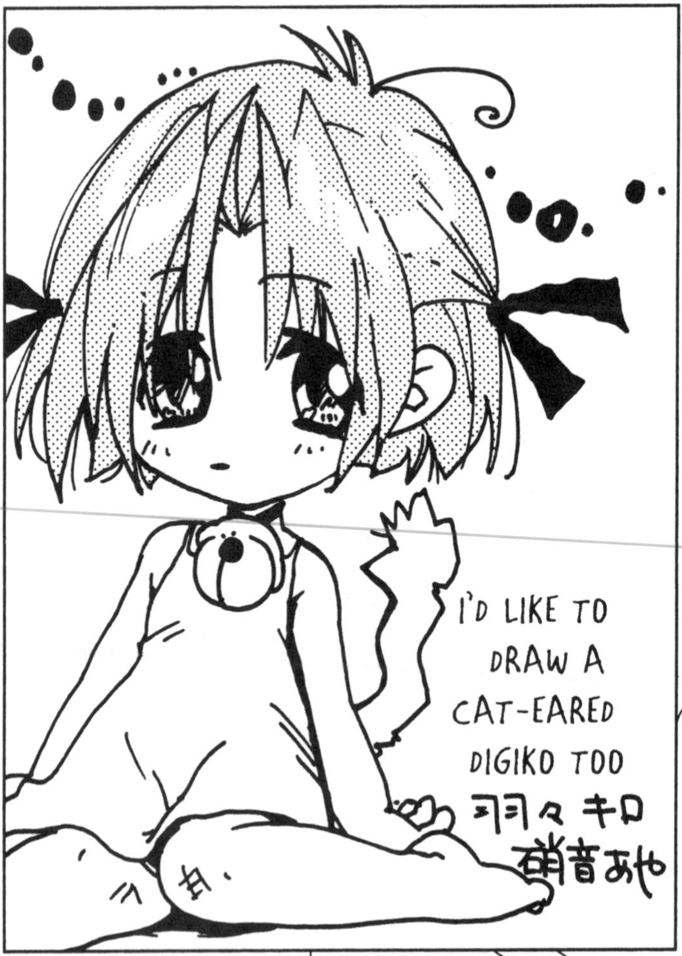
I'D LIKE TO DRAW A CAT-EARED DIGIKO TOO
羽々キロ
硝音あや

KIRO HANEHANE
& AYA SHOUOTO

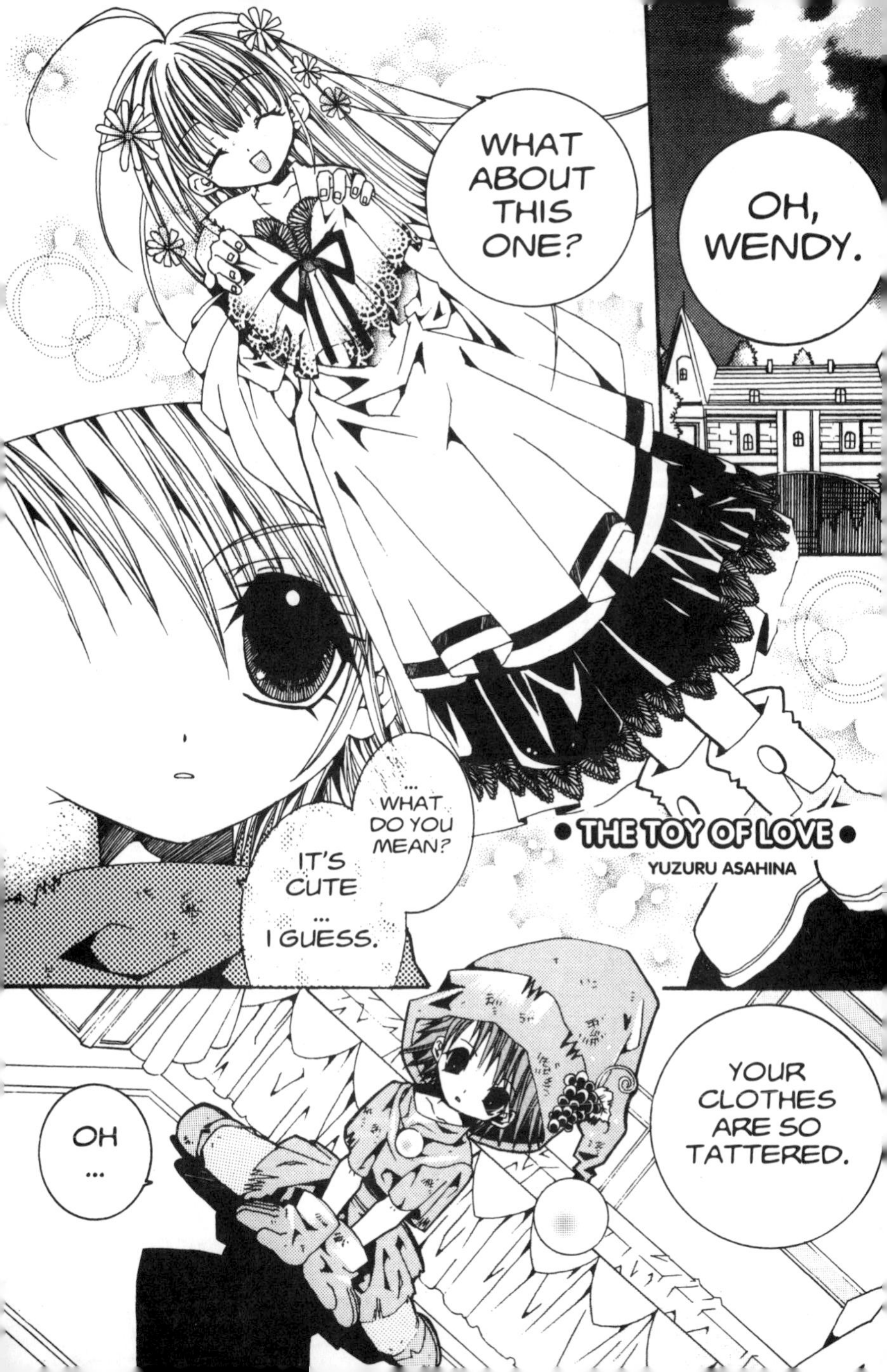
OH, WENDY.
WHAT ABOUT THIS ONE?
... WHAT DO YOU MEAN?
IT'S CUTE ... I GUESS.
• THE TOY OF LOVE •
YUZURU ASAHINA
YOUR CLOTHES ARE SO TATTERED.
OH ...

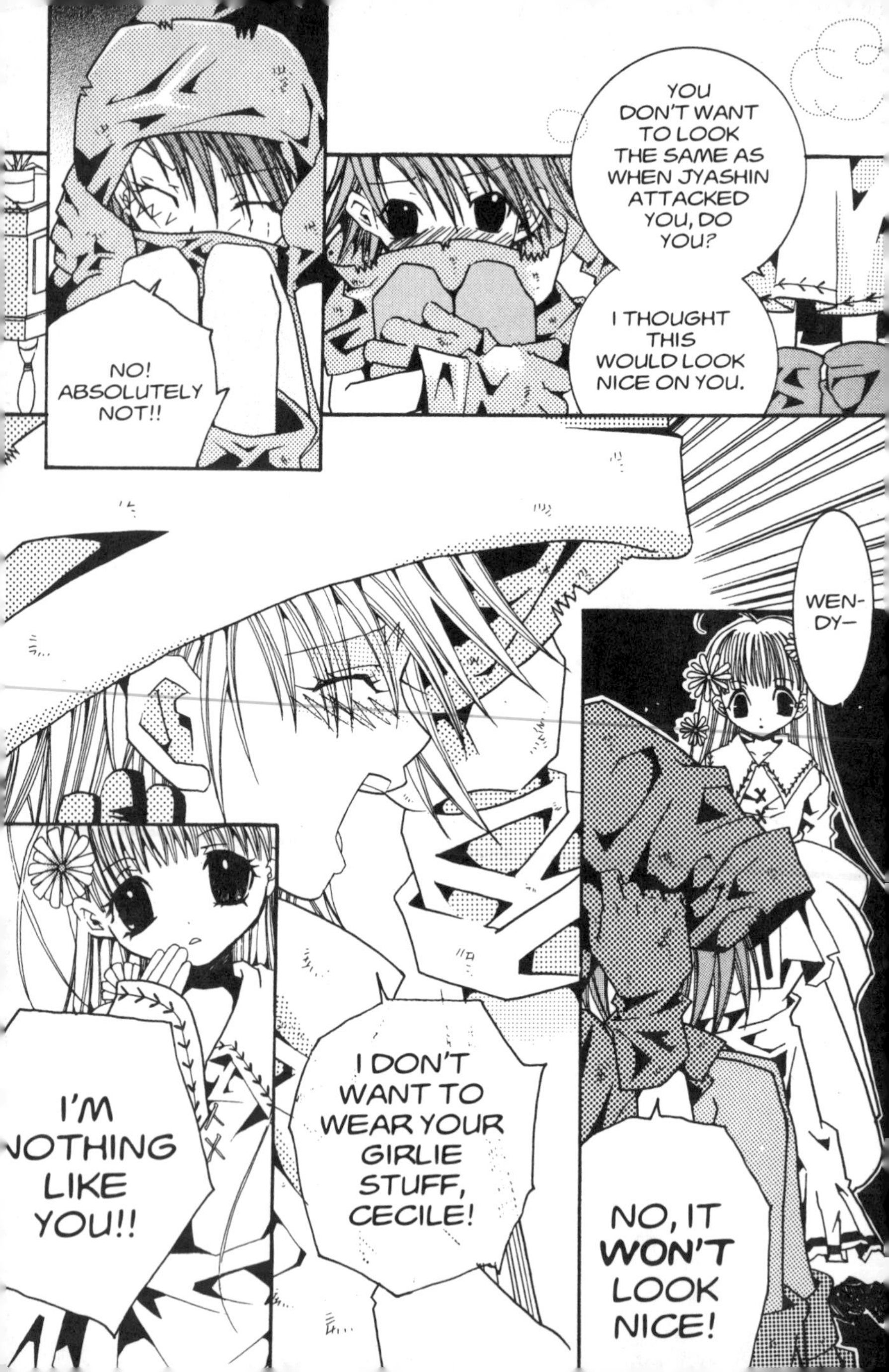
YOU DON'T WANT TO LOOK THE SAME AS WHEN JYASHIN ATTACKED YOU, DO YOU?
I THOUGHT THIS WOULD LOOK NICE ON YOU.
NO! ABSOLUTELY NOT!!
WEN-DY—
NO, IT WON'T LOOK NICE!
I DON'T WANT TO WEAR YOUR GIRLIE STUFF, CECILE!
I'M NOTHING LIKE YOU!!

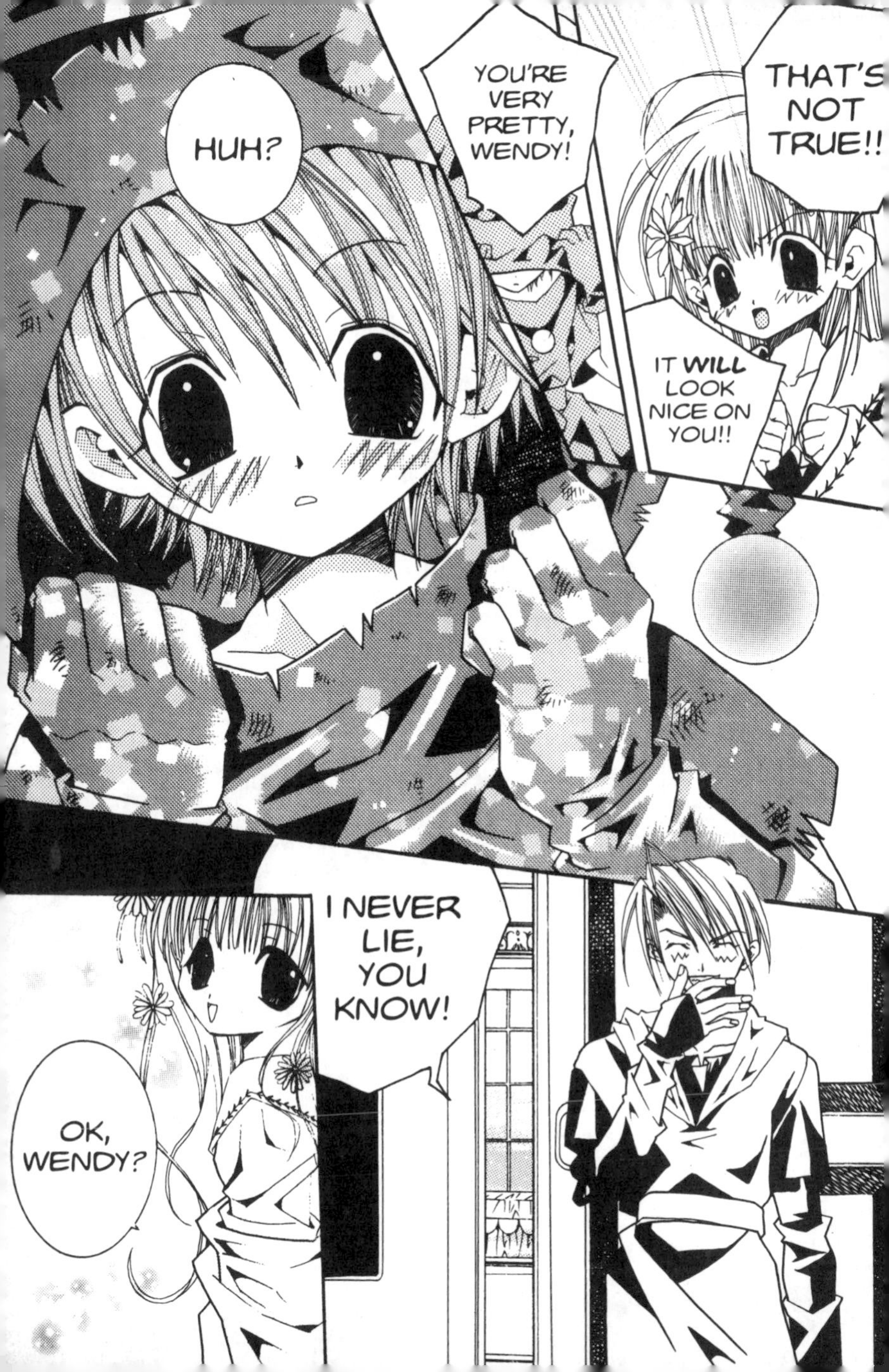
THAT'S NOT TRUE!!
IT WILL LOOK NICE ON YOU!!
YOU'RE VERY PRETTY, WENDY!
HUH?
I NEVER LIE, YOU KNOW!
OK, WENDY?

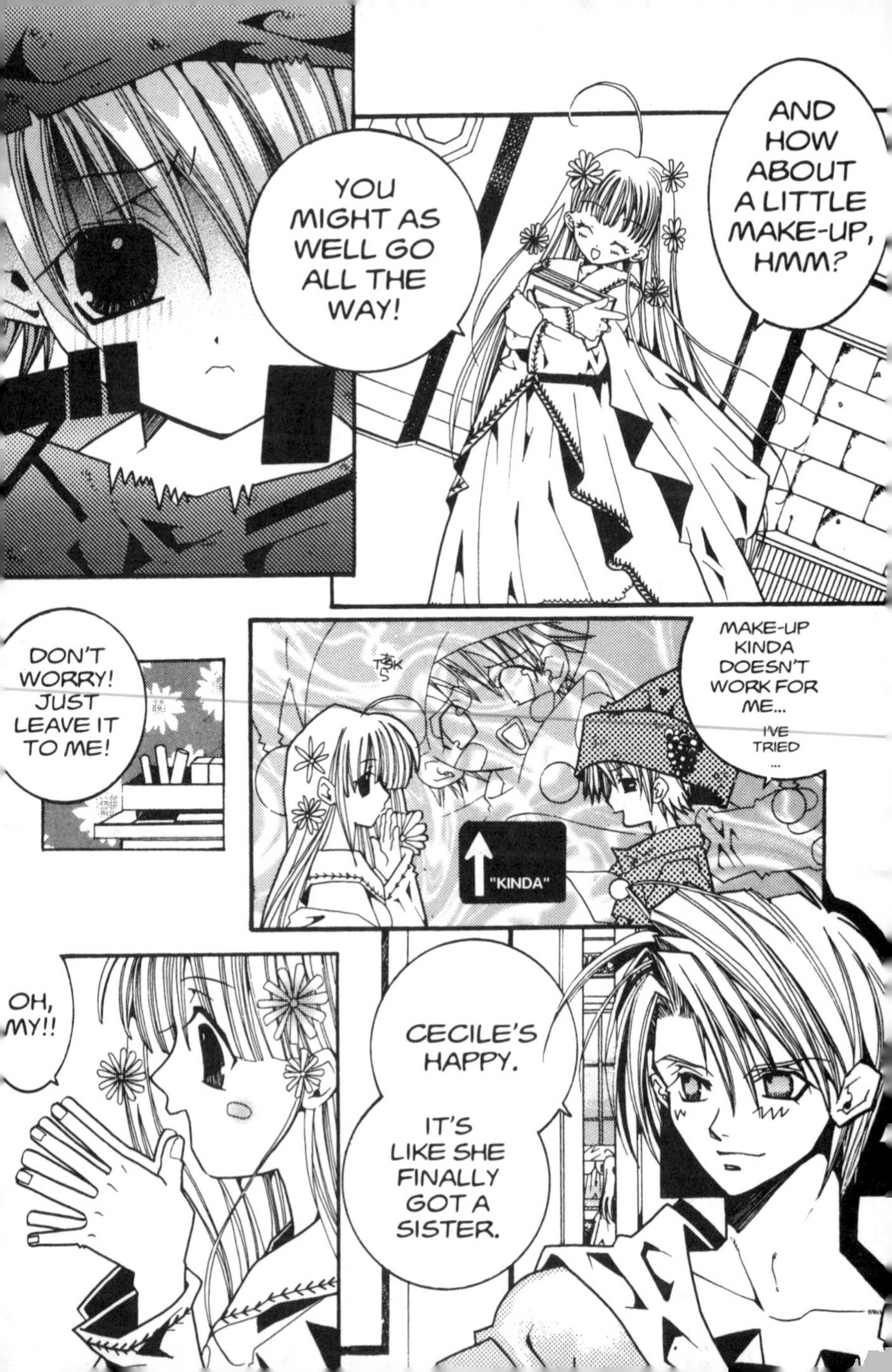
AND HOW ABOUT A LITTLE MAKE-UP, HMM?
YOU MIGHT AS WELL GO ALL THE WAY!
MAKE-UP KINDA DOESN'T WORK FOR ME...
I'VE TRIED ...
TSK
"KINDA"
DON'T WORRY! JUST LEAVE IT TO ME!
CECILE'S HAPPY.
IT'S LIKE SHE FINALLY GOT A SISTER.
OH, MY!!

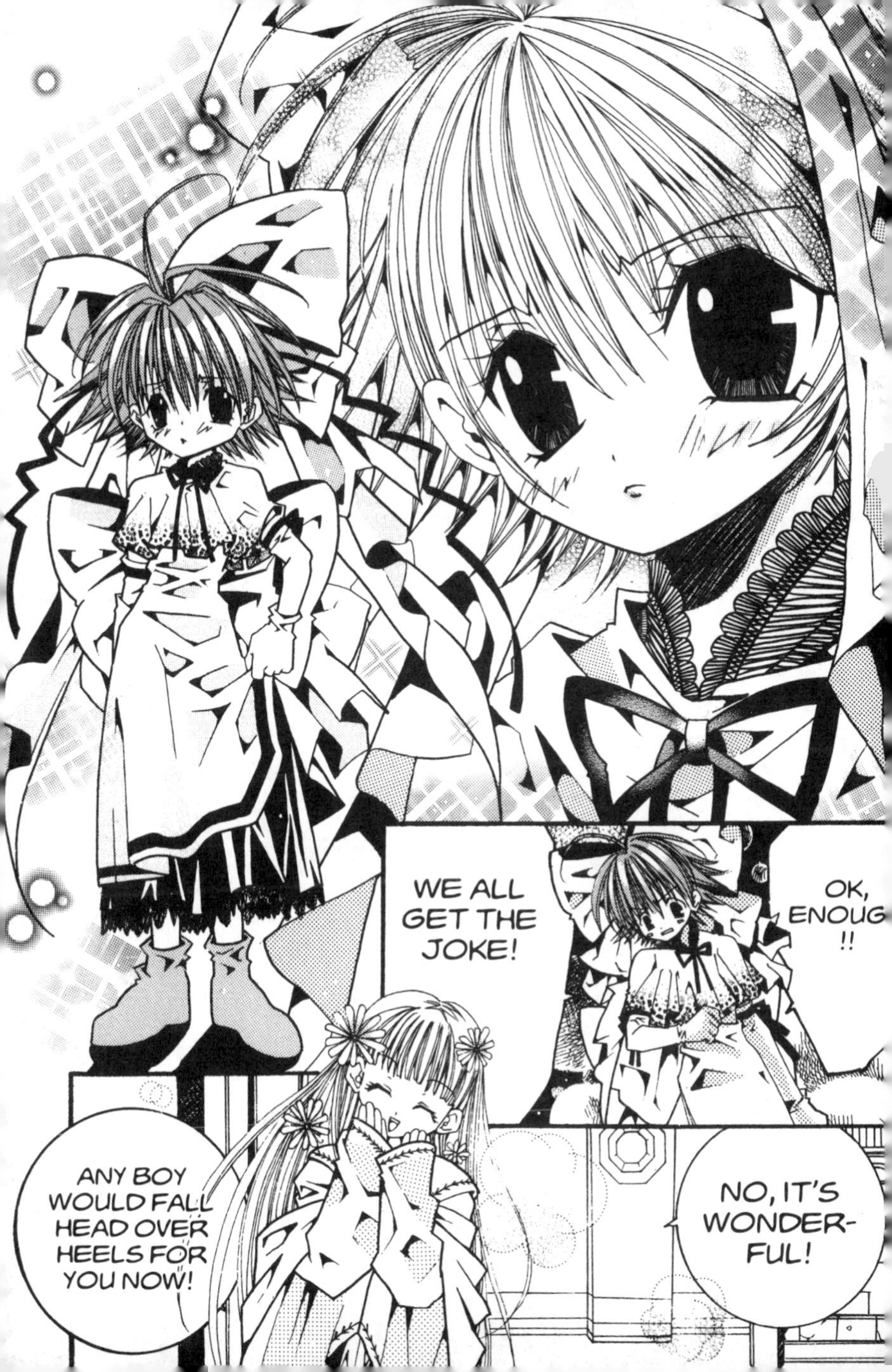
OK, ENOUG !!
WE ALL GET THE JOKE!
NO, IT'S WONDER-FUL!
ANY BOY WOULD FALL HEAD OVER HEELS FOR YOU NOW!

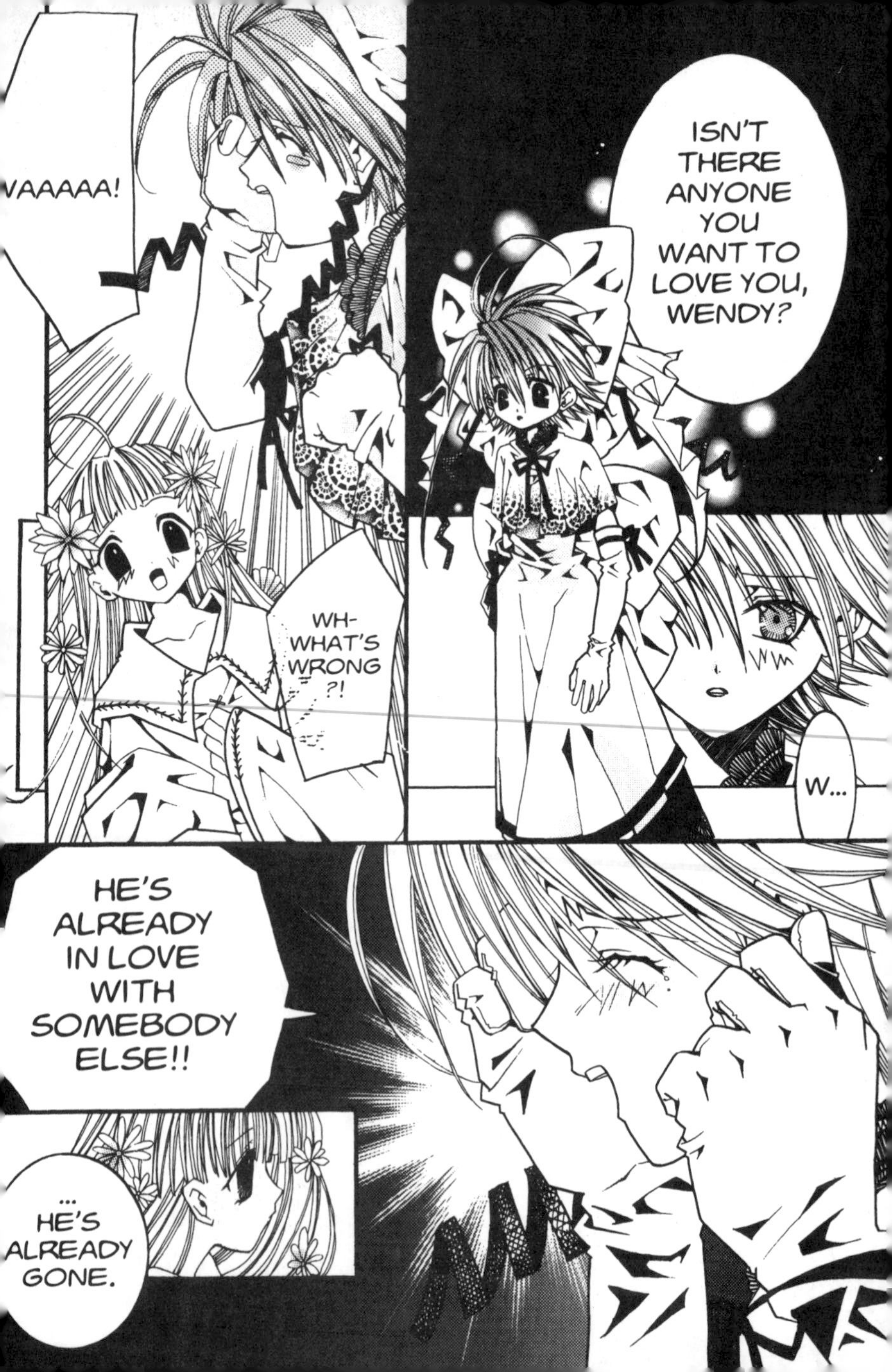
ISN'T THERE ANYONE YOU WANT TO LOVE YOU, WENDY?
W...
VAAAAA!
WH- WHAT'S WRONG ?!
HE'S ALREADY IN LOVE WITH SOMEBODY ELSE!!
... HE'S ALREADY GONE.

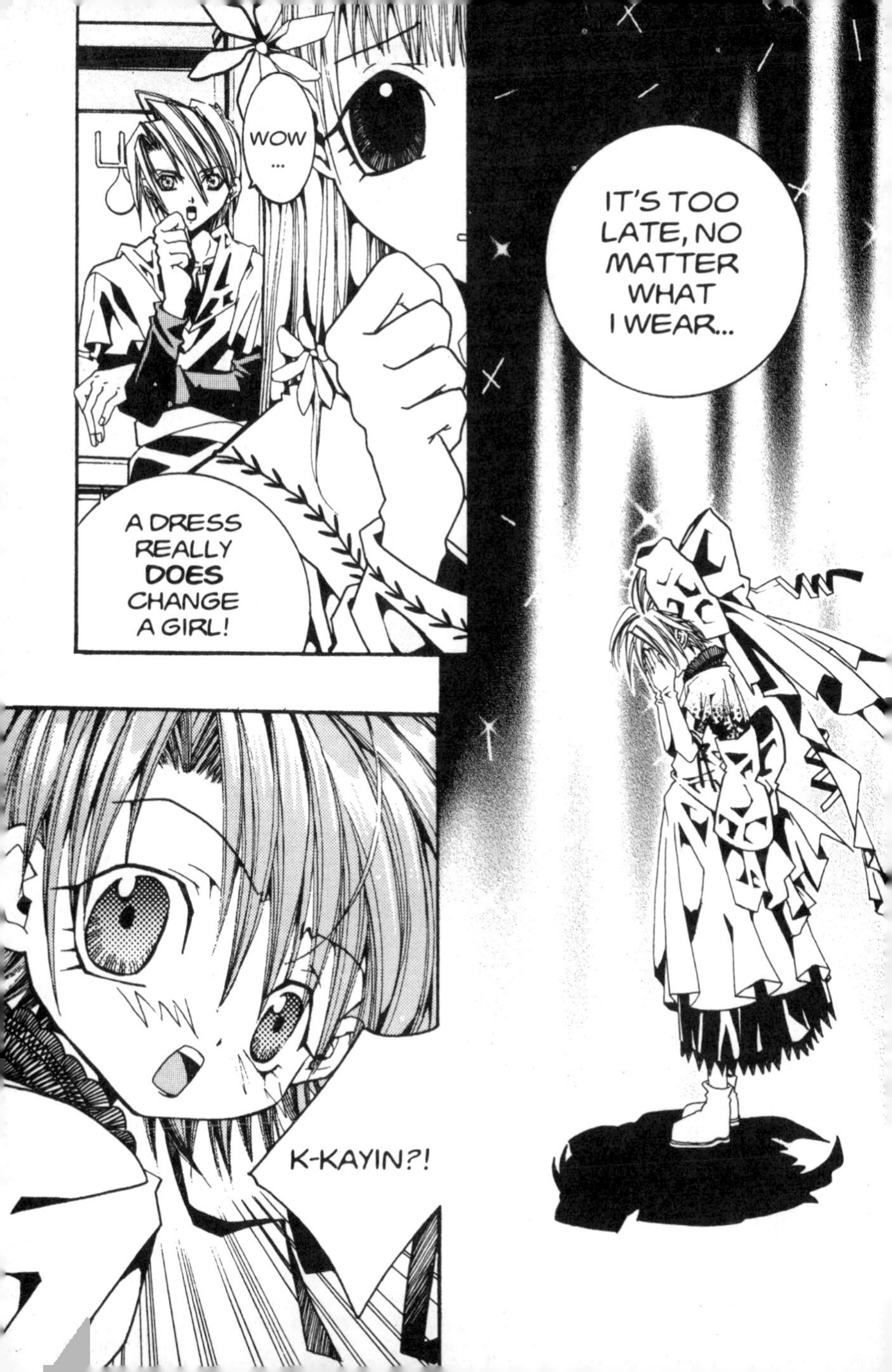
IT'S TOO LATE, NO MATTER WHAT I WEAR...
WOW ...
A DRESS REALLY **DOES** CHANGE A GIRL!
K-KAYIN?!

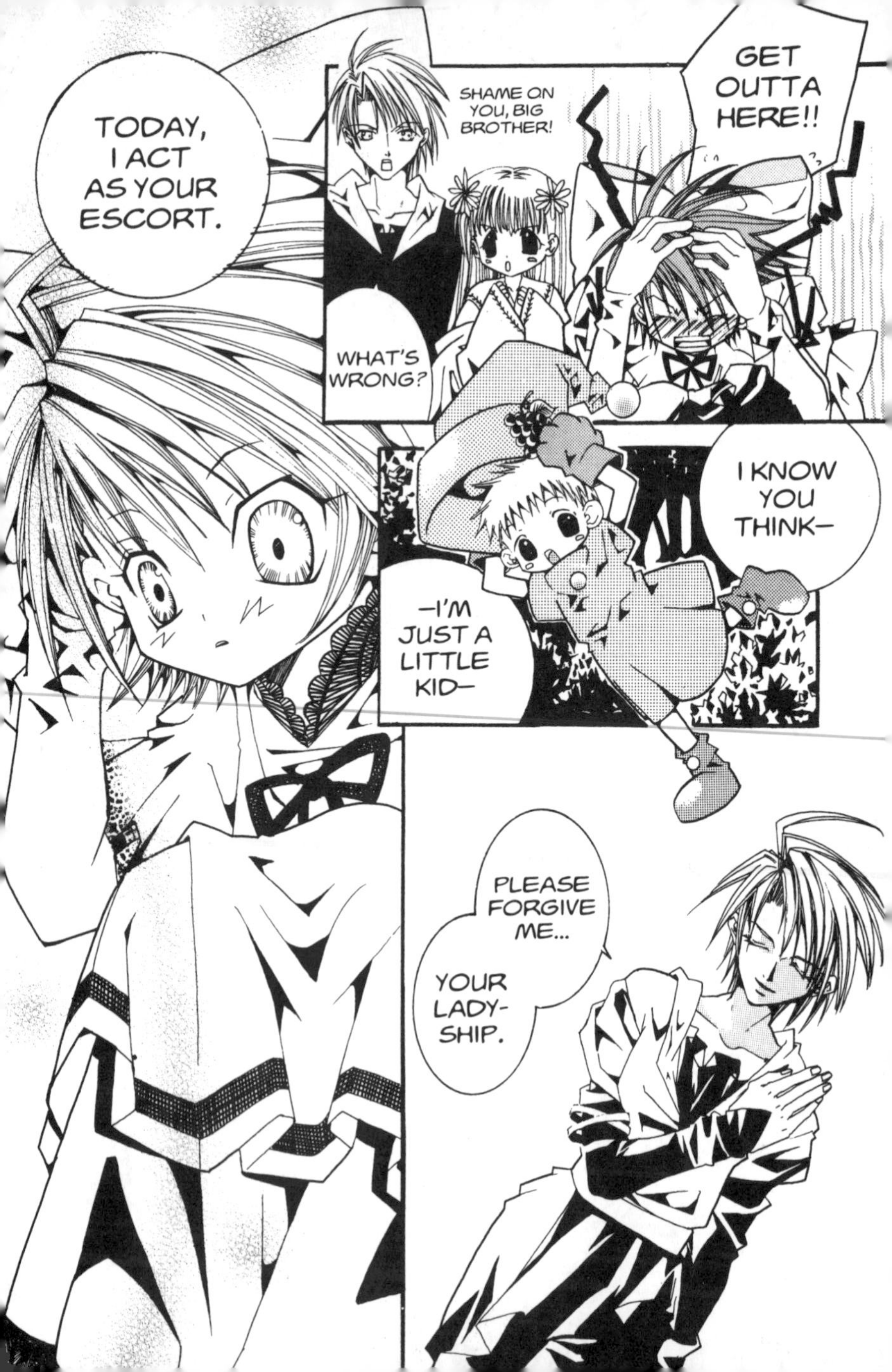
GET OUTTA HERE!!
SHAME ON YOU, BIG BROTHER!
WHAT'S WRONG?
I KNOW YOU THINK—
—I'M JUST A LITTLE KID—
PLEASE FORGIVE ME...
YOUR LADY-SHIP.
TODAY, I ACT AS YOUR ESCORT.

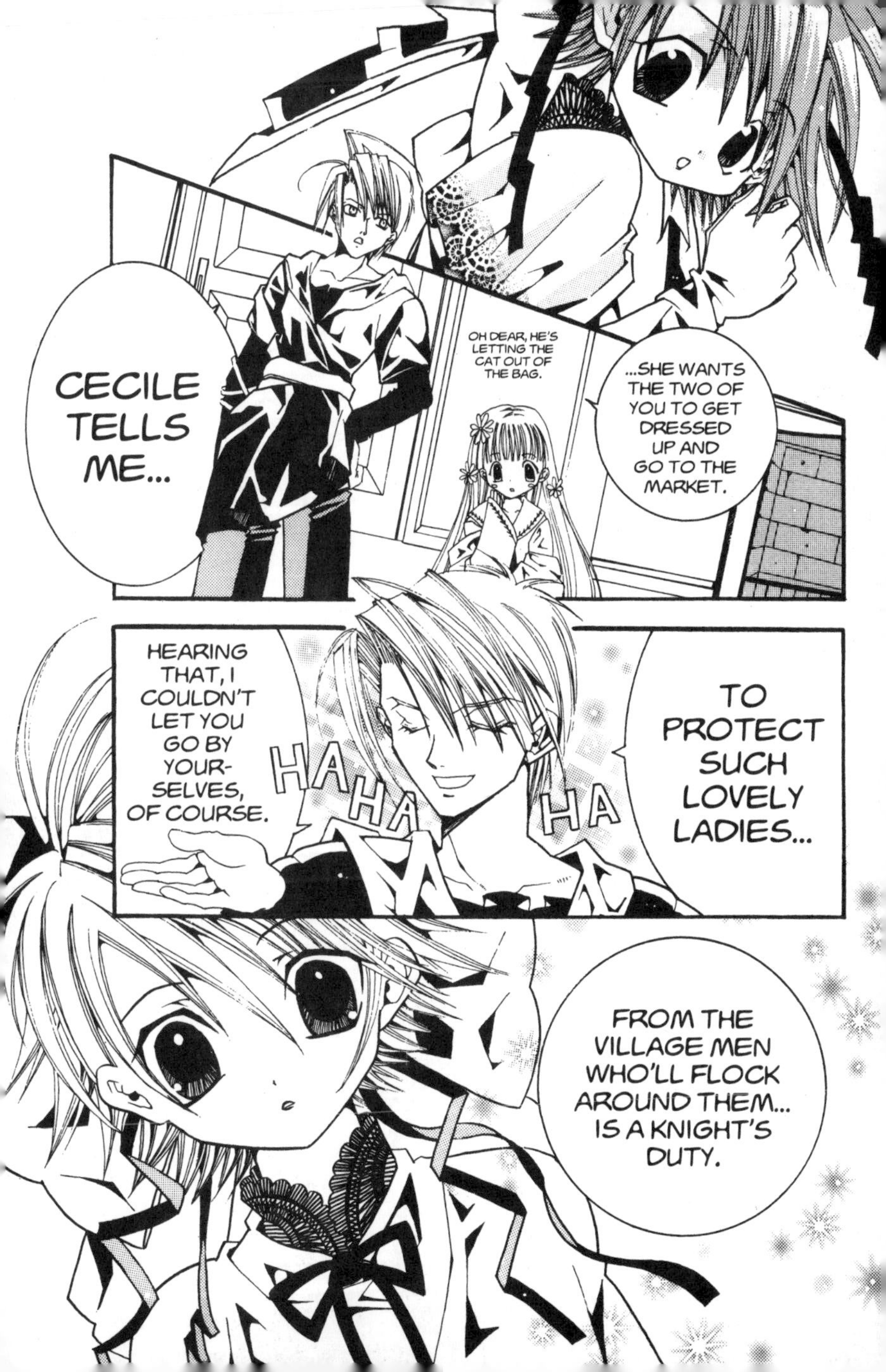
CECILE TELLS ME...
...SHE WANTS THE TWO OF YOU TO GET DRESSED UP AND GO TO THE MARKET.
OH DEAR, HE'S LETTING THE CAT OUT OF THE BAG.
HEARING THAT, I COULDN'T LET YOU GO BY YOUR-SELVES, OF COURSE.
HAHAHA
TO PROTECT SUCH LOVELY LADIES...
FROM THE VILLAGE MEN WHO'LL FLOCK AROUND THEM... IS A KNIGHT'S DUTY.

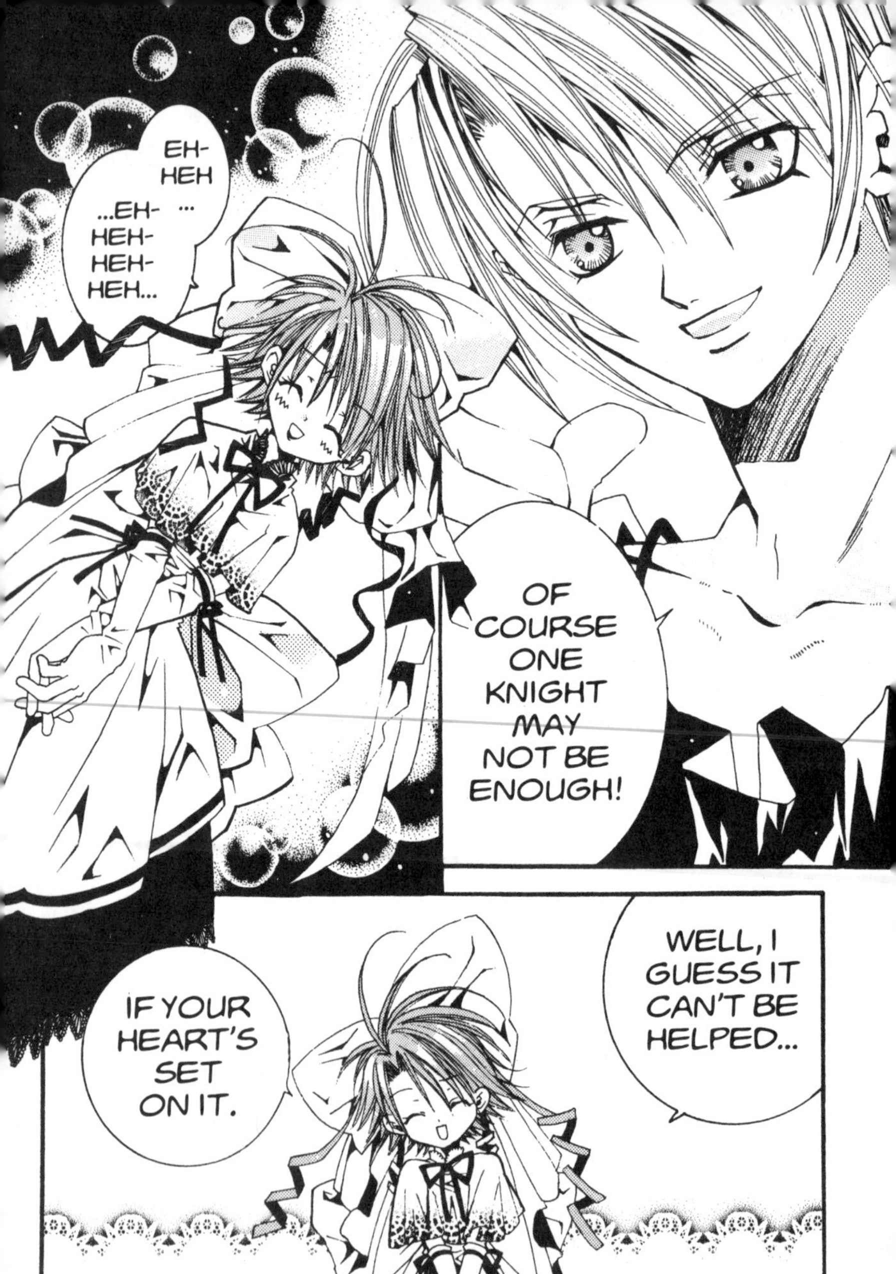
OF COURSE ONE KNIGHT MAY NOT BE ENOUGH!
EH-HEH ...
...EH-HEH-HEH-HEH...
WELL, I GUESS IT CAN'T BE HELPED...
IF YOUR HEART'S SET ON IT.

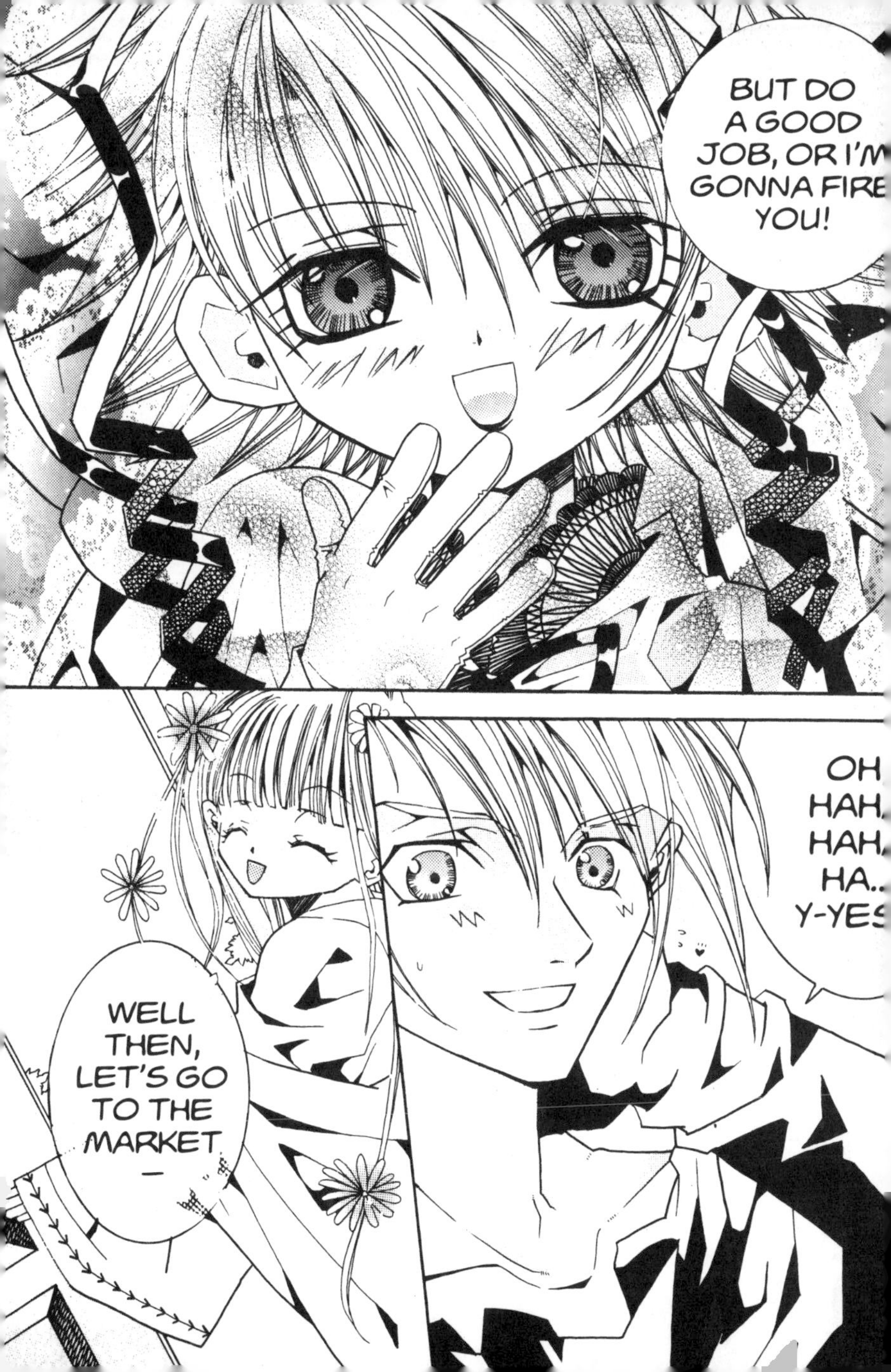
BUT DO A GOOD JOB, OR I'M GONNA FIRE YOU!
OH HAH, HAH, HA... Y-YES
WELL THEN, LET'S GO TO THE MARKET —

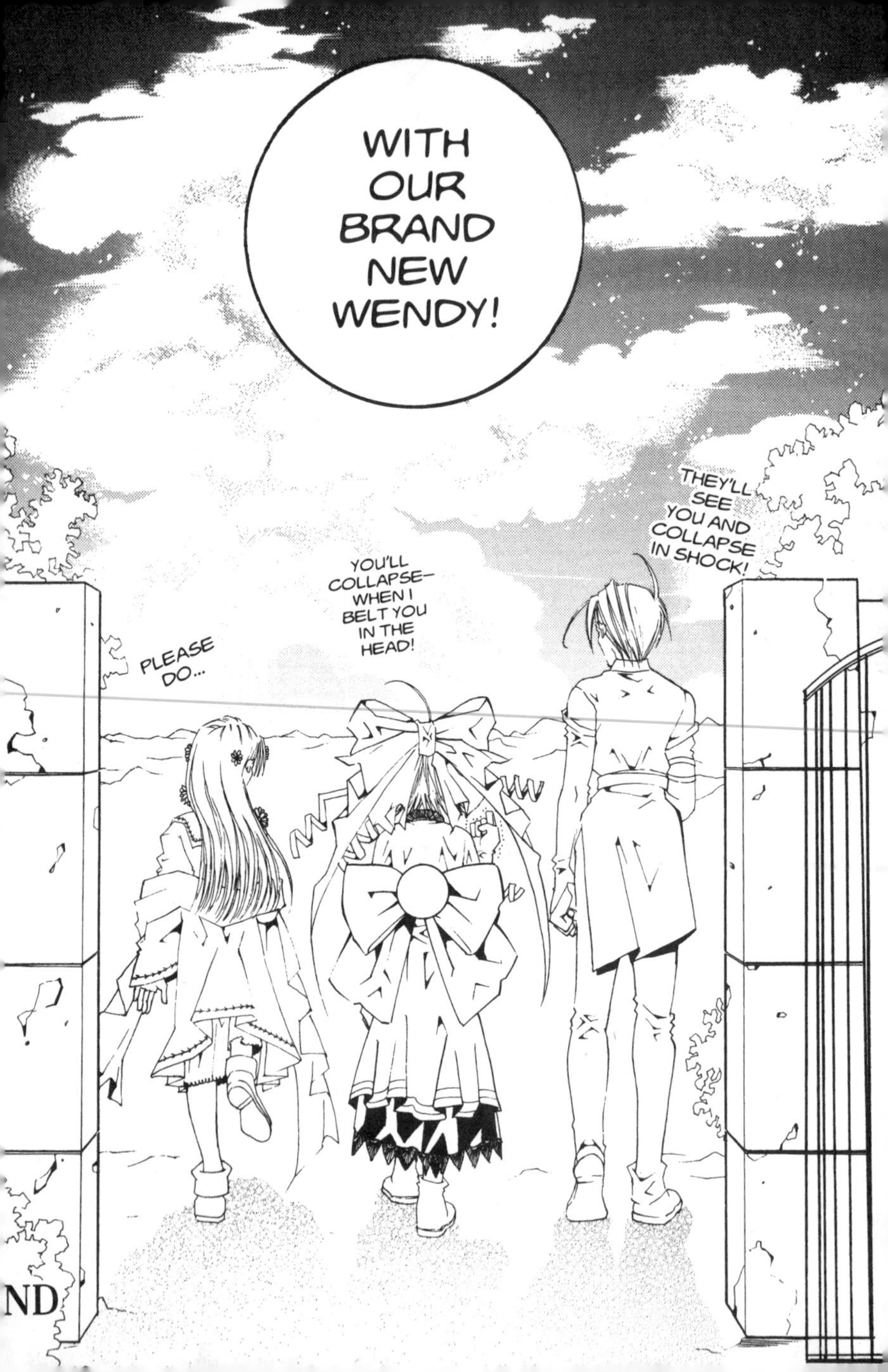
WITH OUR BRAND NEW WENDY!
THEY'LL SEE YOU AND COLLAPSE IN SHOCK!
YOU'LL COLLAPSE— WHEN I BELT YOU IN THE HEAD!
PLEASE DO...
ND

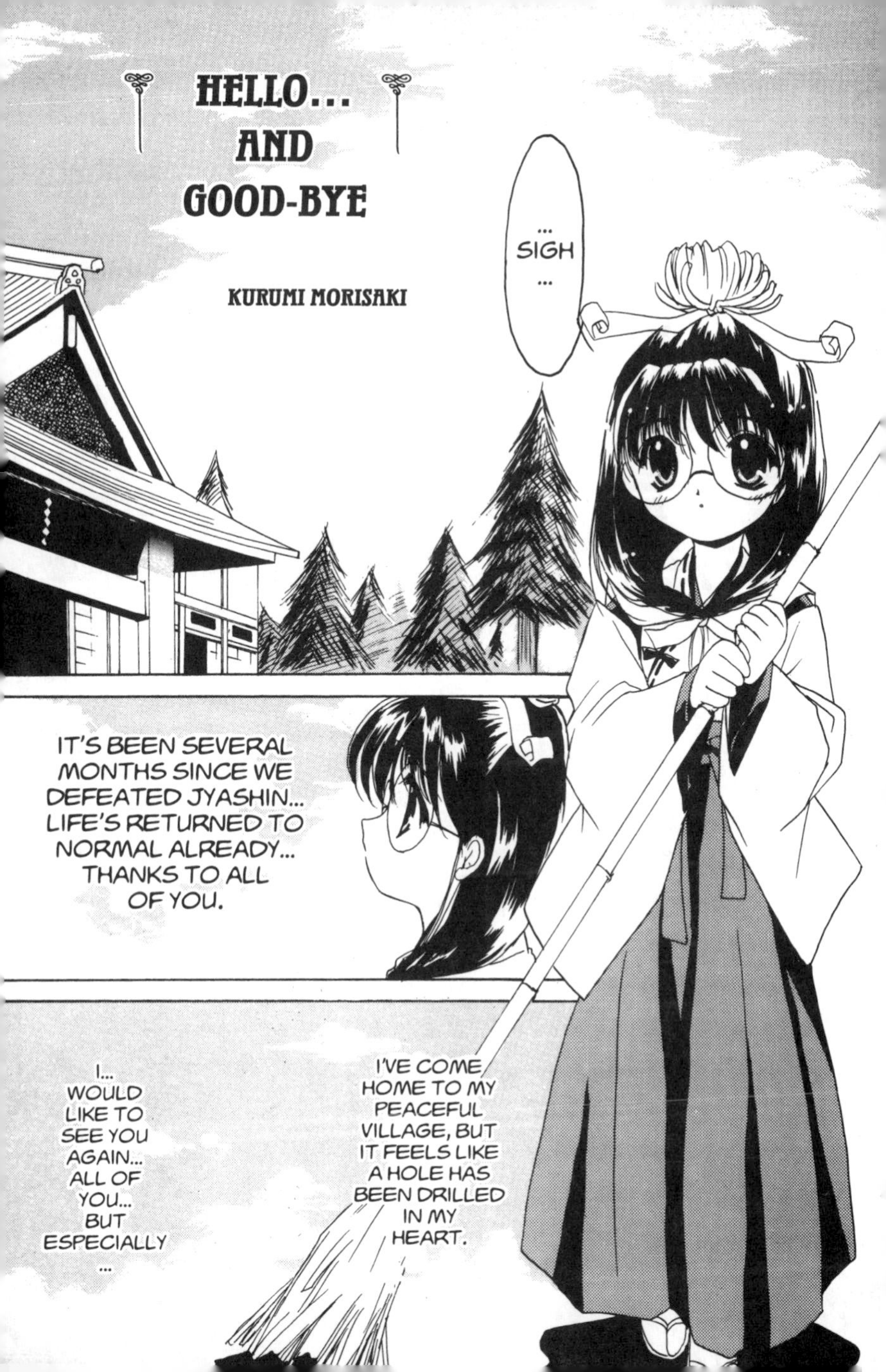
HELLO... AND GOOD-BYE
... SIGH ...
KURUMI MORISAKI
IT'S BEEN SEVERAL MONTHS SINCE WE DEFEATED JYASHIN... LIFE'S RETURNED TO NORMAL ALREADY... THANKS TO ALL OF YOU.
I'VE COME HOME TO MY PEACEFUL VILLAGE, BUT IT FEELS LIKE A HOLE HAS BEEN DRILLED IN MY HEART.
I... WOULD LIKE TO SEE YOU AGAIN... ALL OF YOU... BUT ESPECIALLY ...

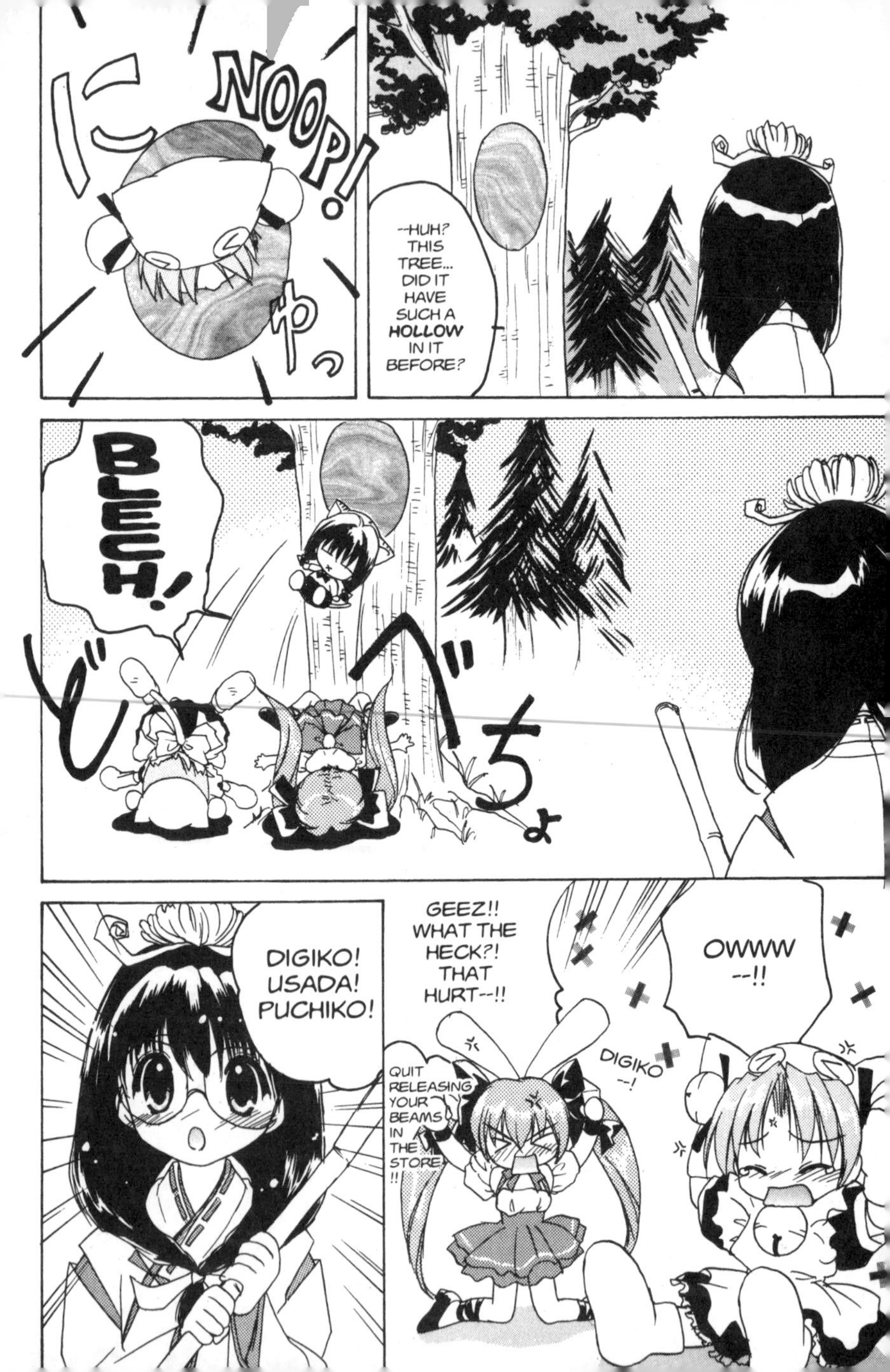
--HUH? THIS TREE... DID IT HAVE SUCH A HOLLOW IN IT BEFORE?
NOOP!
BLECH!
OWWW --!!
GEEZ!! WHAT THE HECK?! THAT HURT--!!
DIGIKO --!
QUIT RELEASING YOUR BEAMS IN THE STORE !!
DIGIKO! USADA! PUCHIKO!

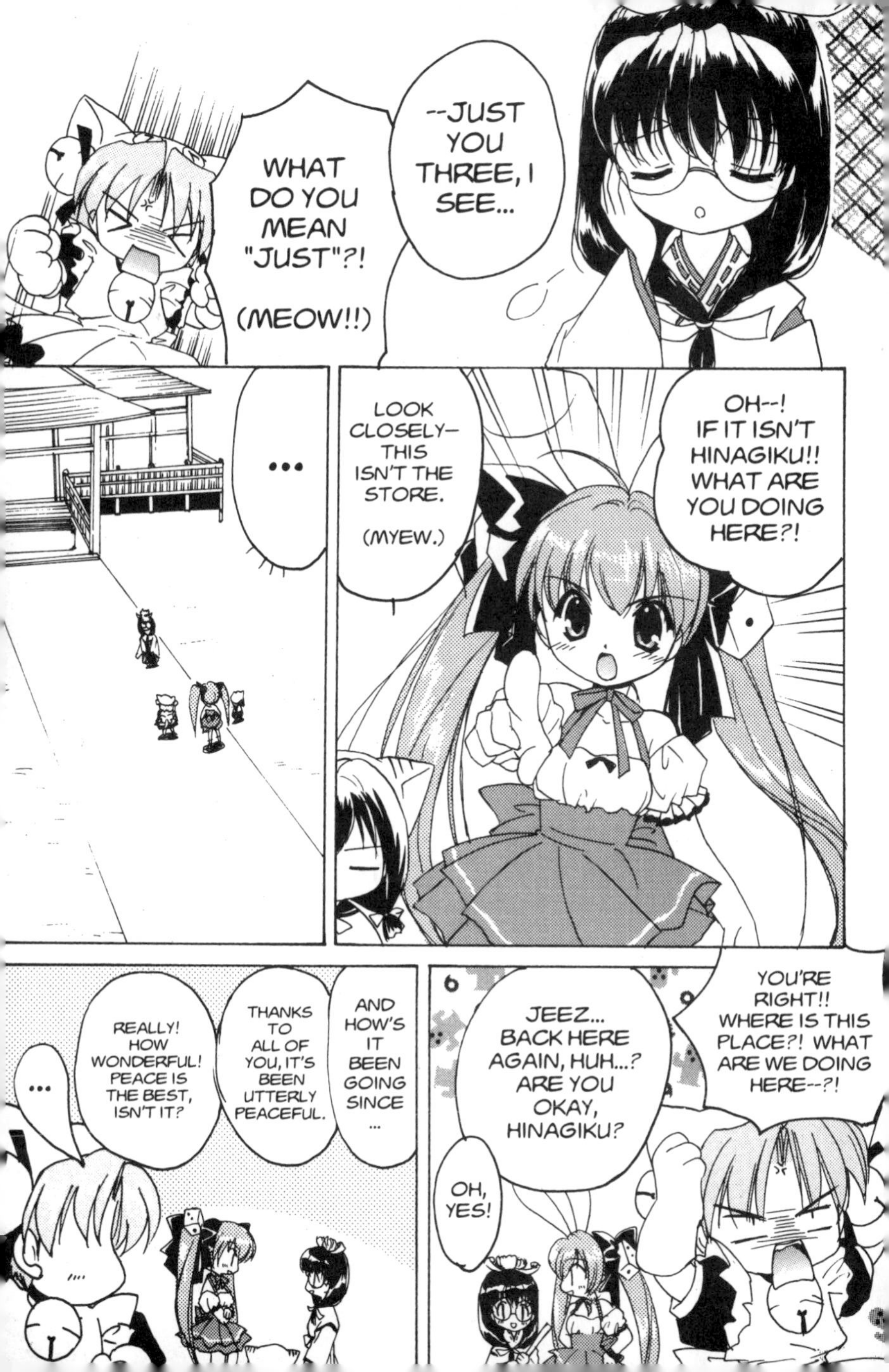

--JUST YOU THREE, I SEE...
WHAT DO YOU MEAN "JUST"?!
(MEOW!!)
OH--! IF IT ISN'T HINAGIKU!! WHAT ARE YOU DOING HERE?!
LOOK CLOSELY— THIS ISN'T THE STORE.
(MYEW.)
...
YOU'RE RIGHT!! WHERE IS THIS PLACE?! WHAT ARE WE DOING HERE--?!
JEEZ... BACK HERE AGAIN, HUH...? ARE YOU OKAY, HINAGIKU?
OH, YES!
AND HOW'S IT BEEN GOING SINCE ...
THANKS TO ALL OF YOU, IT'S BEEN UTTERLY PEACEFUL.
REALLY! HOW WONDERFUL! PEACE IS THE BEST, ISN'T IT?
...

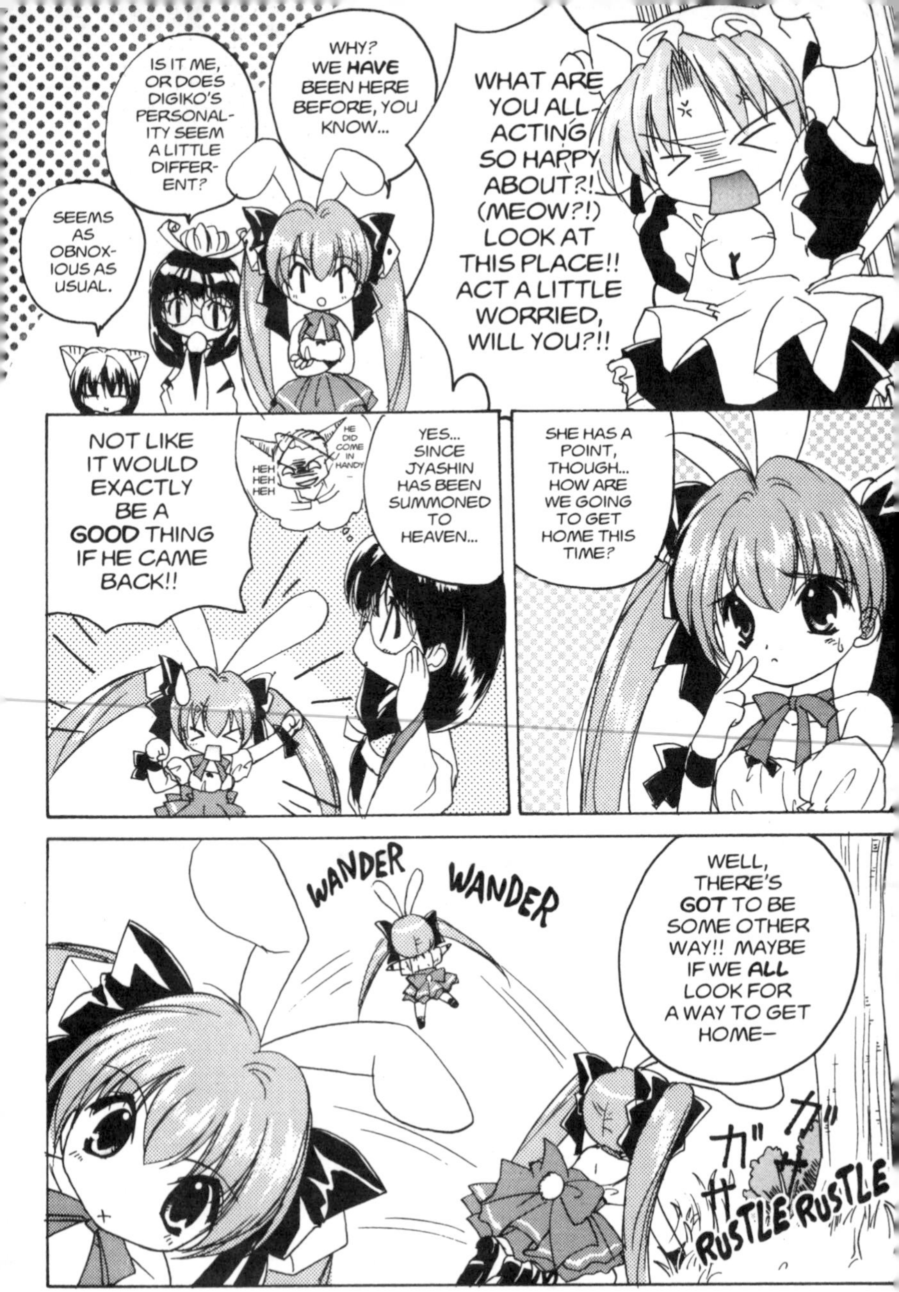
WHAT ARE YOU ALL ACTING SO HAPPY ABOUT?! (MEOW?!) LOOK AT THIS PLACE!! ACT A LITTLE WORRIED, WILL YOU?!!
WHY? WE HAVE BEEN HERE BEFORE, YOU KNOW...
IS IT ME, OR DOES DIGIKO'S PERSONALITY SEEM A LITTLE DIFFERENT?
SEEMS AS OBNOXIOUS AS USUAL.
SHE HAS A POINT, THOUGH... HOW ARE WE GOING TO GET HOME THIS TIME?
YES... SINCE JYASHIN HAS BEEN SUMMONED TO HEAVEN...
HE DID COME IN HANDY
HEH HEH HEH
NOT LIKE IT WOULD EXACTLY BE A GOOD THING IF HE CAME BACK!!
WELL, THERE'S GOT TO BE SOME OTHER WAY!! MAYBE IF WE ALL LOOK FOR A WAY TO GET HOME–
WANDER WANDER
RUSTLE RUSTLE

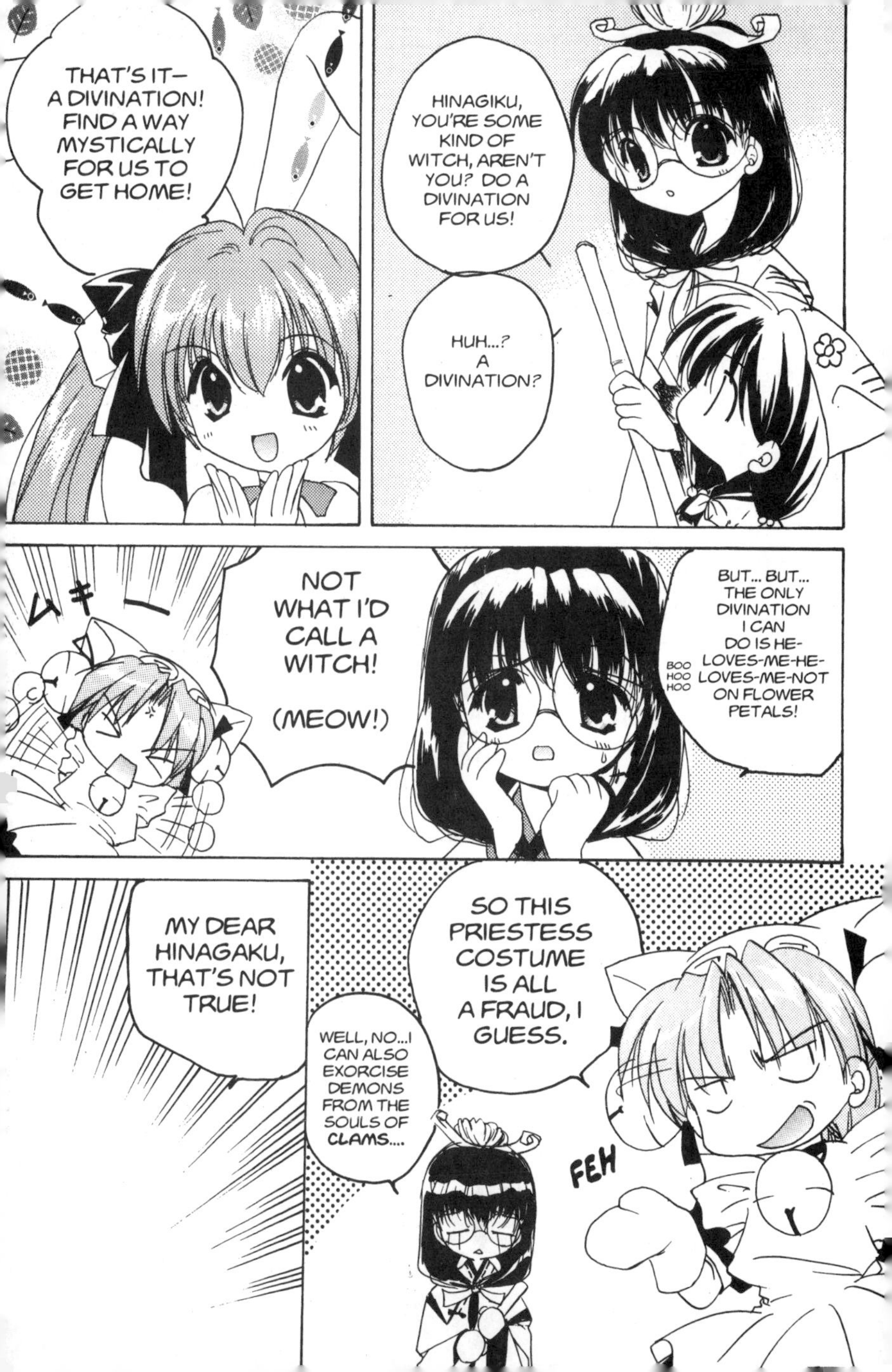
HINAGIKU, YOU'RE SOME KIND OF WITCH, AREN'T YOU? DO A DIVINATION FOR US!
HUH...? A DIVINATION?
THAT'S IT— A DIVINATION! FIND A WAY MYSTICALLY FOR US TO GET HOME!
BUT... BUT... THE ONLY DIVINATION I CAN DO IS HE-LOVES-ME-HE-LOVES-ME-NOT ON FLOWER PETALS!
BOO HOO HOO
NOT WHAT I'D CALL A WITCH!
(MEOW!)
ムキー
SO THIS PRIESTESS COSTUME IS ALL A FRAUD, I GUESS.
FEH
WELL, NO...I CAN ALSO EXORCISE DEMONS FROM THE SOULS OF **CLAMS**....
MY DEAR HINAGAKU, THAT'S NOT TRUE!

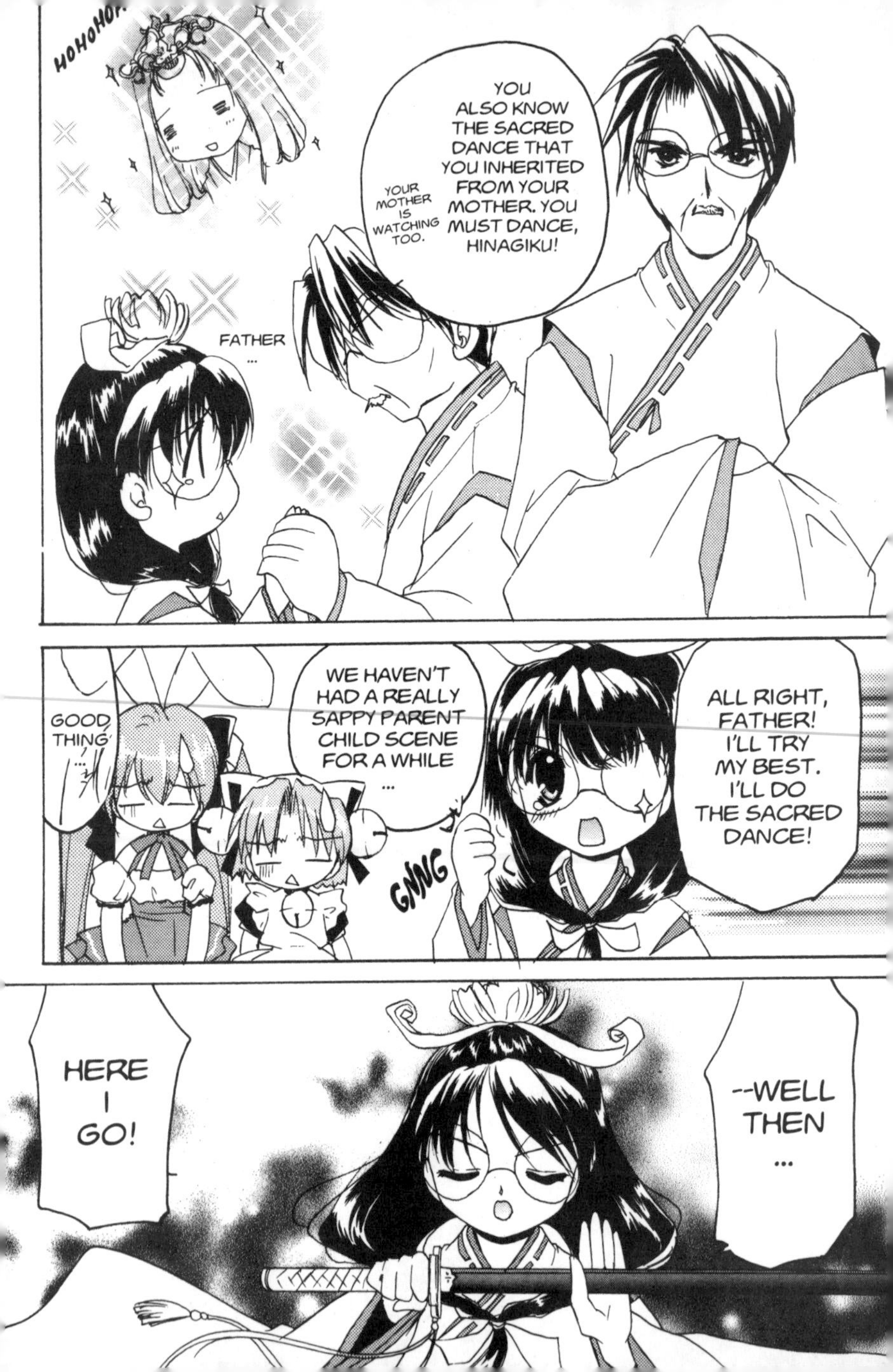
YOU ALSO KNOW THE SACRED DANCE THAT YOU INHERITED FROM YOUR MOTHER. YOU MUST DANCE, HINAGIKU!
YOUR MOTHER IS WATCHING TOO.
FATHER ...
HOHOHOH
ALL RIGHT, FATHER! I'LL TRY MY BEST. I'LL DO THE SACRED DANCE!
GNNG
WE HAVEN'T HAD A REALLY SAPPY PARENT CHILD SCENE FOR A WHILE ...
GOOD THING ...
--WELL THEN ...
HERE I GO!

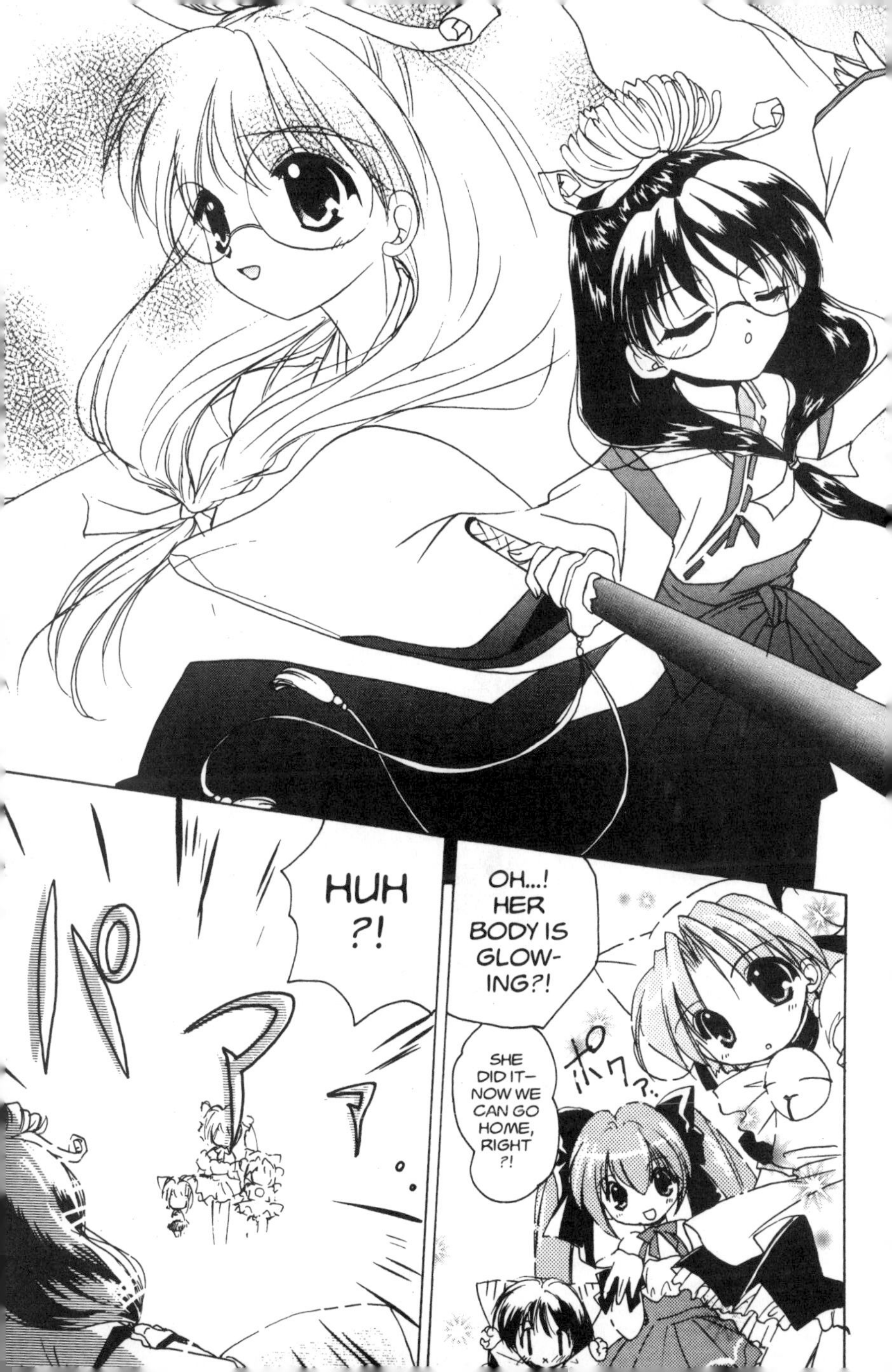
OH...! HER BODY IS GLOW-ING?!
SHE DID IT—NOW WE CAN GO HOME, RIGHT ?!
HUH ?!

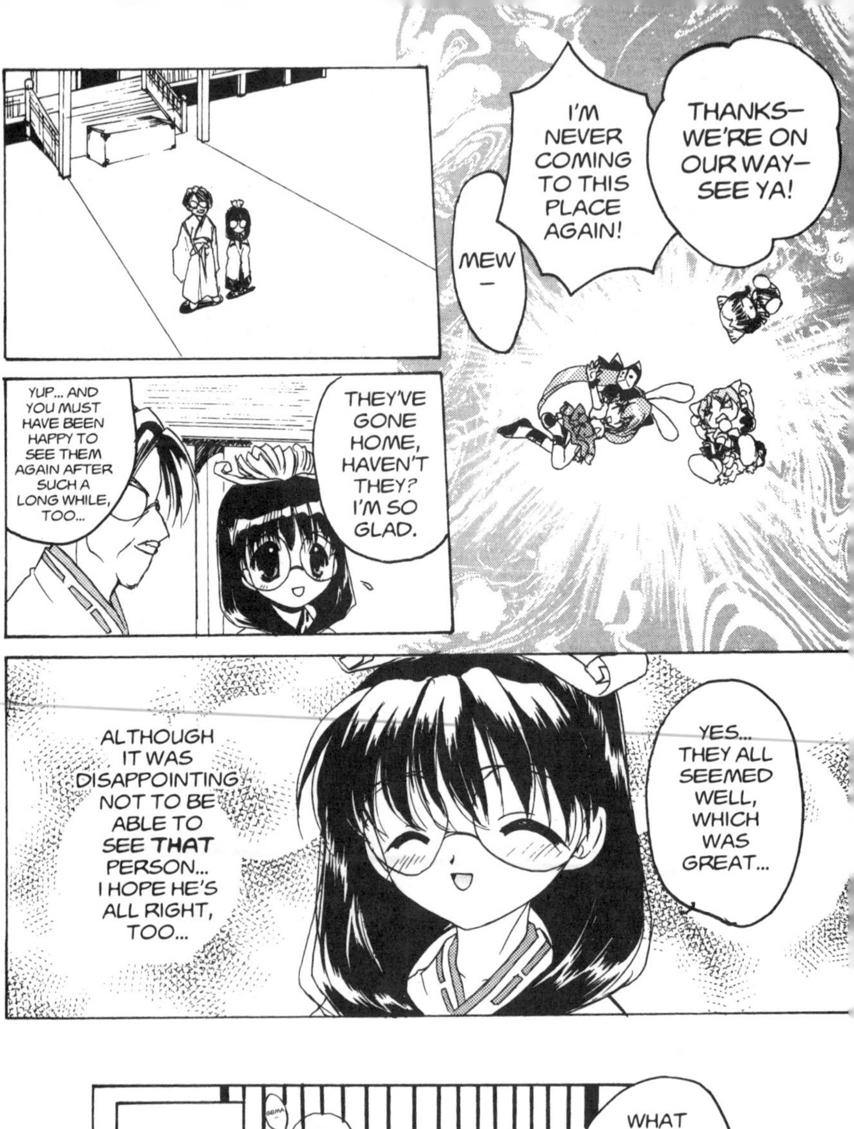
THANKS— WE'RE ON OUR WAY— SEE YA!
I'M NEVER COMING TO THIS PLACE AGAIN!
MEW —
THEY'VE GONE HOME, HAVEN'T THEY? I'M SO GLAD.
YUP... AND YOU MUST HAVE BEEN HAPPY TO SEE THEM AGAIN AFTER SUCH A LONG WHILE, TOO...
YES... THEY ALL SEEMED WELL, WHICH WAS GREAT...
ALTHOUGH IT WAS DISAPPOINTING NOT TO BE ABLE TO SEE THAT PERSON... I HOPE HE'S ALL RIGHT, TOO...
WHAT AM I DOING IN A PLACE LIKE THIS...?
GEMA
LEFT BEHIND ...

END

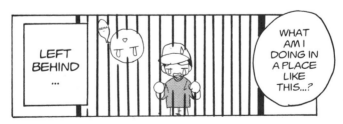

A WORD ABOUT "DI-GI-CHARAT"!

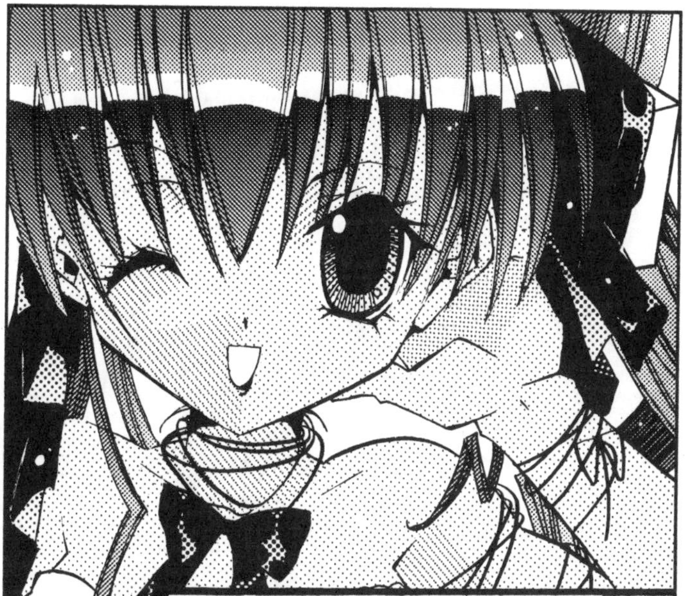

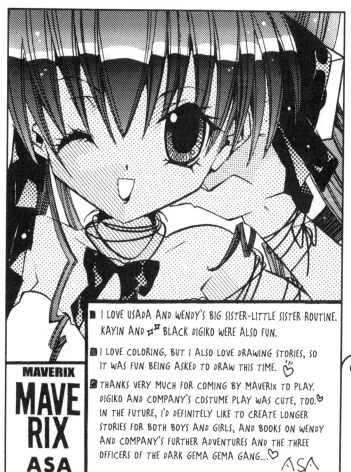

MAVERIX

MAVE
RIX

ASA

- I LOVE USADA AND WENDY'S BIG SISTER-LITTLE SISTER ROUTINE. KAYIN AND BLACK DIGIKO WERE ALSO FUN.
- I LOVE COLORING, BUT I ALSO LOVE DRAWING STORIES, SO IT WAS FUN BEING ASKED TO DRAW THIS TIME. ♡
- THANKS VERY MUCH FOR COMING BY MAVERIX TO PLAY. DIGIKO AND COMPANY'S COSTUME PLAY WAS CUTE, TOO.♡ IN THE FUTURE, I'D DEFINITELY LIKE TO CREATE LONGER STORIES FOR BOTH BOYS AND GIRLS, AND BOOKS ON WENDY AND COMPANY'S FURTHER ADVENTURES AND THE THREE OFFICERS OF THE DARK GEMA GEMA GANG...♡

ASA

YUZURU ASAHINA

A WORD ABOUT "DI-GI-CHARAT"!

CONCERNING DiGiCHARAT— THANKS TO THE ANIME, THE IMAGE OF DIGIKO IN MY MIND HAS COMPLETELY BECOME LIKE THIS... ◊

TO ALL YOU DIGIKO FANS, I'M SORRY... ◊

FEH

I WAS HAPPY THAT THE MOVIE WITHIN THE GAME WAS THE SAME AS THE ANIME. ♥

Morisaki. k

KURUMI MORISAKI

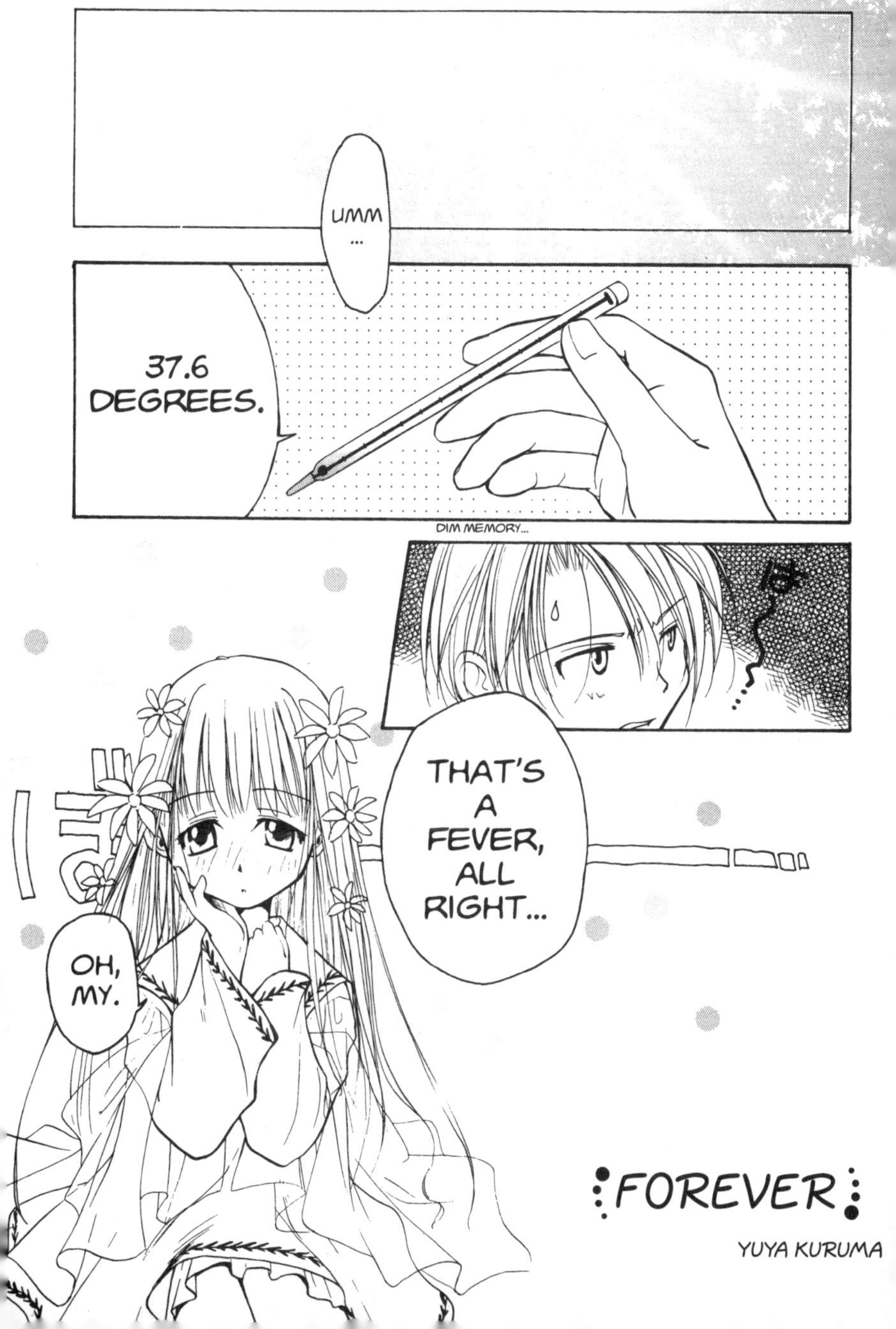
UMM ...
37.6 DEGREES.
DIM MEMORY...
THAT'S A FEVER, ALL RIGHT...
OH, MY.
FOREVER
YUYA KURUMA

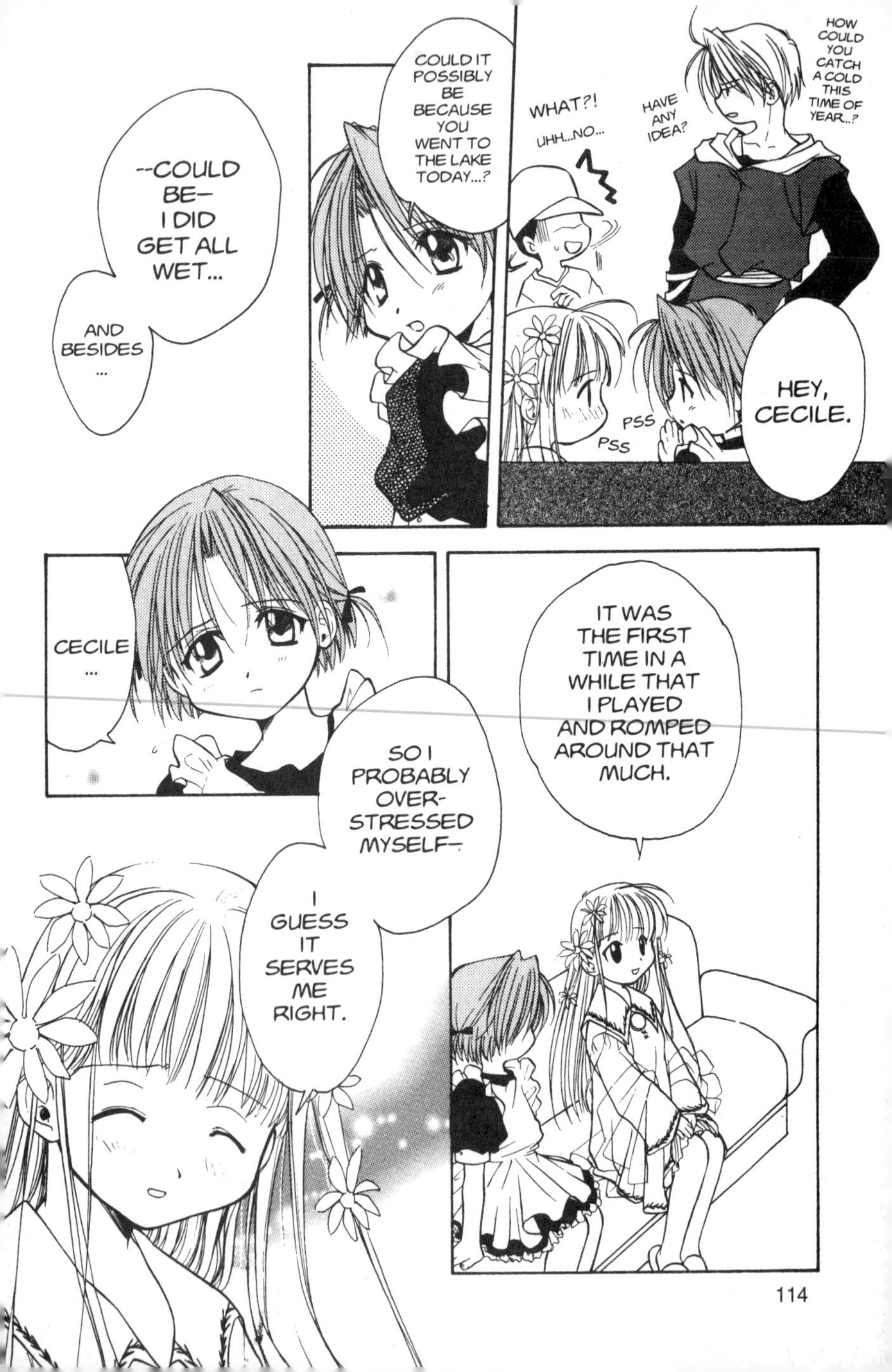

HOW COULD YOU CATCH A COLD THIS TIME OF YEAR...?
HAVE ANY IDEA?
WHAT?!
UHH...NO...
HEY, CECILE.
PSS
PSS
COULD IT POSSIBLY BE BECAUSE YOU WENT TO THE LAKE TODAY...?
--COULD BE— I DID GET ALL WET...
AND BESIDES ...
IT WAS THE FIRST TIME IN A WHILE THAT I PLAYED AND ROMPED AROUND THAT MUCH.
CECILE ...
SO I PROBABLY OVER-STRESSED MYSELF—
I GUESS IT SERVES ME RIGHT.

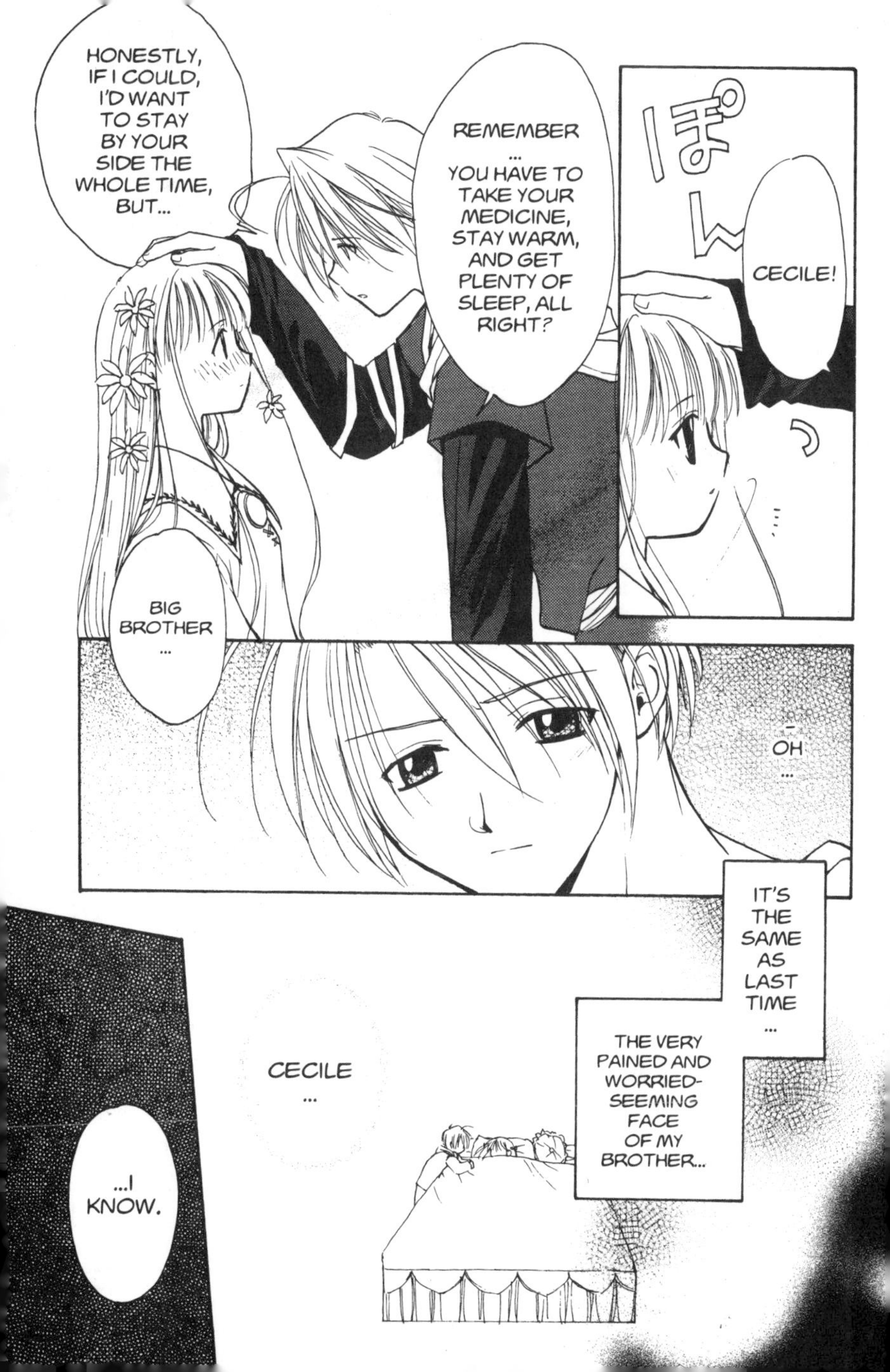

ぽん
CECILE!
…
REMEMBER ... YOU HAVE TO TAKE YOUR MEDICINE, STAY WARM, AND GET PLENTY OF SLEEP, ALL RIGHT?
HONESTLY, IF I COULD, I'D WANT TO STAY BY YOUR SIDE THE WHOLE TIME, BUT...
BIG BROTHER ...
– OH ...
IT'S THE SAME AS LAST TIME ...
THE VERY PAINED AND WORRIED-SEEMING FACE OF MY BROTHER...
CECILE ...
...I KNOW.

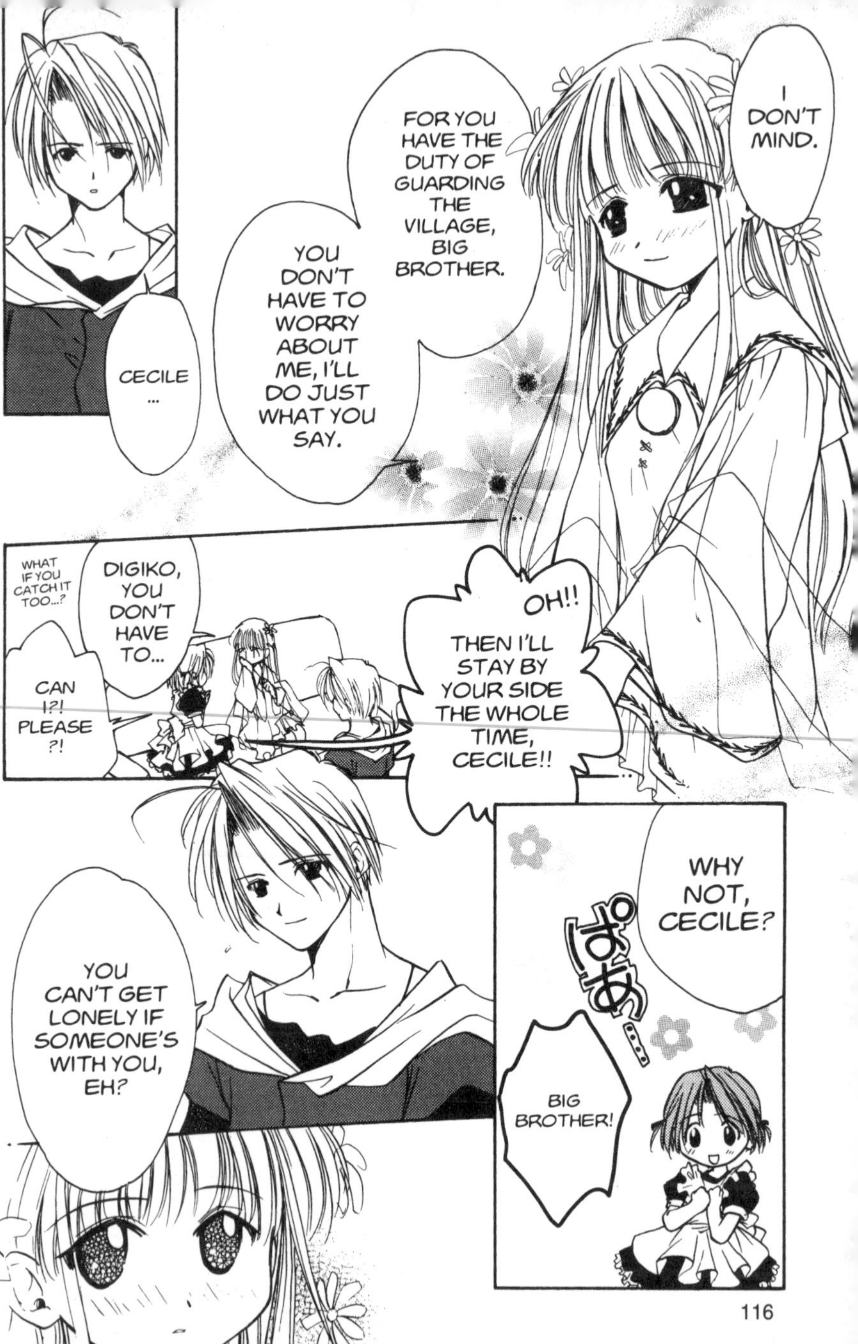
I DON'T MIND.
FOR YOU HAVE THE DUTY OF GUARDING THE VILLAGE, BIG BROTHER.
YOU DON'T HAVE TO WORRY ABOUT ME, I'LL DO JUST WHAT YOU SAY.
CECILE ...
OH!!
THEN I'LL STAY BY YOUR SIDE THE WHOLE TIME, CECILE!!
DIGIKO, YOU DON'T HAVE TO...
WHAT IF YOU CATCH IT TOO...?
CAN I?! PLEASE?!
WHY NOT, CECILE?
ぱあ…
BIG BROTHER!
YOU CAN'T GET LONELY IF SOMEONE'S WITH YOU, EH?

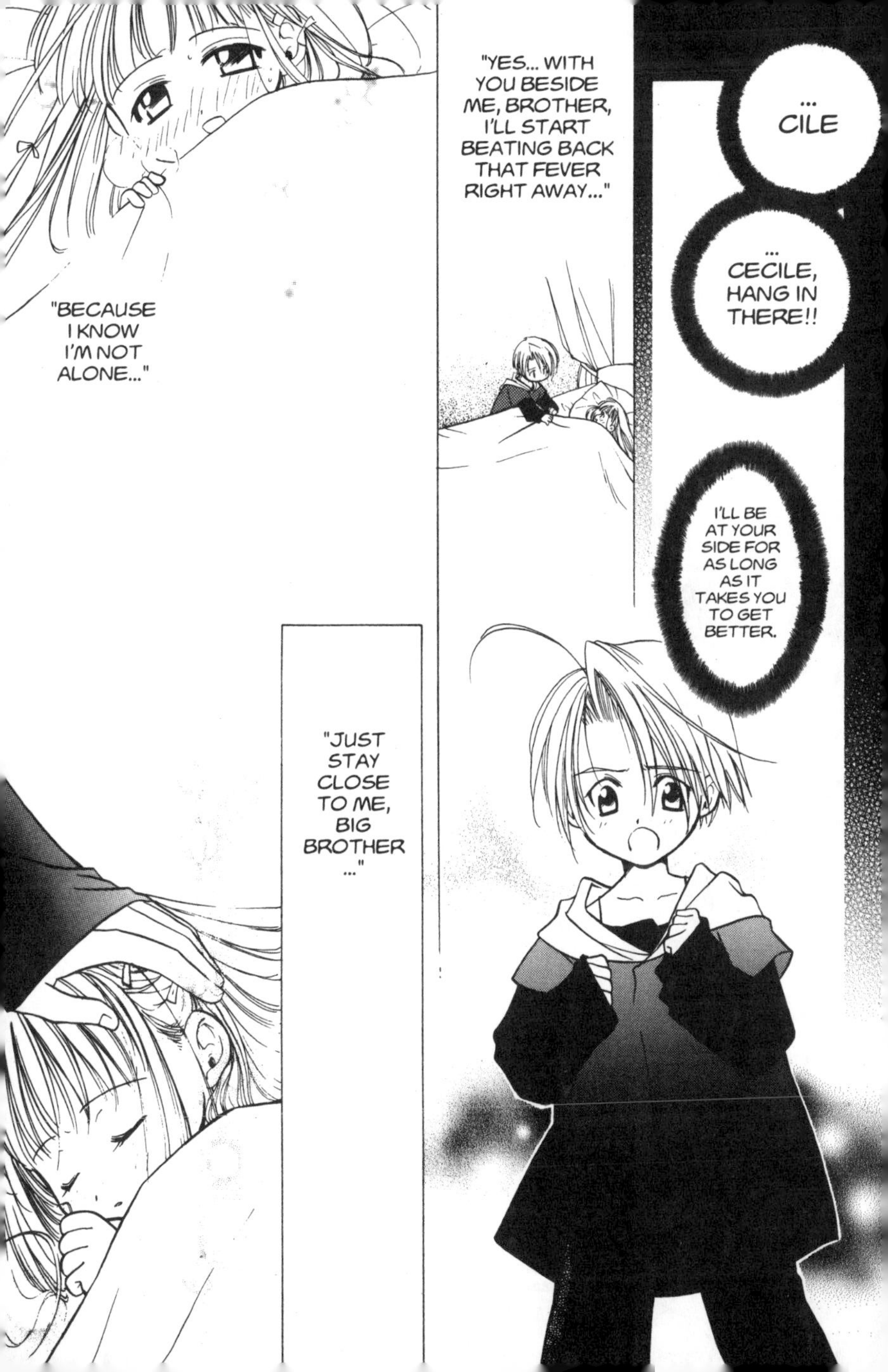
...CILE
...CECILE, HANG IN THERE!!
I'LL BE AT YOUR SIDE FOR AS LONG AS IT TAKES YOU TO GET BETTER.
"YES... WITH YOU BESIDE ME, BROTHER, I'LL START BEATING BACK THAT FEVER RIGHT AWAY..."
"BECAUSE I KNOW I'M NOT ALONE..."
"JUST STAY CLOSE TO ME, BIG BROTHER..."

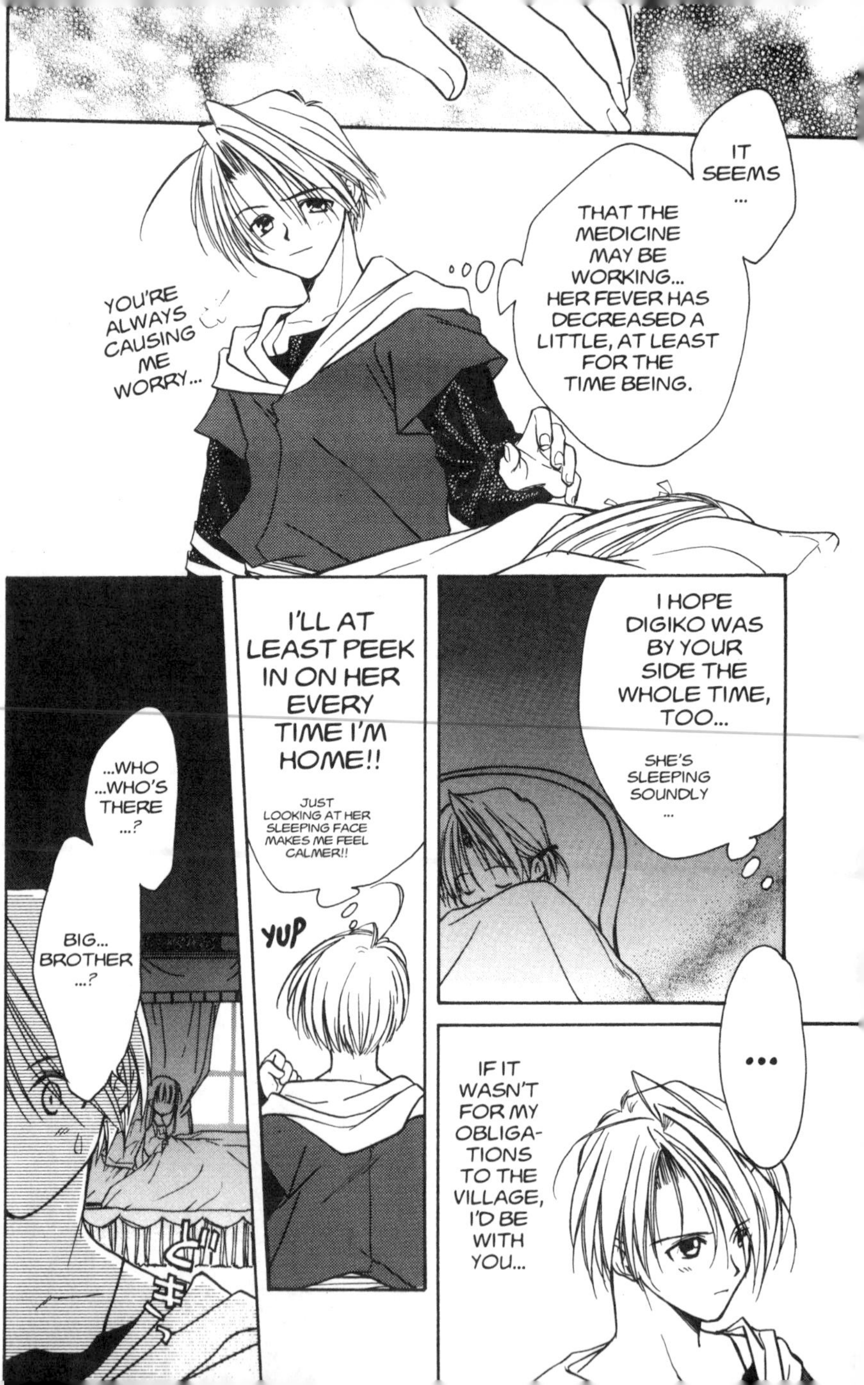
IT SEEMS ...
THAT THE MEDICINE MAY BE WORKING... HER FEVER HAS DECREASED A LITTLE, AT LEAST FOR THE TIME BEING.
YOU'RE ALWAYS CAUSING ME WORRY...
I HOPE DIGIKO WAS BY YOUR SIDE THE WHOLE TIME, TOO...
SHE'S SLEEPING SOUNDLY ...
...
IF IT WASN'T FOR MY OBLIGA-TIONS TO THE VILLAGE, I'D BE WITH YOU...
I'LL AT LEAST PEEK IN ON HER EVERY TIME I'M HOME!!
JUST LOOKING AT HER SLEEPING FACE MAKES ME FEEL CALMER!!
YUP
...WHO ...WHO'S THERE ...?
BIG... BROTHER ...?
ドキッ

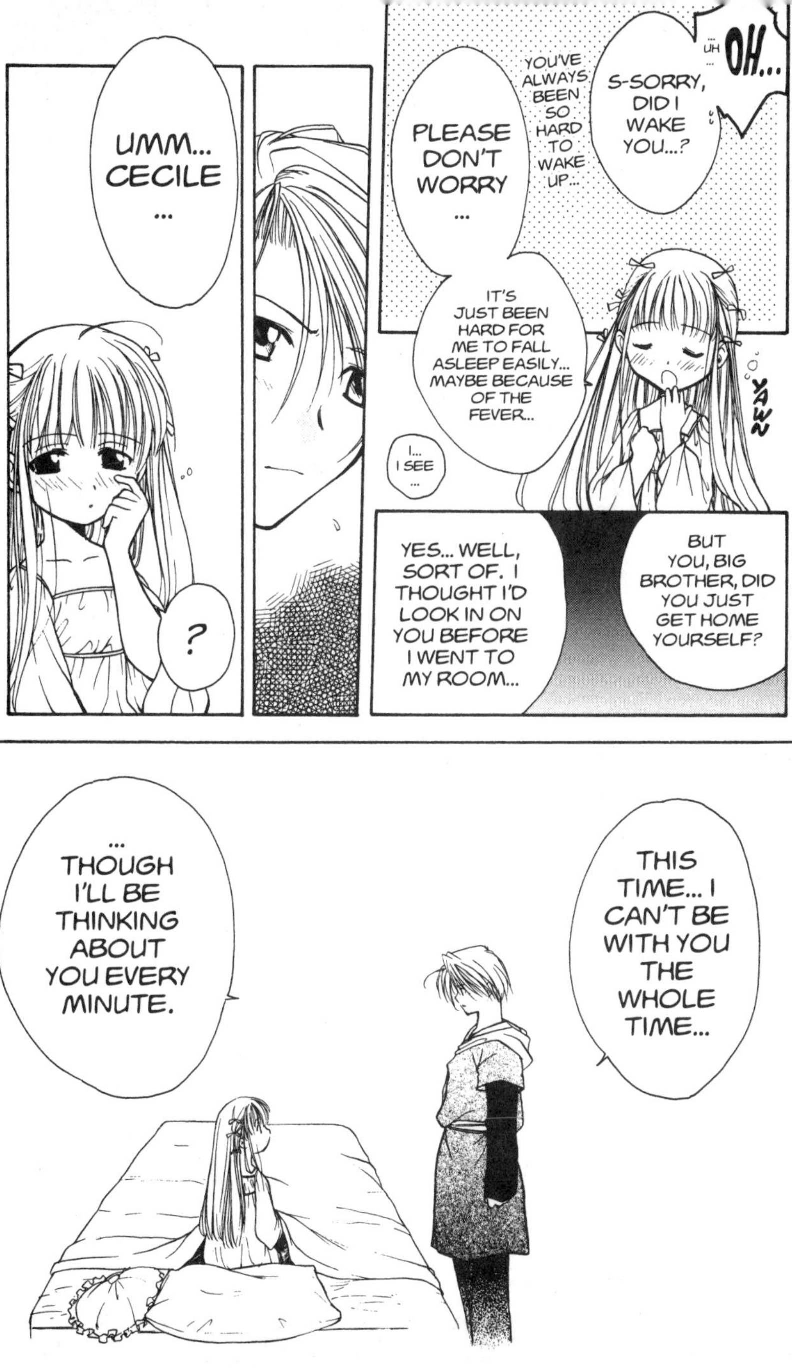

OH...
... UH ...
S-SORRY, DID I WAKE YOU...?
YOU'VE ALWAYS BEEN SO HARD TO WAKE UP...
PLEASE DON'T WORRY ...
IT'S JUST BEEN HARD FOR ME TO FALL ASLEEP EASILY... MAYBE BECAUSE OF THE FEVER...
YAWN
I... I SEE ...
BUT YOU, BIG BROTHER, DID YOU JUST GET HOME YOURSELF?
YES... WELL, SORT OF. I THOUGHT I'D LOOK IN ON YOU BEFORE I WENT TO MY ROOM...
UMM... CECILE ...
?
THIS TIME... I CAN'T BE WITH YOU THE WHOLE TIME...
... THOUGH I'LL BE THINKING ABOUT YOU EVERY MINUTE.

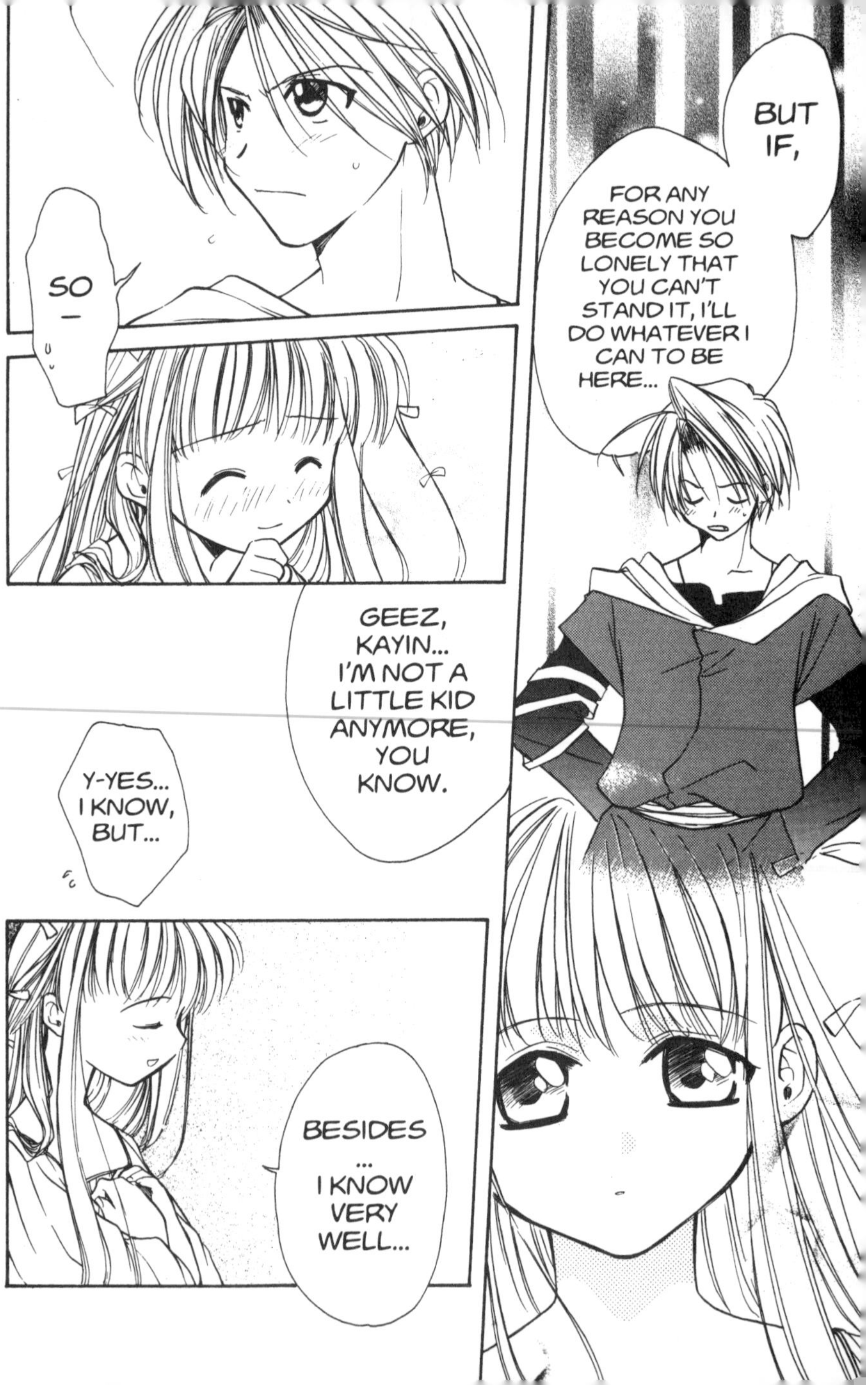
BUT IF,
FOR ANY REASON YOU BECOME SO LONELY THAT YOU CAN'T STAND IT, I'LL DO WHATEVER I CAN TO BE HERE...
SO —
GEEZ, KAYIN... I'M NOT A LITTLE KID ANYMORE, YOU KNOW.
Y-YES... I KNOW, BUT...
BESIDES ... I KNOW VERY WELL...

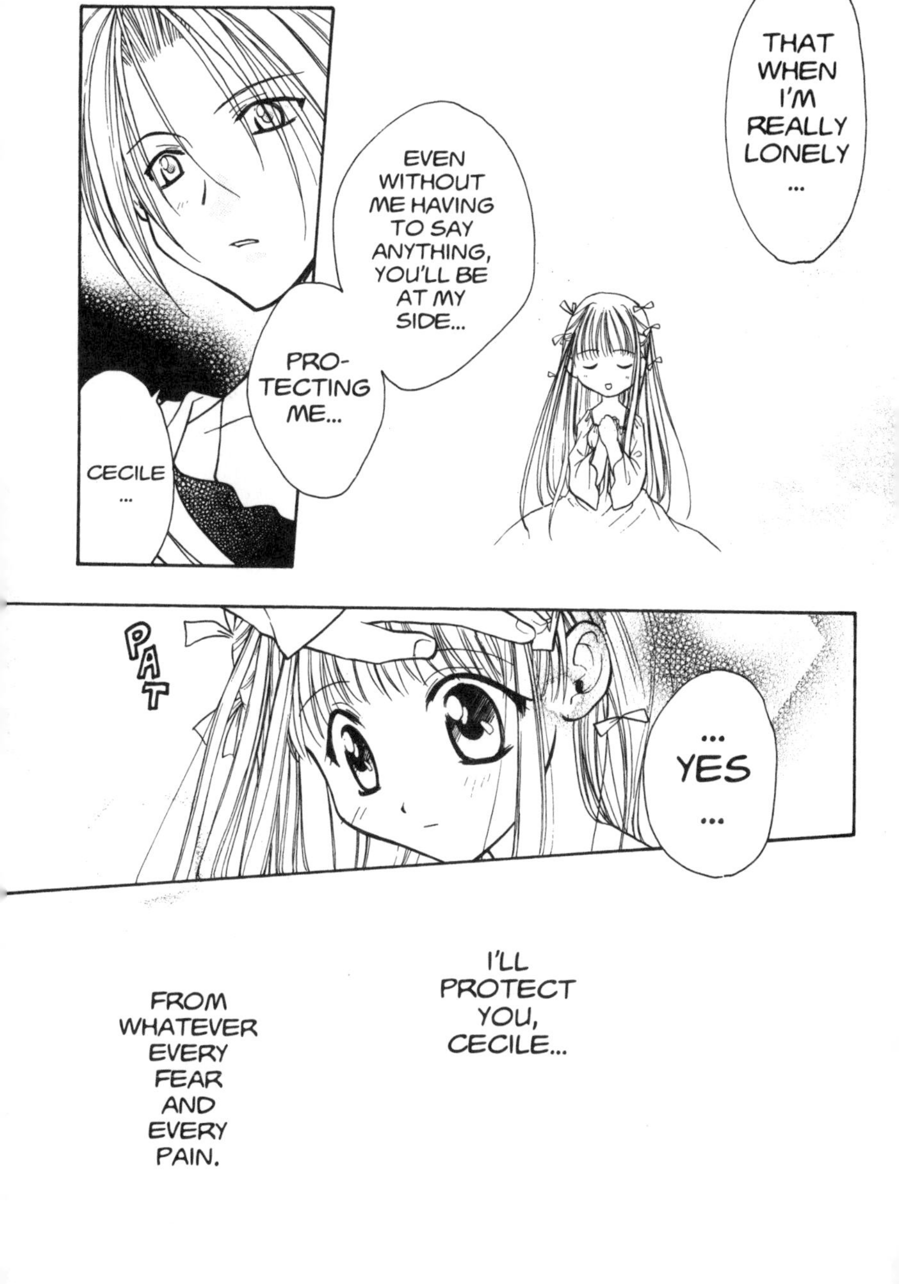
THAT WHEN I'M REALLY LONELY...
EVEN WITHOUT ME HAVING TO SAY ANYTHING, YOU'LL BE AT MY SIDE...
PROTECTING ME...
CECILE...
... YES ...
PAT
I'LL PROTECT YOU, CECILE...
FROM WHATEVER EVERY FEAR AND EVERY PAIN.

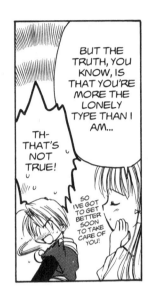

BUT THE TRUTH, YOU KNOW, IS THAT YOU'RE MORE THE LONELY TYPE THAN I AM...
TH- THAT'S NOT TRUE!
SO I'VE GOT TO GET BETTER SOON TO TAKE CARE OF YOU!

I'LL PROTECT YOU—

—FOREVER—

○EXTRA○

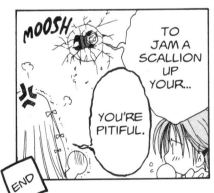

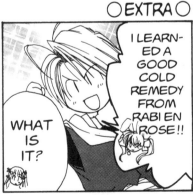

I LEARN-ED A GOOD COLD REMEDY FROM RABI EN ROSE!!
WHAT IS IT?

TO JAM A SCALLION UP YOUR...
YOU'RE PITIFUL.
MOOSH
END

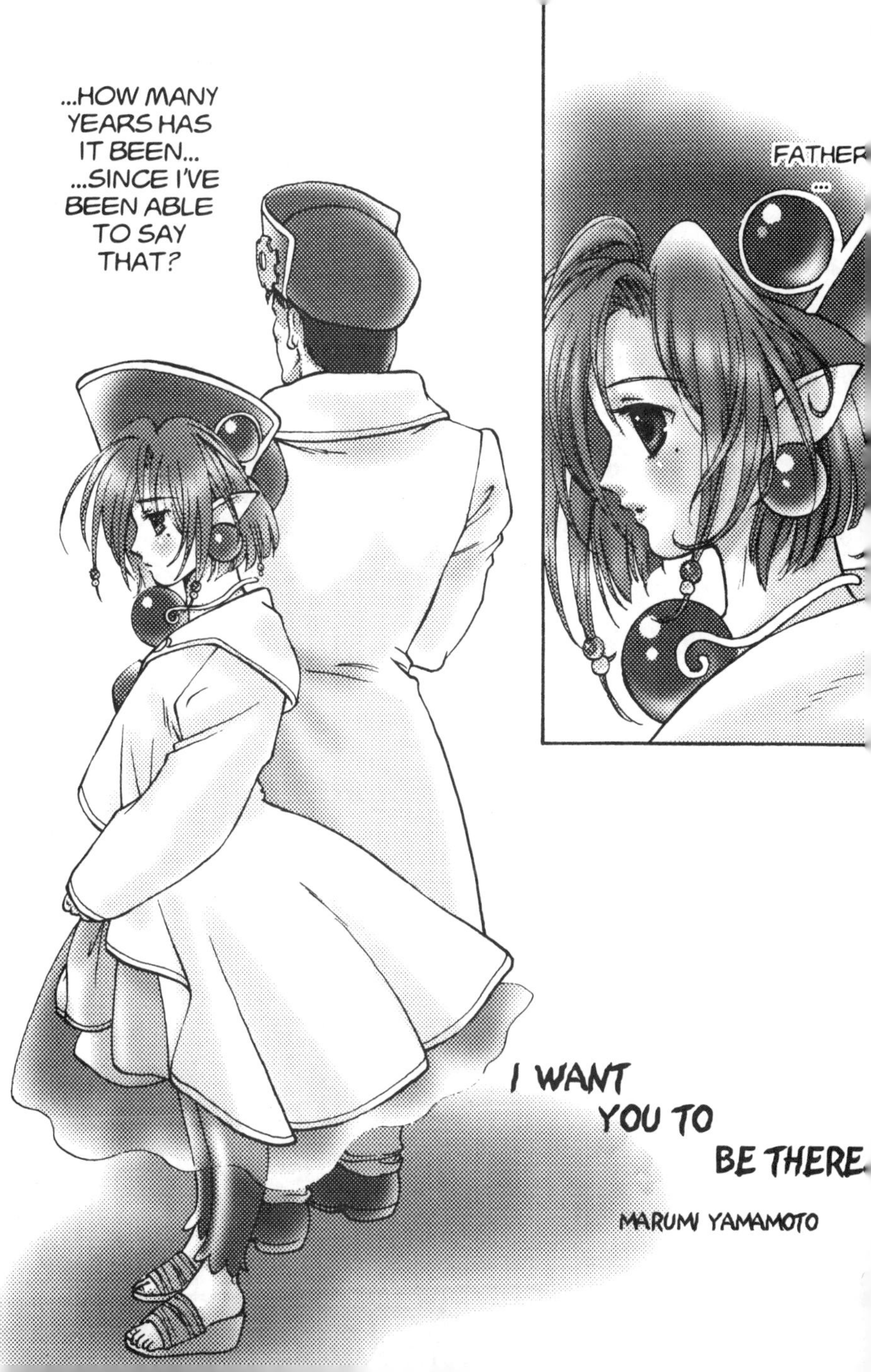
FATHER ...
...HOW MANY YEARS HAS IT BEEN... ...SINCE I'VE BEEN ABLE TO SAY THAT?
I WANT YOU TO BE THERE
MARUMI YAMAMOTO

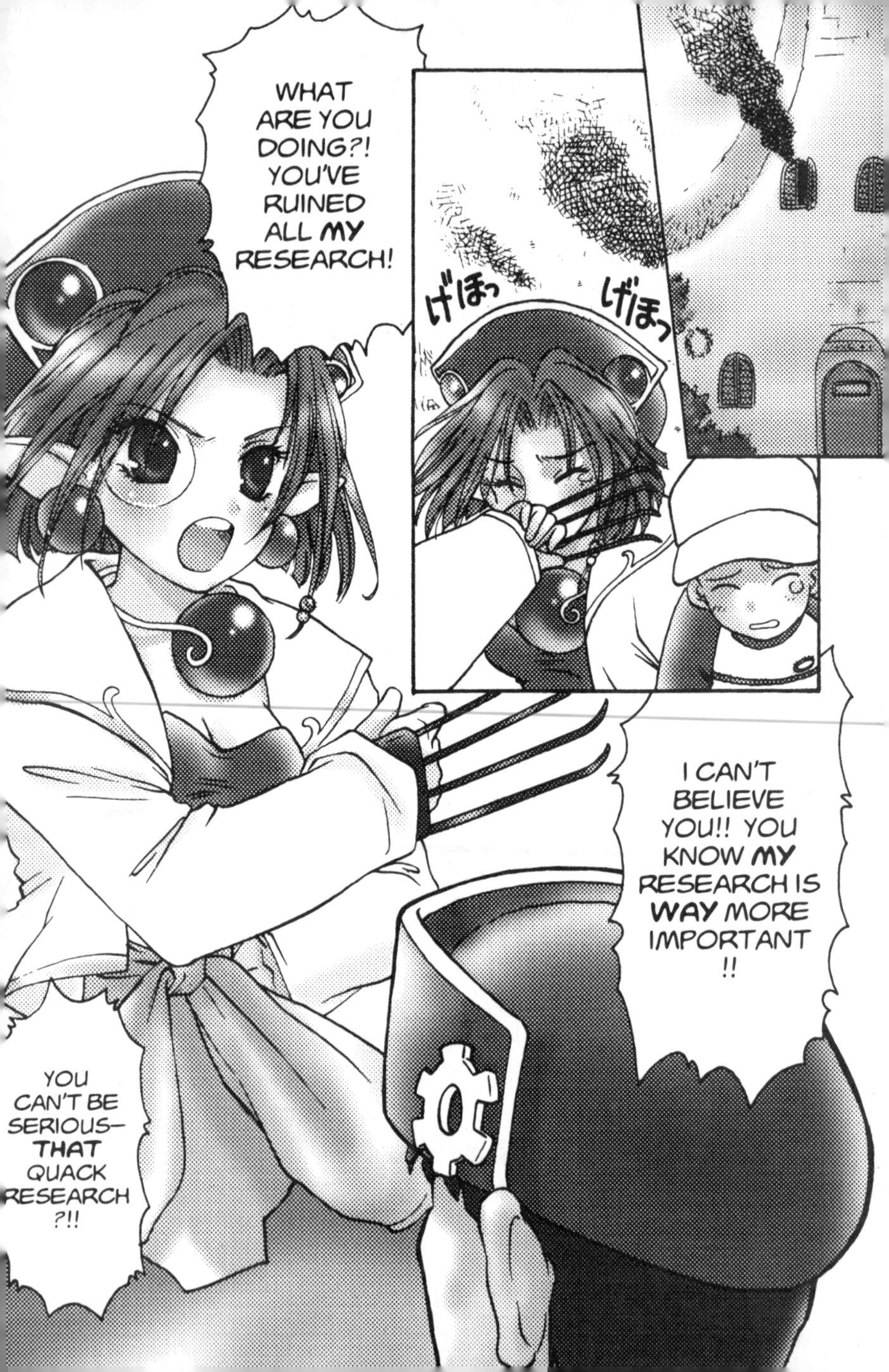

げほっ げほっ
WHAT ARE YOU DOING?! YOU'VE RUINED ALL **MY** RESEARCH!
I CAN'T BELIEVE YOU!! YOU KNOW **MY** RESEARCH IS **WAY** MORE IMPORTANT !!
YOU CAN'T BE SERIOUS— **THAT** QUACK RESEARCH ?!!

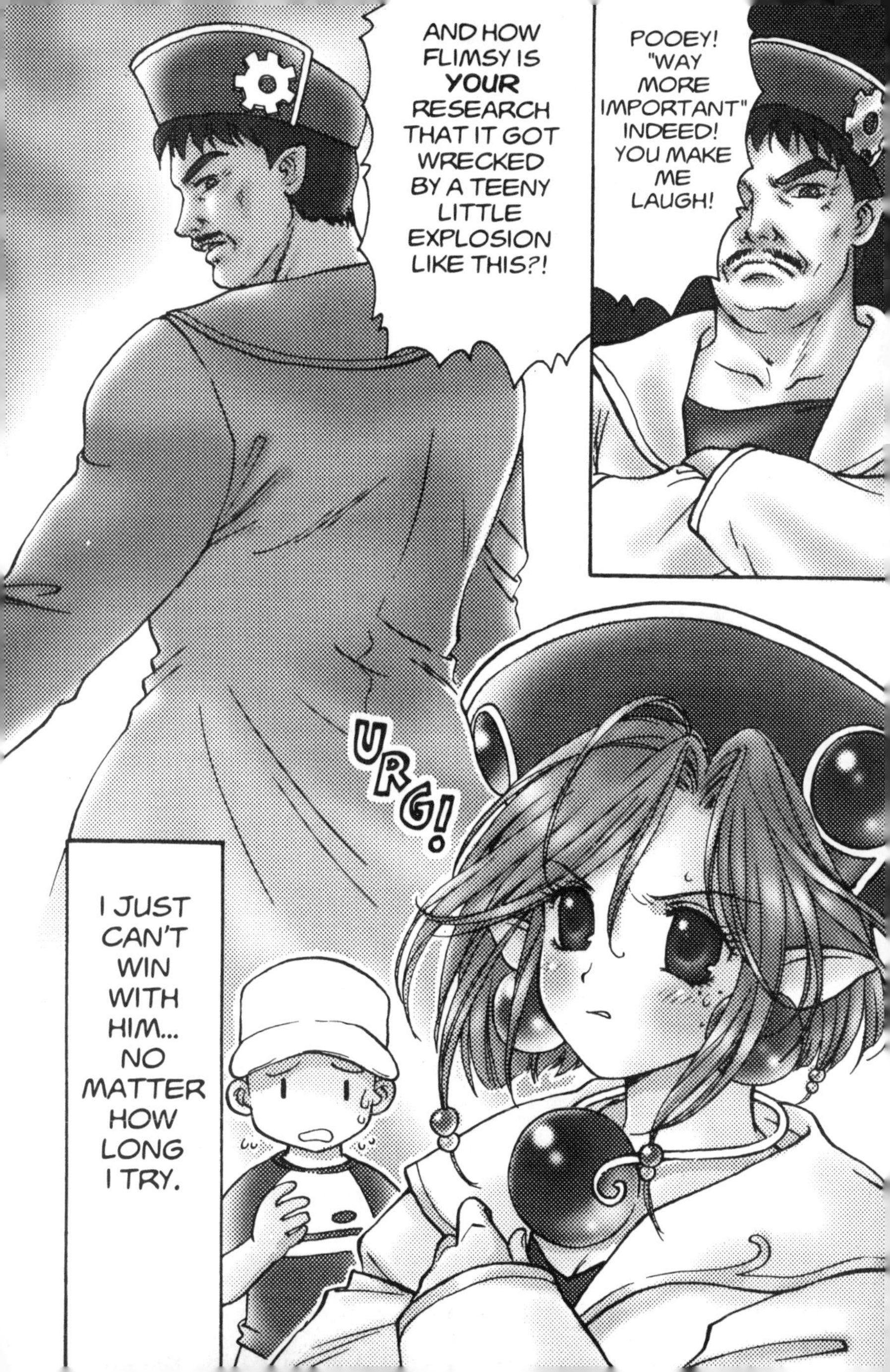
POOEY! "WAY MORE IMPORTANT" INDEED! YOU MAKE ME LAUGH!
AND HOW FLIMSY IS **YOUR** RESEARCH THAT IT GOT WRECKED BY A TEENY LITTLE EXPLOSION LIKE THIS?!
URG!
I JUST CAN'T WIN WITH HIM... NO MATTER HOW LONG I TRY.

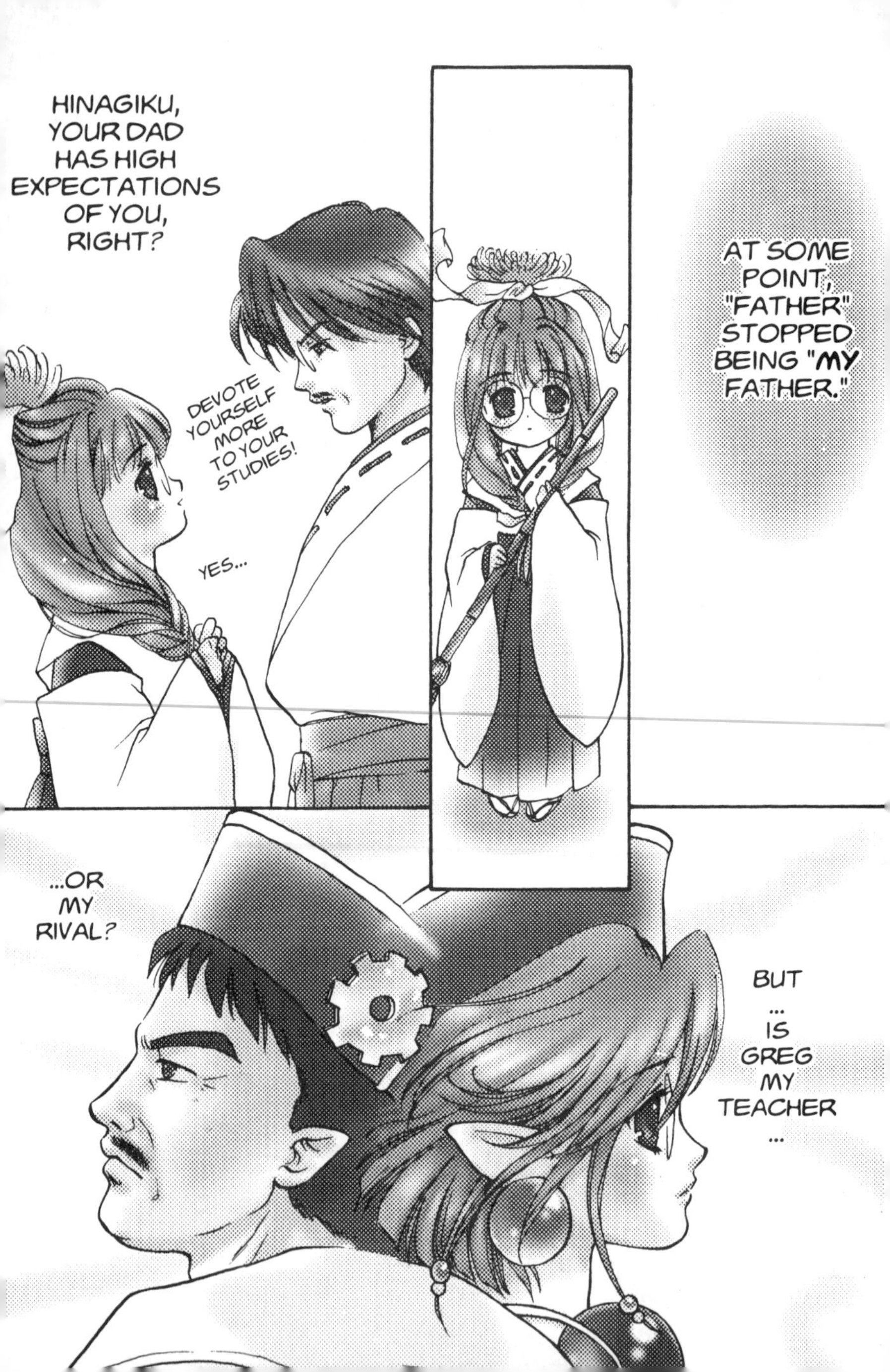
AT SOME POINT, "FATHER" STOPPED BEING "**MY** FATHER."
HINAGIKU, YOUR DAD HAS HIGH EXPECTATIONS OF YOU, RIGHT?
DEVOTE YOURSELF MORE TO YOUR STUDIES!
YES...
BUT ... IS GREG MY TEACHER ...
...OR MY RIVAL?

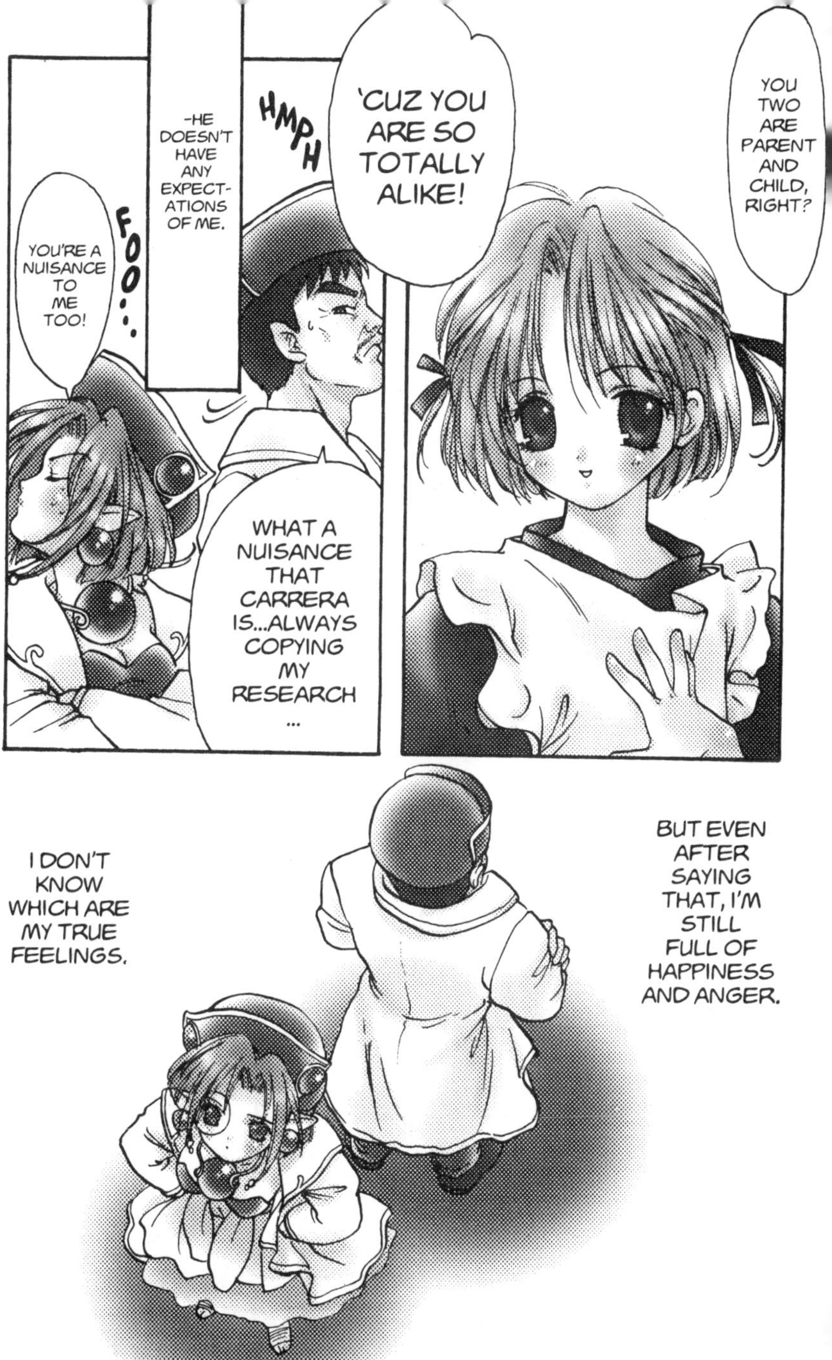
YOU TWO ARE PARENT AND CHILD, RIGHT?
'CUZ YOU ARE SO TOTALLY ALIKE!
HMPH
-HE DOESN'T HAVE ANY EXPECTATIONS OF ME.
WHAT A NUISANCE THAT CARRERA IS...ALWAYS COPYING MY RESEARCH...
FOO...
YOU'RE A NUISANCE TO ME TOO!
BUT EVEN AFTER SAYING THAT, I'M STILL FULL OF HAPPINESS AND ANGER.
I DON'T KNOW WHICH ARE MY TRUE FEELINGS.

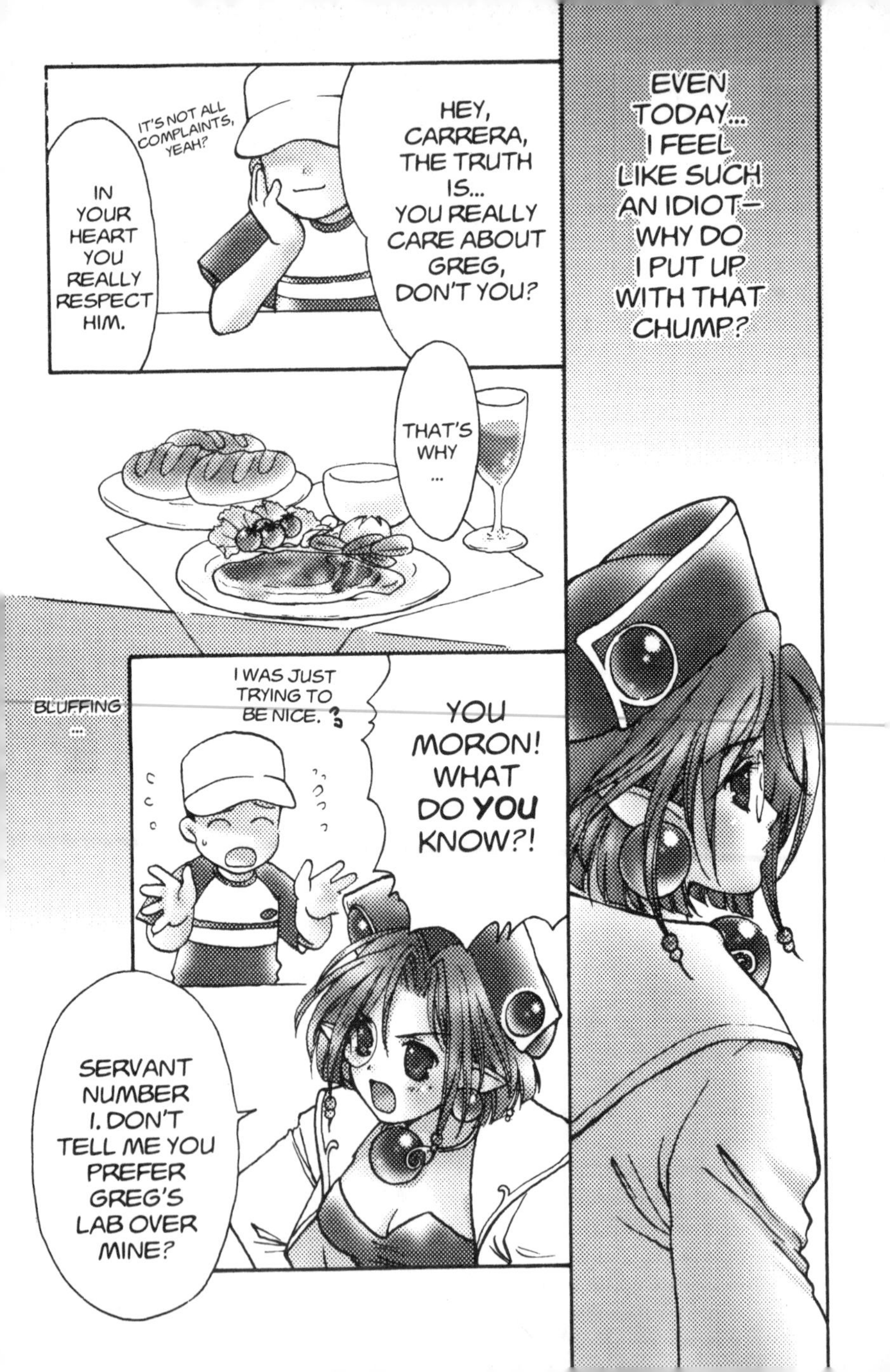
EVEN TODAY... I FEEL LIKE SUCH AN IDIOT— WHY DO I PUT UP WITH THAT CHUMP?
HEY, CARRERA, THE TRUTH IS... YOU REALLY CARE ABOUT GREG, DON'T YOU?
IT'S NOT ALL COMPLAINTS, YEAH?
IN YOUR HEART YOU REALLY RESPECT HIM.
THAT'S WHY ...
YOU MORON! WHAT DO **YOU** KNOW?!
I WAS JUST TRYING TO BE NICE.
BLUFFING ...
SERVANT NUMBER 1. DON'T TELL ME YOU PREFER GREG'S LAB OVER MINE?

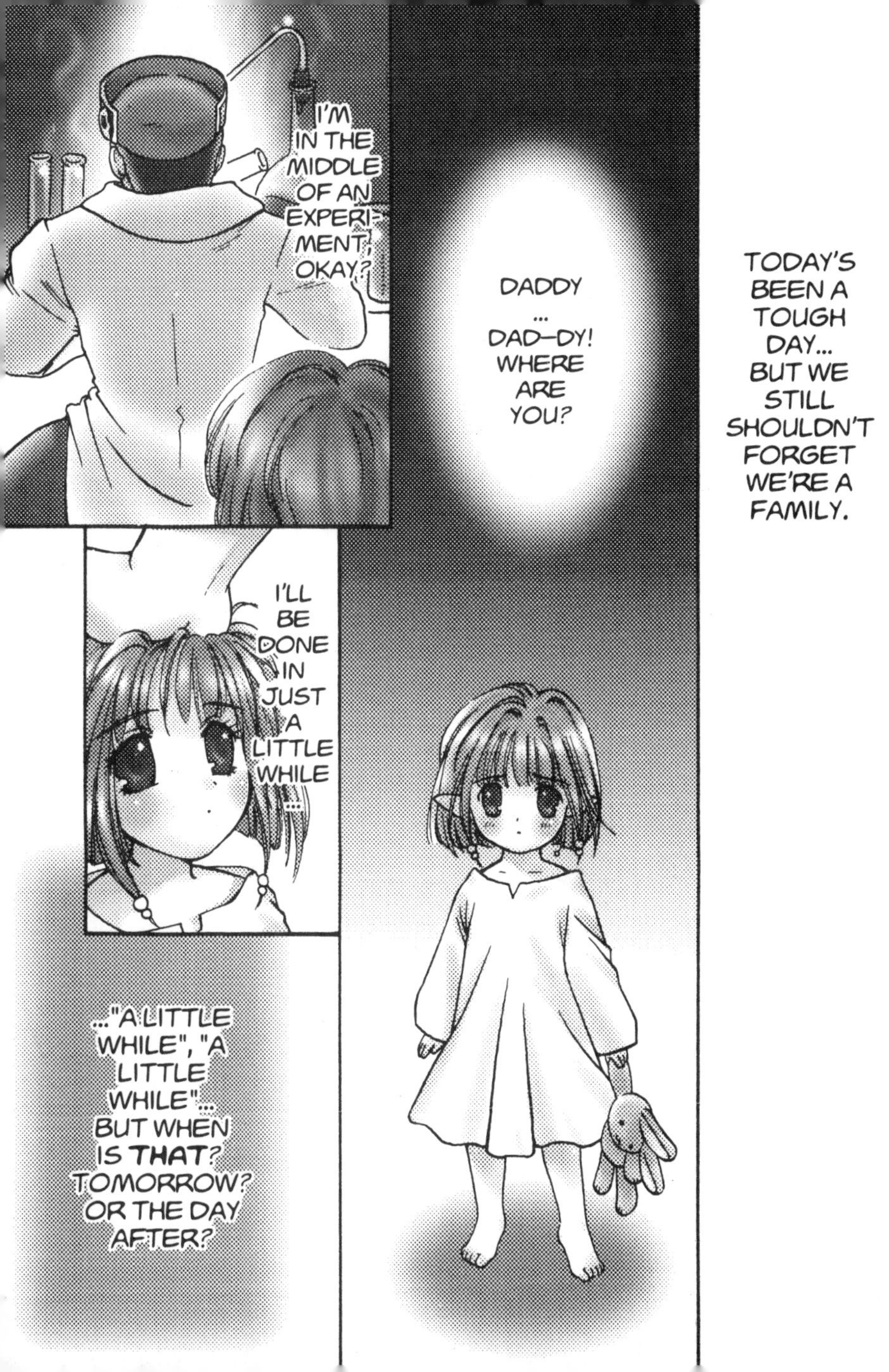
TODAY'S BEEN A TOUGH DAY... BUT WE STILL SHOULDN'T FORGET WE'RE A FAMILY.
DADDY ... DAD-DY! WHERE ARE YOU?
I'M IN THE MIDDLE OF AN EXPERIMENT, OKAY?
I'LL BE DONE IN JUST A LITTLE WHILE ...
..."A LITTLE WHILE", "A LITTLE WHILE"... BUT WHEN IS **THAT**? TOMORROW? OR THE DAY AFTER?

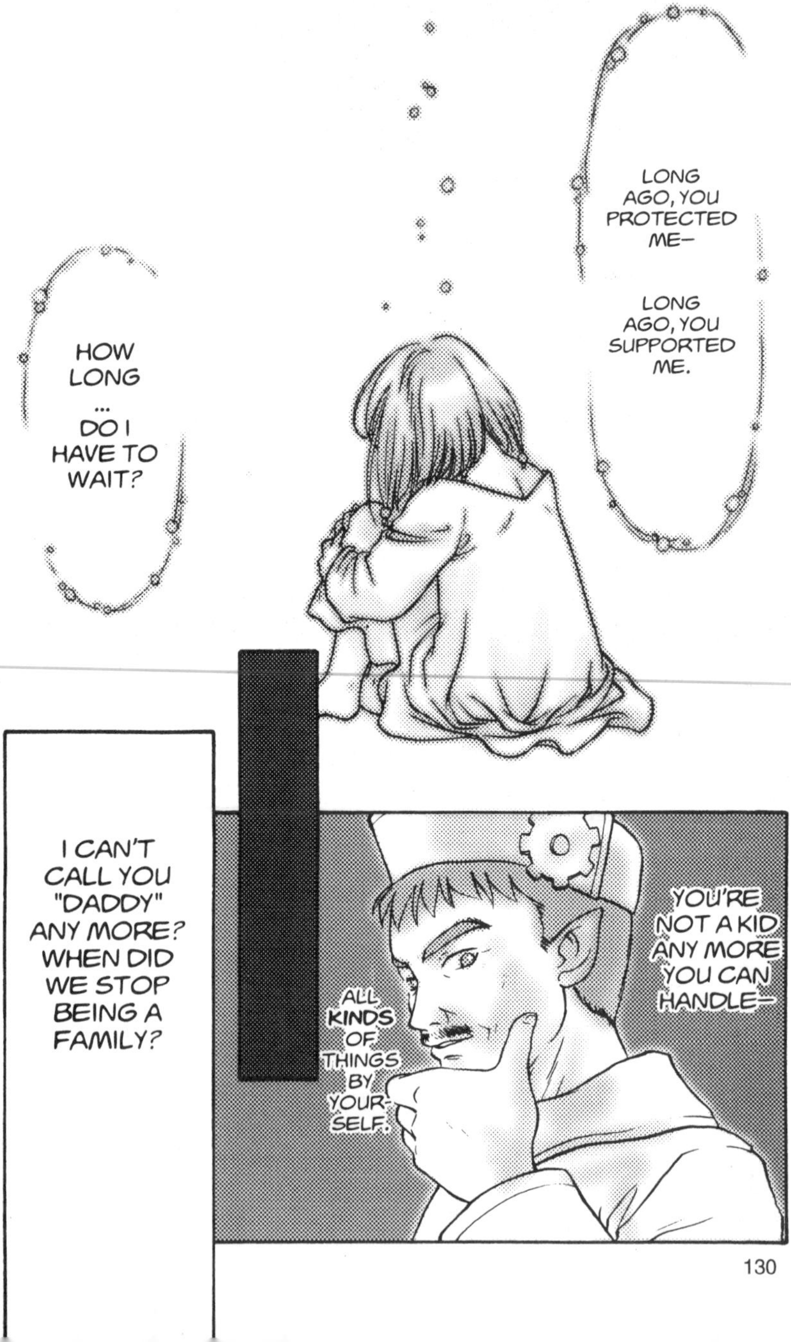

LONG AGO, YOU PROTECTED ME—
LONG AGO, YOU SUPPORTED ME.
HOW LONG ... DO I HAVE TO WAIT?
YOU'RE NOT A KID ANY MORE YOU CAN HANDLE—
ALL KINDS OF THINGS BY YOURSELF.
I CAN'T CALL YOU "DADDY" ANY MORE? WHEN DID WE STOP BEING A FAMILY?

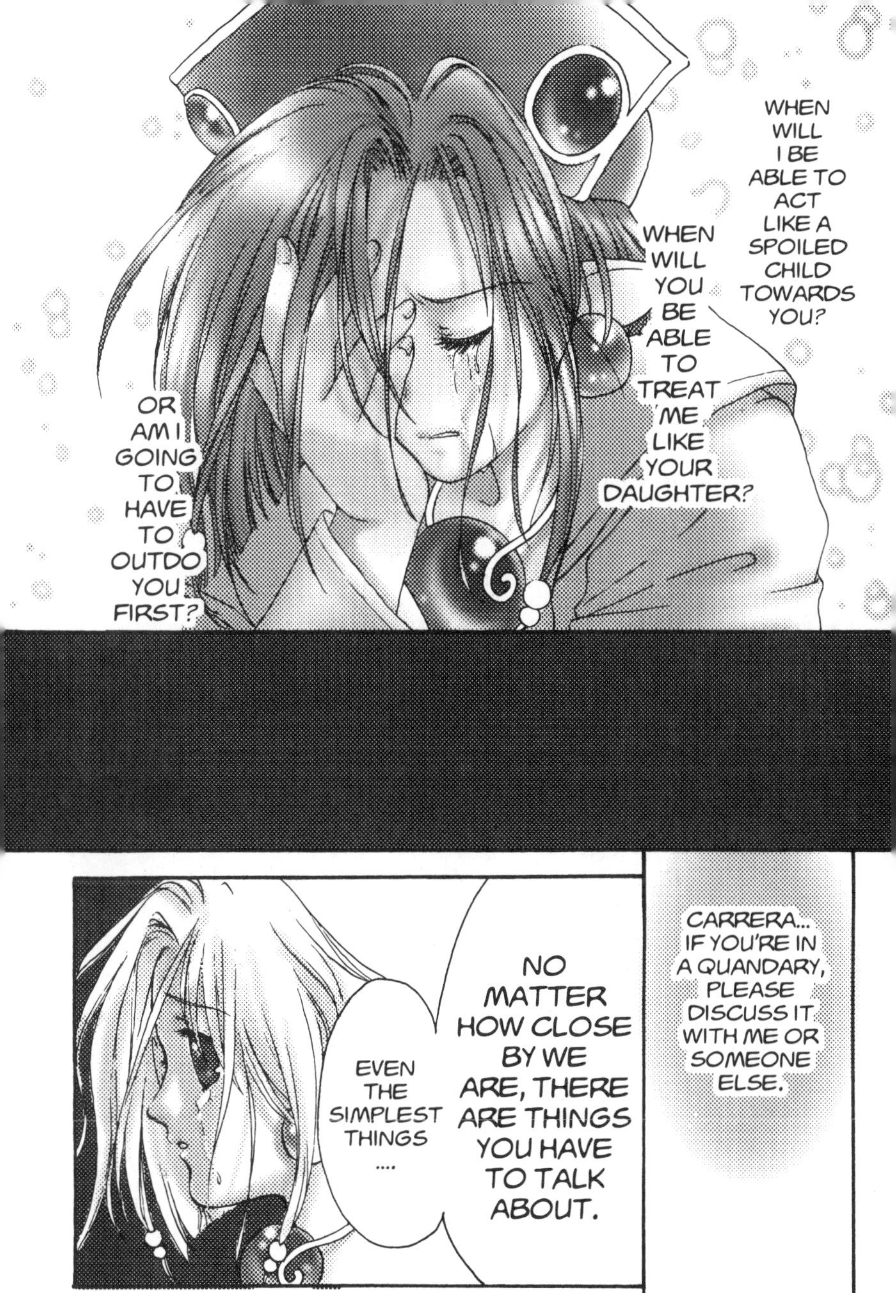
WHEN WILL I BE ABLE TO ACT LIKE A SPOILED CHILD TOWARDS YOU?
WHEN WILL YOU BE ABLE TO TREAT ME LIKE YOUR DAUGHTER?
OR AM I GOING TO HAVE TO OUTDO YOU FIRST?
CARRERA... IF YOU'RE IN A QUANDARY, PLEASE DISCUSS IT WITH ME OR SOMEONE ELSE.
NO MATTER HOW CLOSE BY WE ARE, THERE ARE THINGS YOU HAVE TO TALK ABOUT.
EVEN THE SIMPLEST THINGS ....

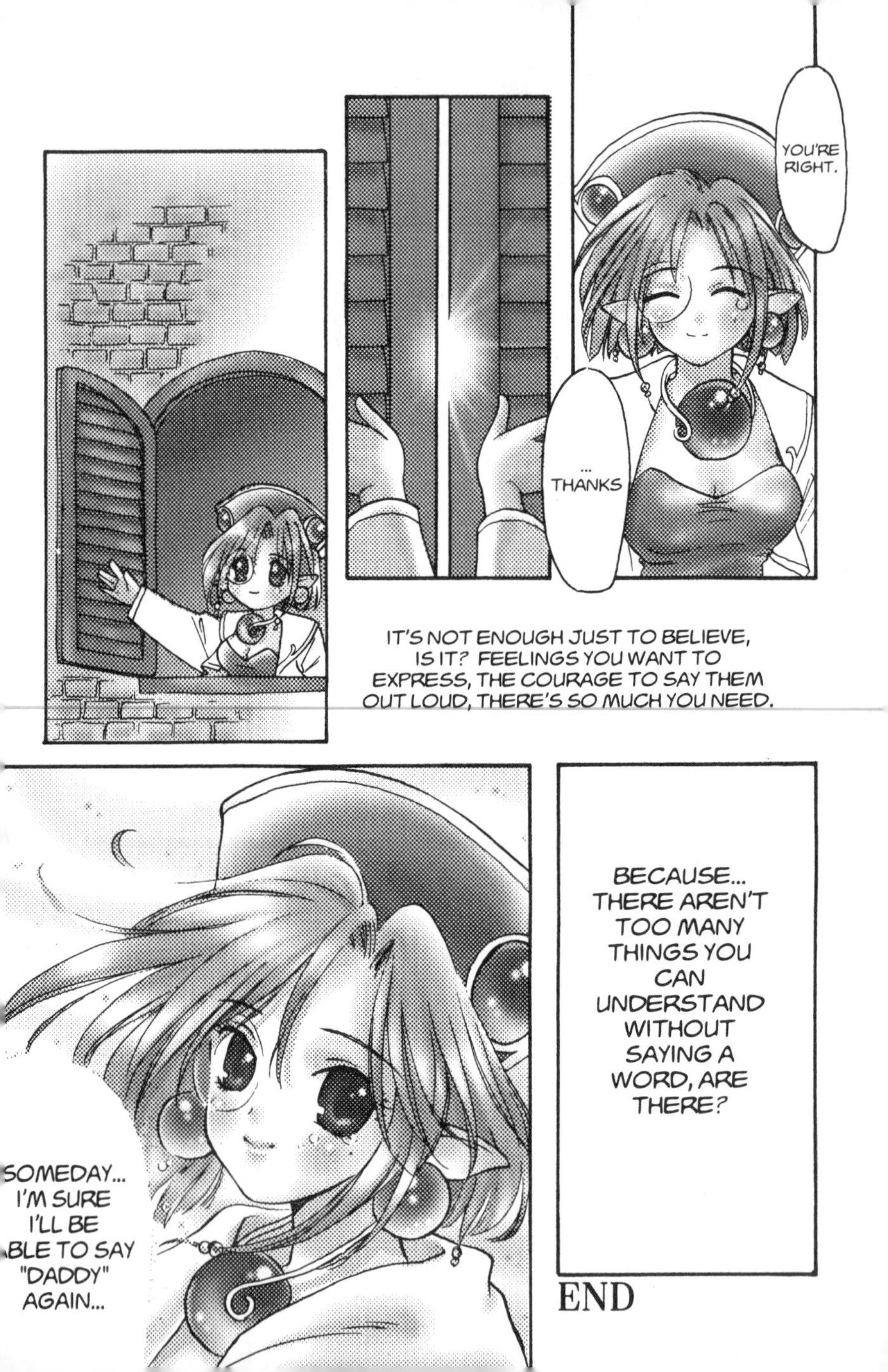
YOU'RE RIGHT.
... THANKS
IT'S NOT ENOUGH JUST TO BELIEVE, IS IT? FEELINGS YOU WANT TO EXPRESS, THE COURAGE TO SAY THEM OUT LOUD, THERE'S SO MUCH YOU NEED.
BECAUSE... THERE AREN'T TOO MANY THINGS YOU CAN UNDERSTAND WITHOUT SAYING A WORD, ARE THERE?
SOMEDAY... I'M SURE I'LL BE ABLE TO SAY "DADDY" AGAIN...
END

A WORD ABOUT "DI-GI-CHARAT"!

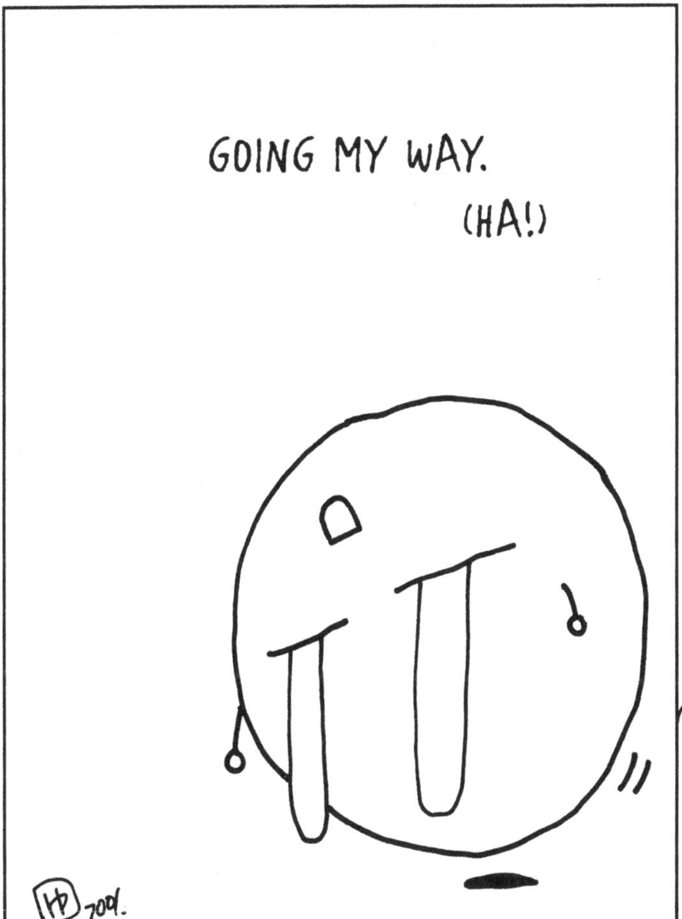
GOING MY WAY.
(HA!)

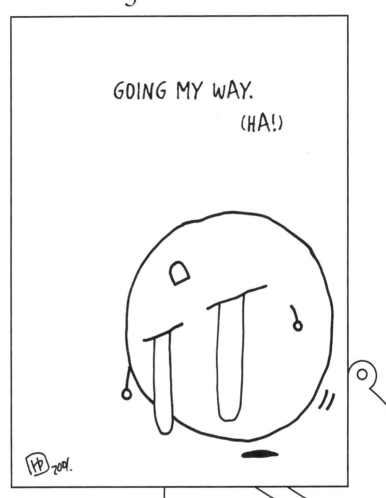

YUYA KURUMA

A WORD ABOUT "DI-GI-CHARAT"!

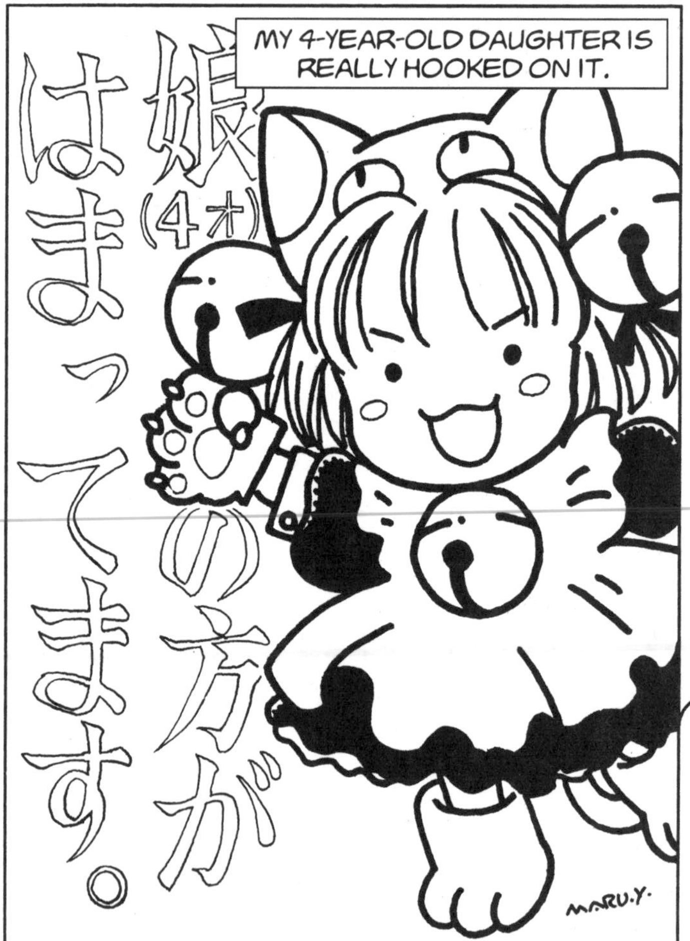
MY 4-YEAR-OLD DAUGHTER IS REALLY HOOKED ON IT.
娘(4才)の方がはまってます。
MARU.Y.

MARUMI YAMAMOTO

HOLD MY HAND

KAZUKI☆SHU

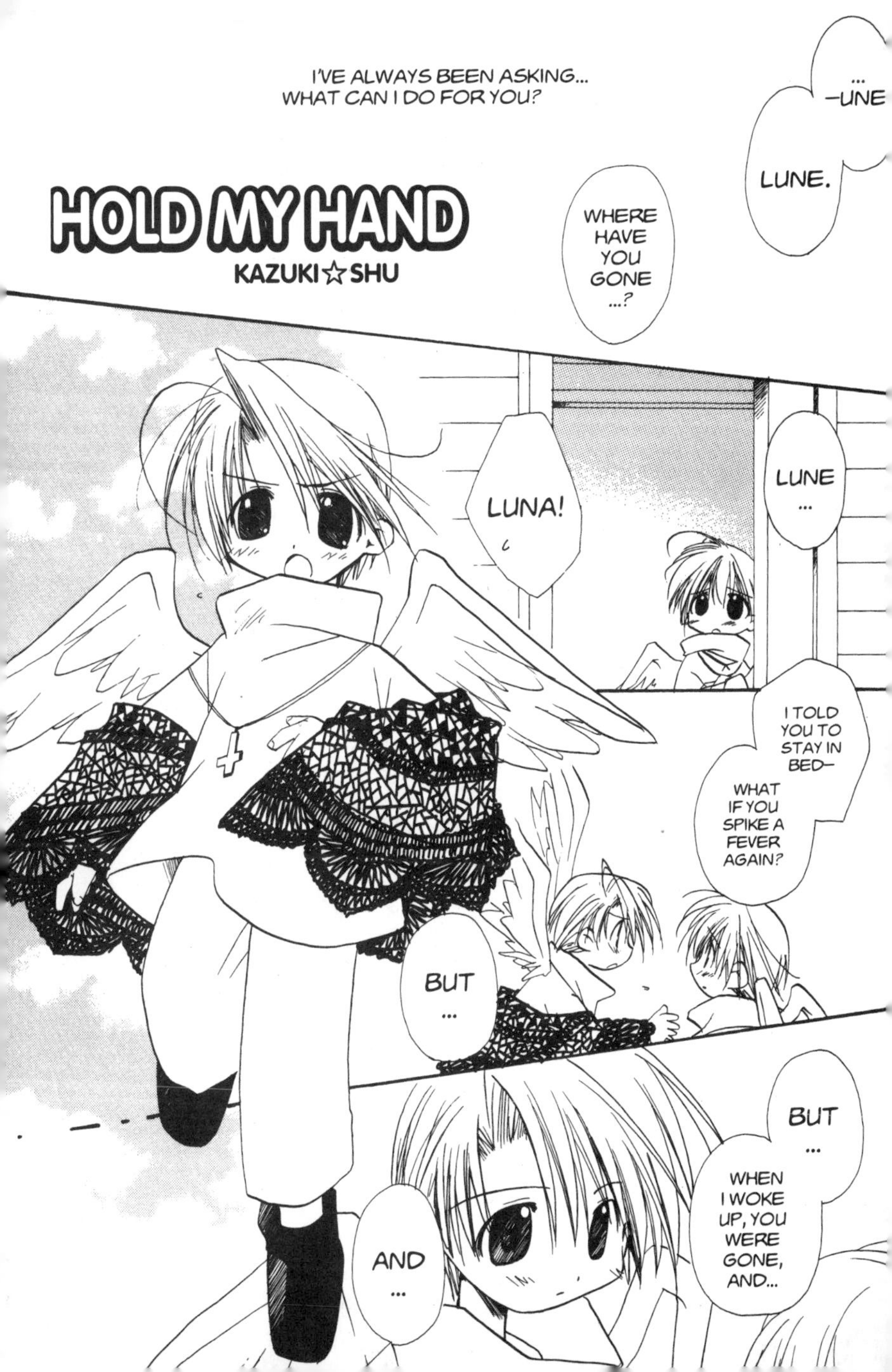
... —UNE
LUNE.
WHERE HAVE YOU GONE ...?
I'VE ALWAYS BEEN ASKING... WHAT CAN I DO FOR YOU?
LUNE ...
LUNA!
I TOLD YOU TO STAY IN BED—
WHAT IF YOU SPIKE A FEVER AGAIN?
BUT ...
BUT ...
WHEN I WOKE UP, YOU WERE GONE, AND...
AND ...

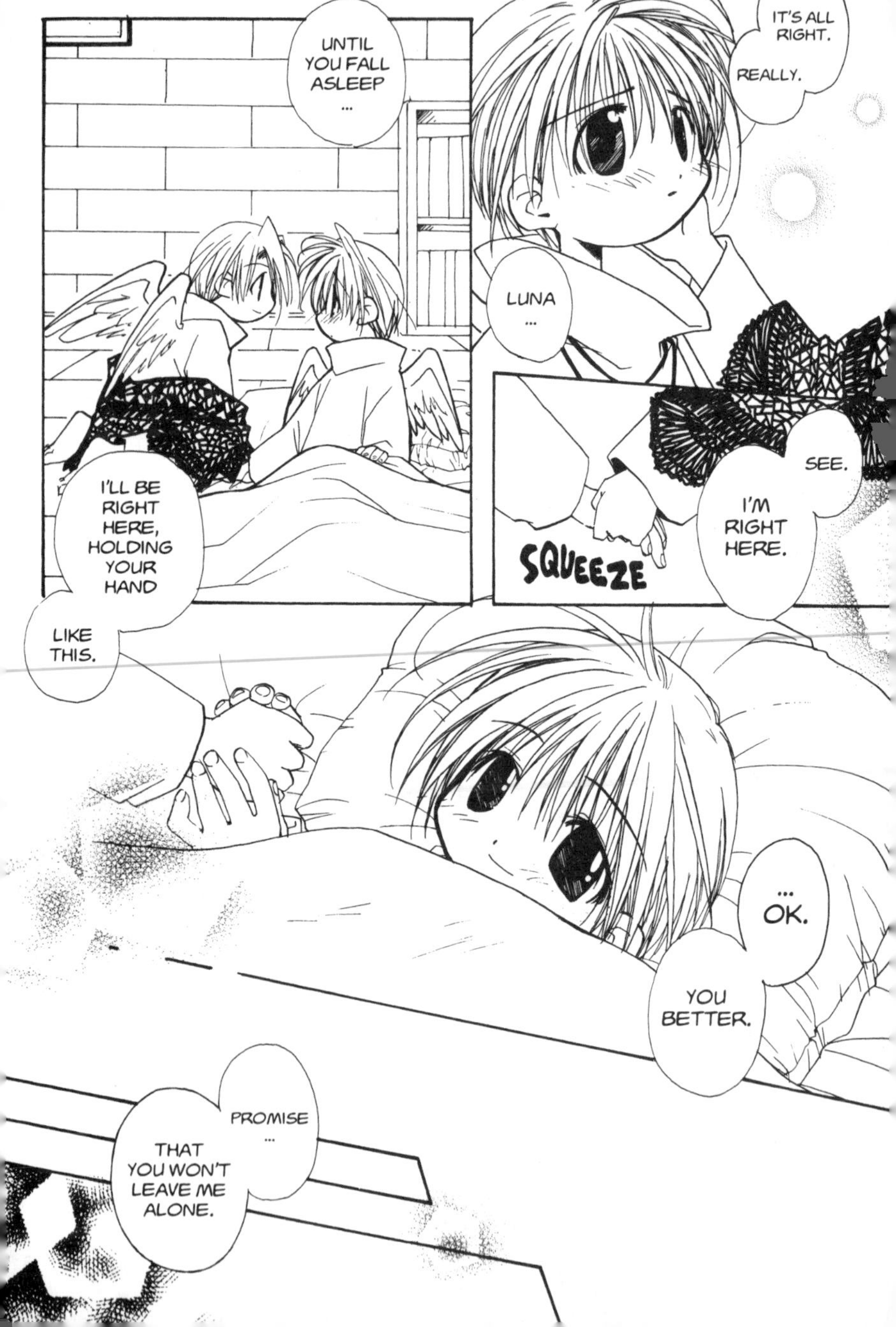
IT'S ALL RIGHT.
REALLY.
LUNA ...
SEE.
I'M RIGHT HERE.
SQUEEZE
UNTIL YOU FALL ASLEEP ...
I'LL BE RIGHT HERE, HOLDING YOUR HAND
LIKE THIS.
... OK.
YOU BETTER.
PROMISE ...
THAT YOU WON'T LEAVE ME ALONE.

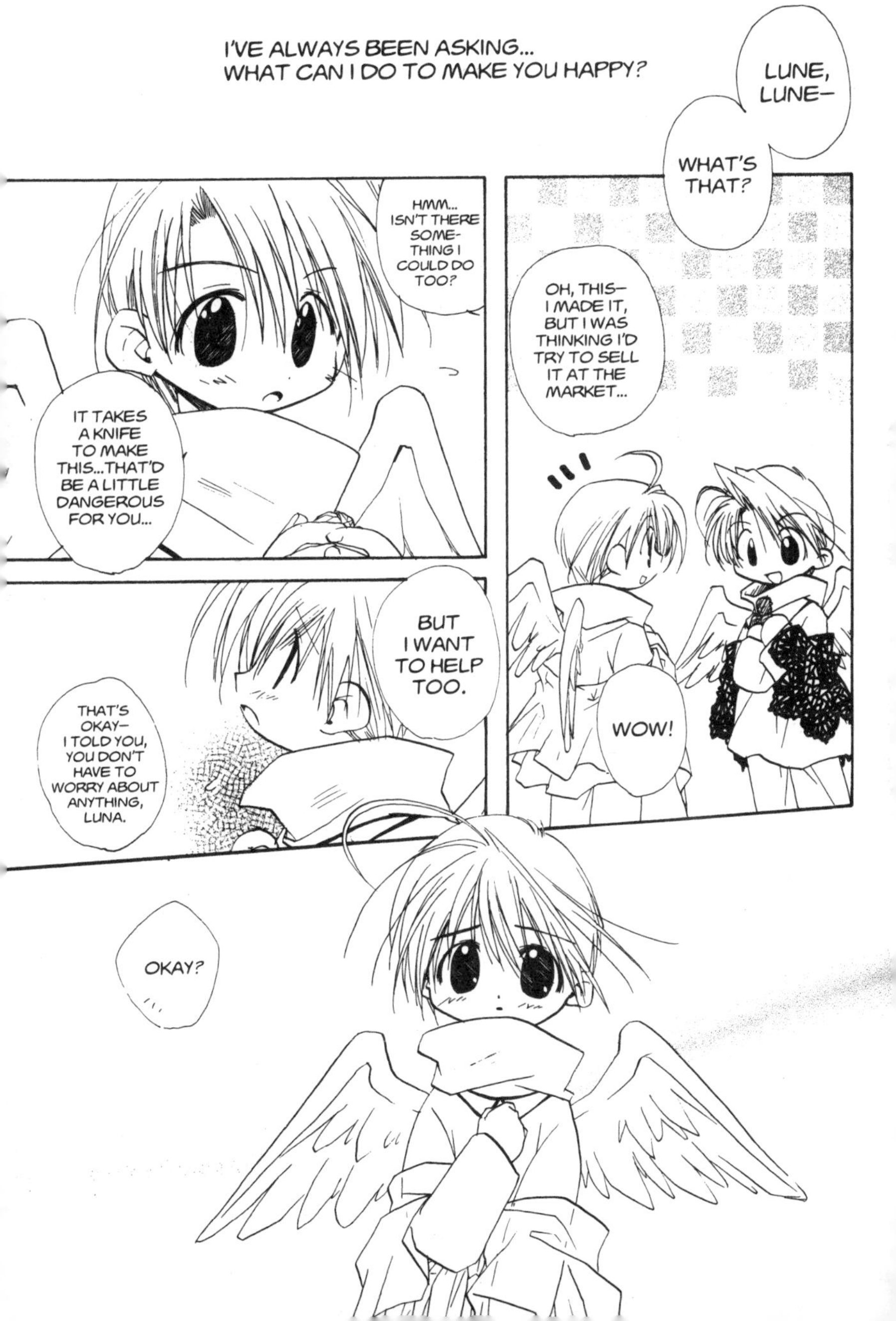
I'VE ALWAYS BEEN ASKING...
WHAT CAN I DO TO MAKE YOU HAPPY?
LUNE, LUNE—
WHAT'S THAT?
OH, THIS— I MADE IT, BUT I WAS THINKING I'D TRY TO SELL IT AT THE MARKET...
WOW!
HMM... ISN'T THERE SOME-THING I COULD DO TOO?
IT TAKES A KNIFE TO MAKE THIS...THAT'D BE A LITTLE DANGEROUS FOR YOU...
BUT I WANT TO HELP TOO.
THAT'S OKAY— I TOLD YOU, YOU DON'T HAVE TO WORRY ABOUT ANYTHING, LUNA.
OKAY?

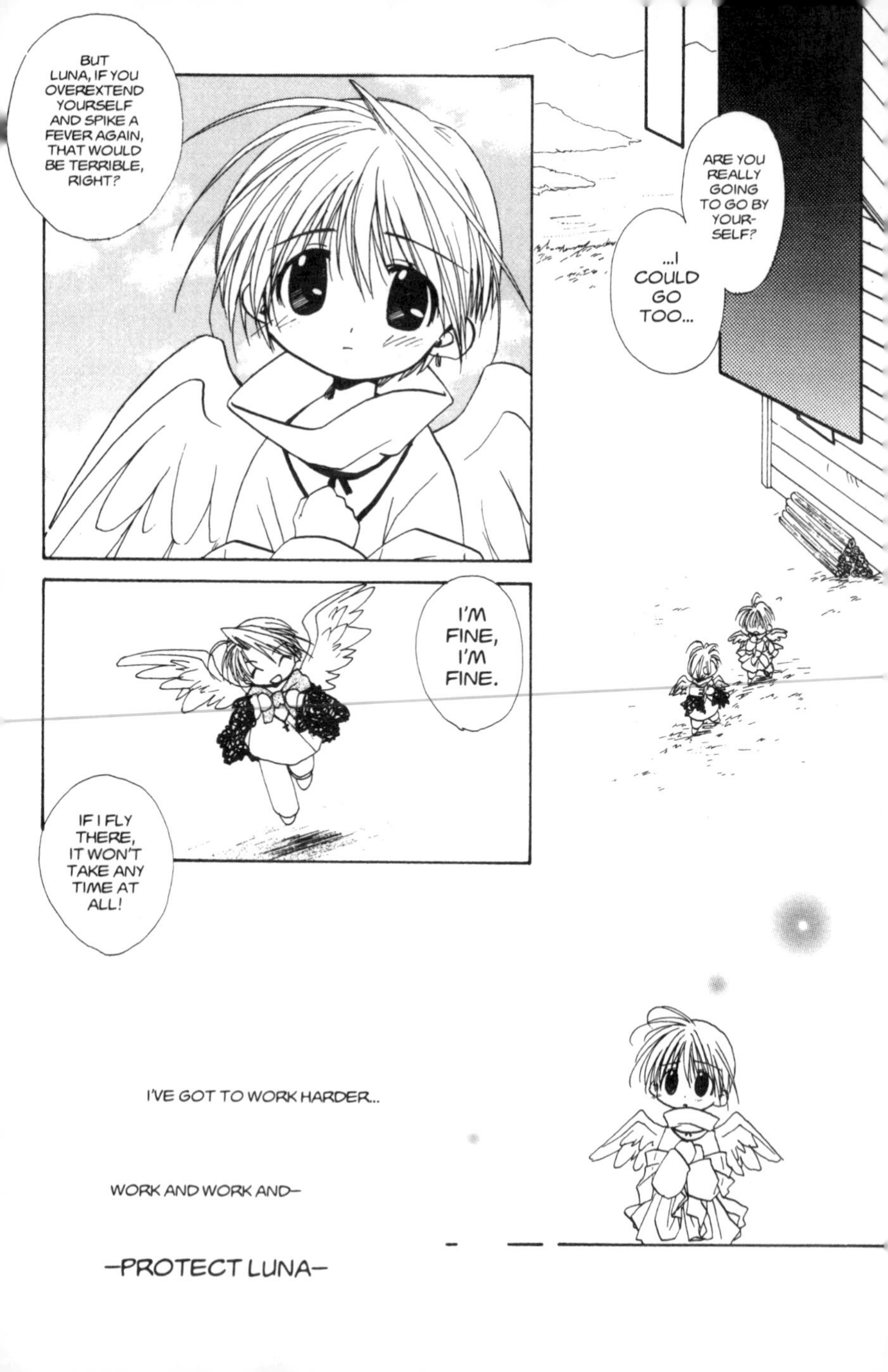
ARE YOU REALLY GOING TO GO BY YOURSELF?
...I COULD GO TOO...
BUT LUNA, IF YOU OVEREXTEND YOURSELF AND SPIKE A FEVER AGAIN, THAT WOULD BE TERRIBLE, RIGHT?
I'M FINE, I'M FINE.
IF I FLY THERE, IT WON'T TAKE ANY TIME AT ALL!
I'VE GOT TO WORK HARDER..
WORK AND WORK AND—
—PROTECT LUNA—

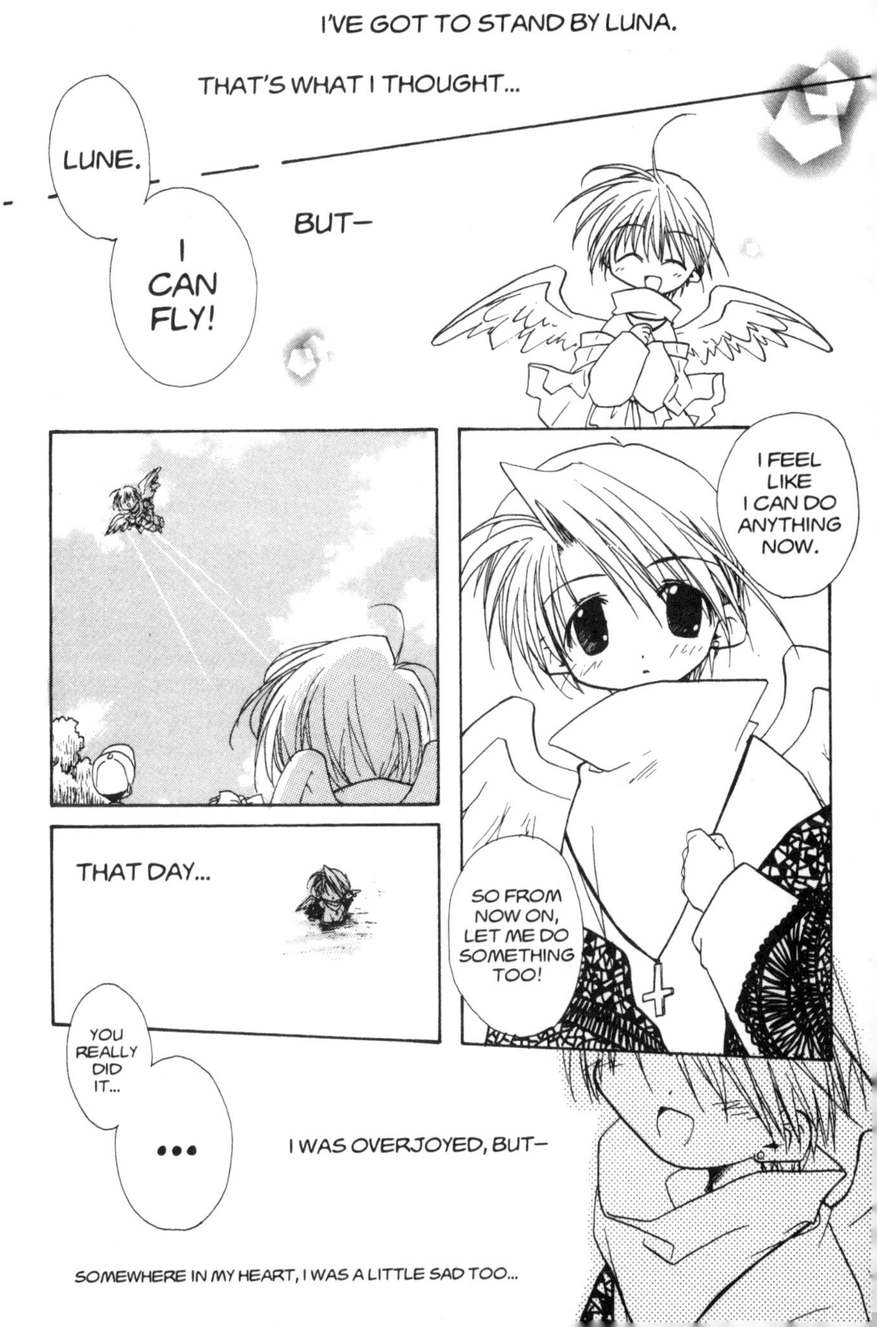
I'VE GOT TO STAND BY LUNA.
THAT'S WHAT I THOUGHT...
BUT—
LUNE.
I CAN FLY!
I FEEL LIKE I CAN DO ANYTHING NOW.
SO FROM NOW ON, LET ME DO SOMETHING TOO!
THAT DAY...
YOU REALLY DID IT...
•••
I WAS OVERJOYED, BUT—
SOMEWHERE IN MY HEART, I WAS A LITTLE SAD TOO...

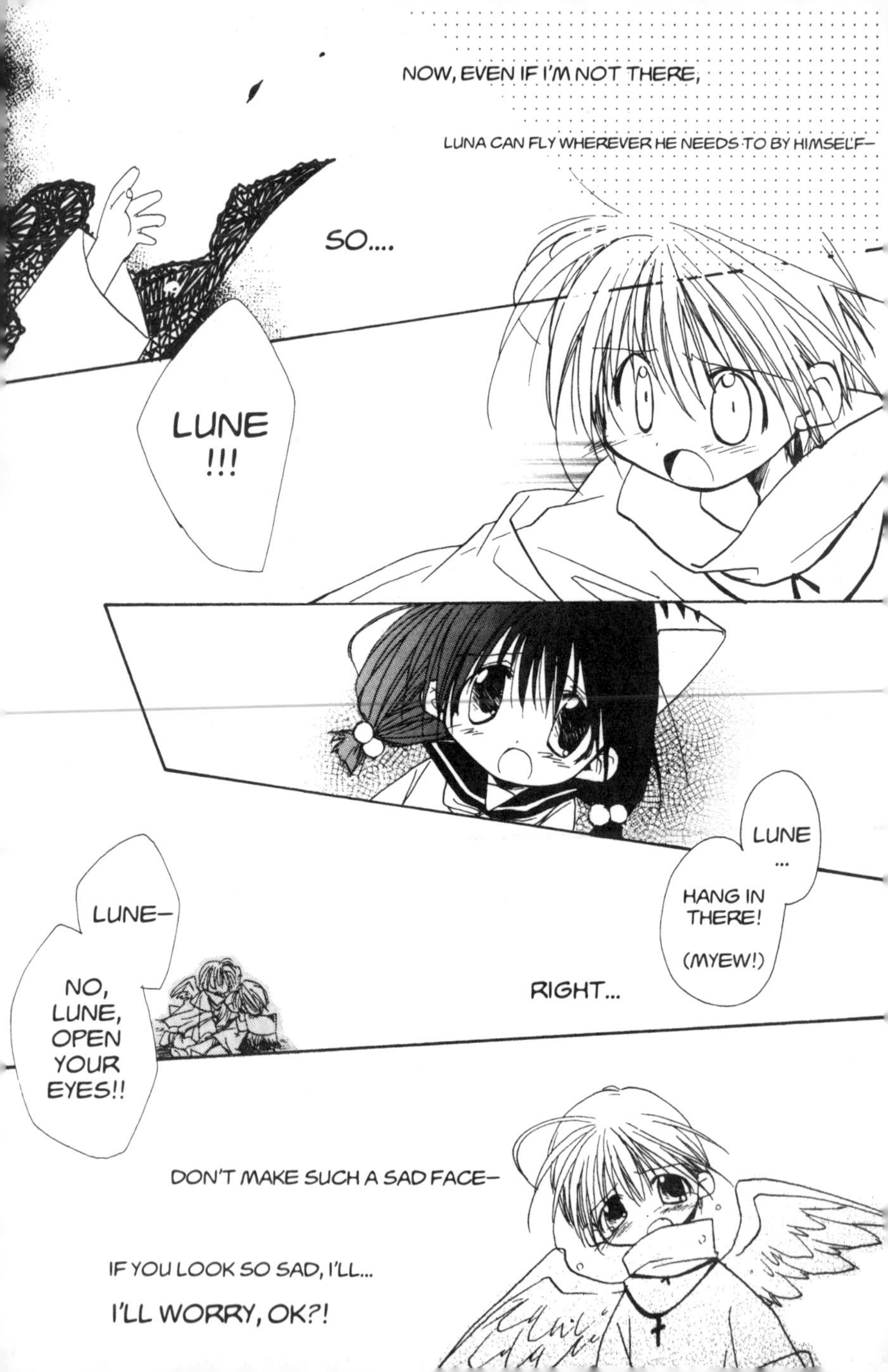
NOW, EVEN IF I'M NOT THERE,
LUNA CAN FLY WHEREVER HE NEEDS TO BY HIMSELF—
SO....
LUNE !!!
LUNE ... HANG IN THERE! (MYEW!)
RIGHT...
LUNE—
NO, LUNE, OPEN YOUR EYES!!
DON'T MAKE SUCH A SAD FACE—
IF YOU LOOK SO SAD, I'LL...
I'LL WORRY, OK?!

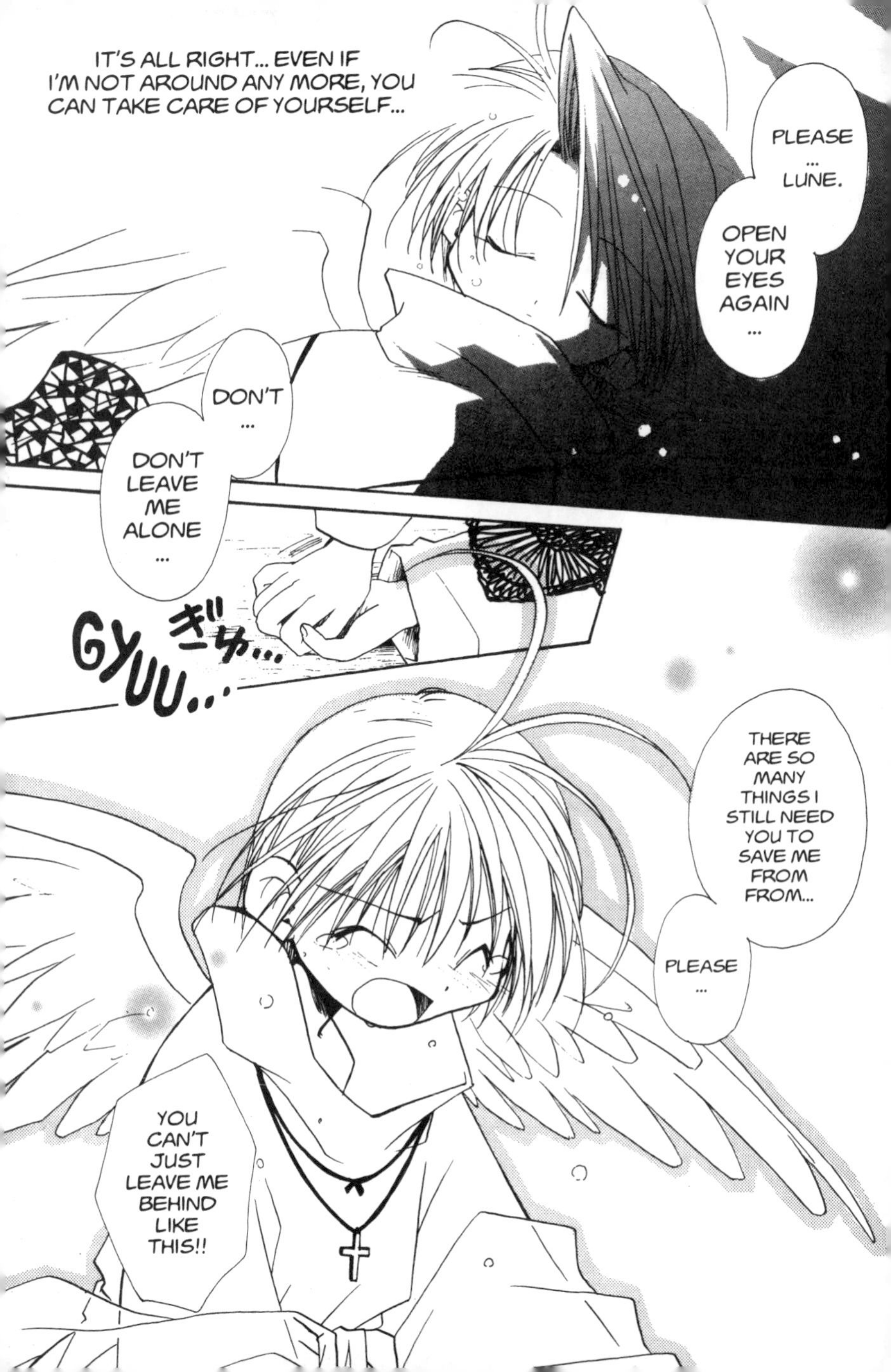
PLEASE ... LUNE.
OPEN YOUR EYES AGAIN ...
IT'S ALL RIGHT... EVEN IF I'M NOT AROUND ANY MORE, YOU CAN TAKE CARE OF YOURSELF...
DON'T ...
DON'T LEAVE ME ALONE ...
ぎゅ…
GYUU...
THERE ARE SO MANY THINGS I STILL NEED YOU TO SAVE ME FROM FROM...
PLEASE ...
YOU CAN'T JUST LEAVE ME BEHIND LIKE THIS!!

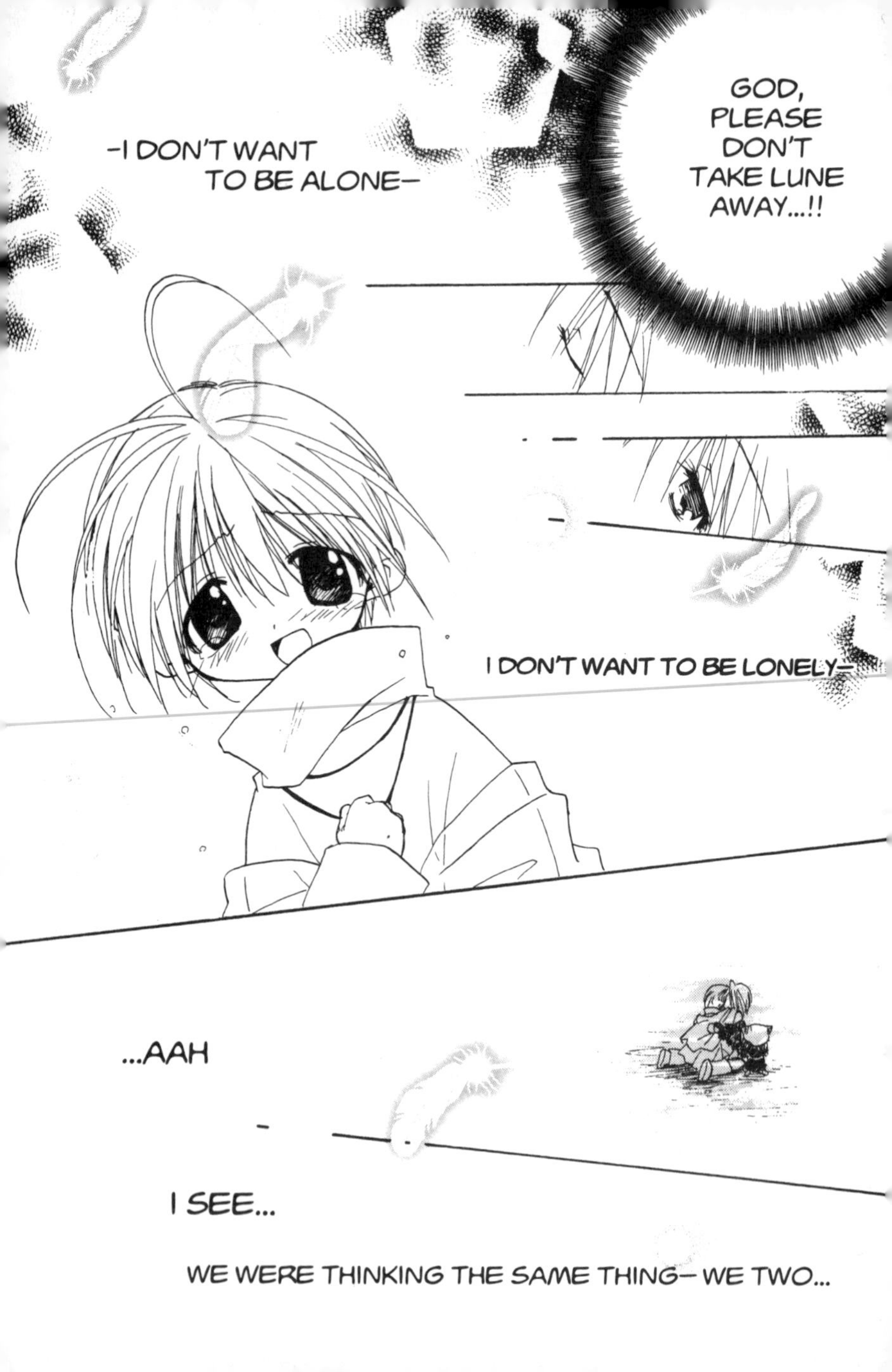
GOD, PLEASE DON'T TAKE LUNE AWAY...!!
-I DON'T WANT TO BE ALONE-
I DON'T WANT TO BE LONELY-
...AAH
I SEE...
WE WERE THINKING THE SAME THING- WE TWO...

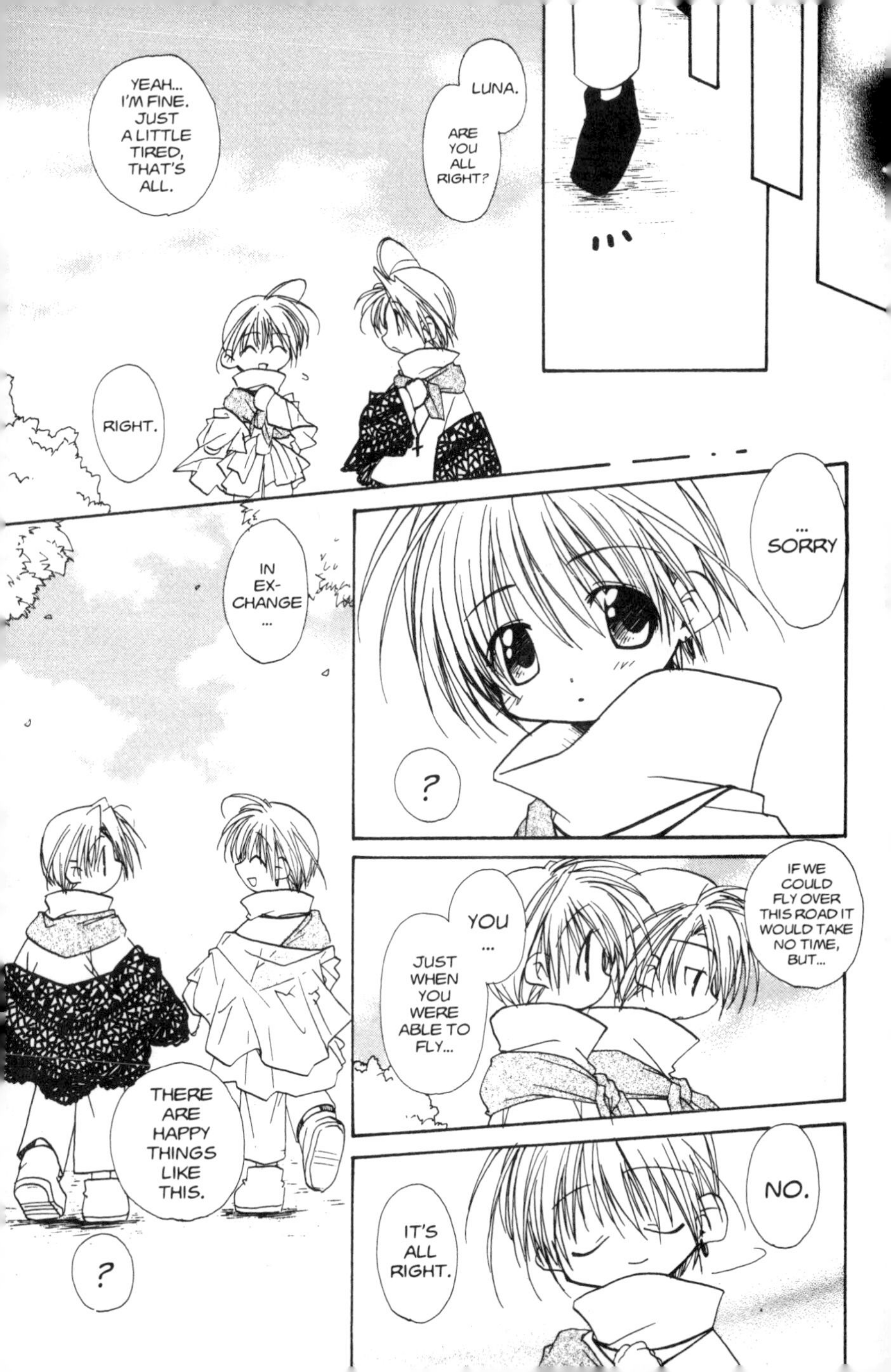
...
LUNA.
ARE YOU ALL RIGHT?
YEAH... I'M FINE. JUST A LITTLE TIRED, THAT'S ALL.
RIGHT.
... SORRY
?
IF WE COULD FLY OVER THIS ROAD IT WOULD TAKE NO TIME, BUT...
YOU ...
JUST WHEN YOU WERE ABLE TO FLY...
NO.
IT'S ALL RIGHT.
IN EX-CHANGE ...
THERE ARE HAPPY THINGS LIKE THIS.
?

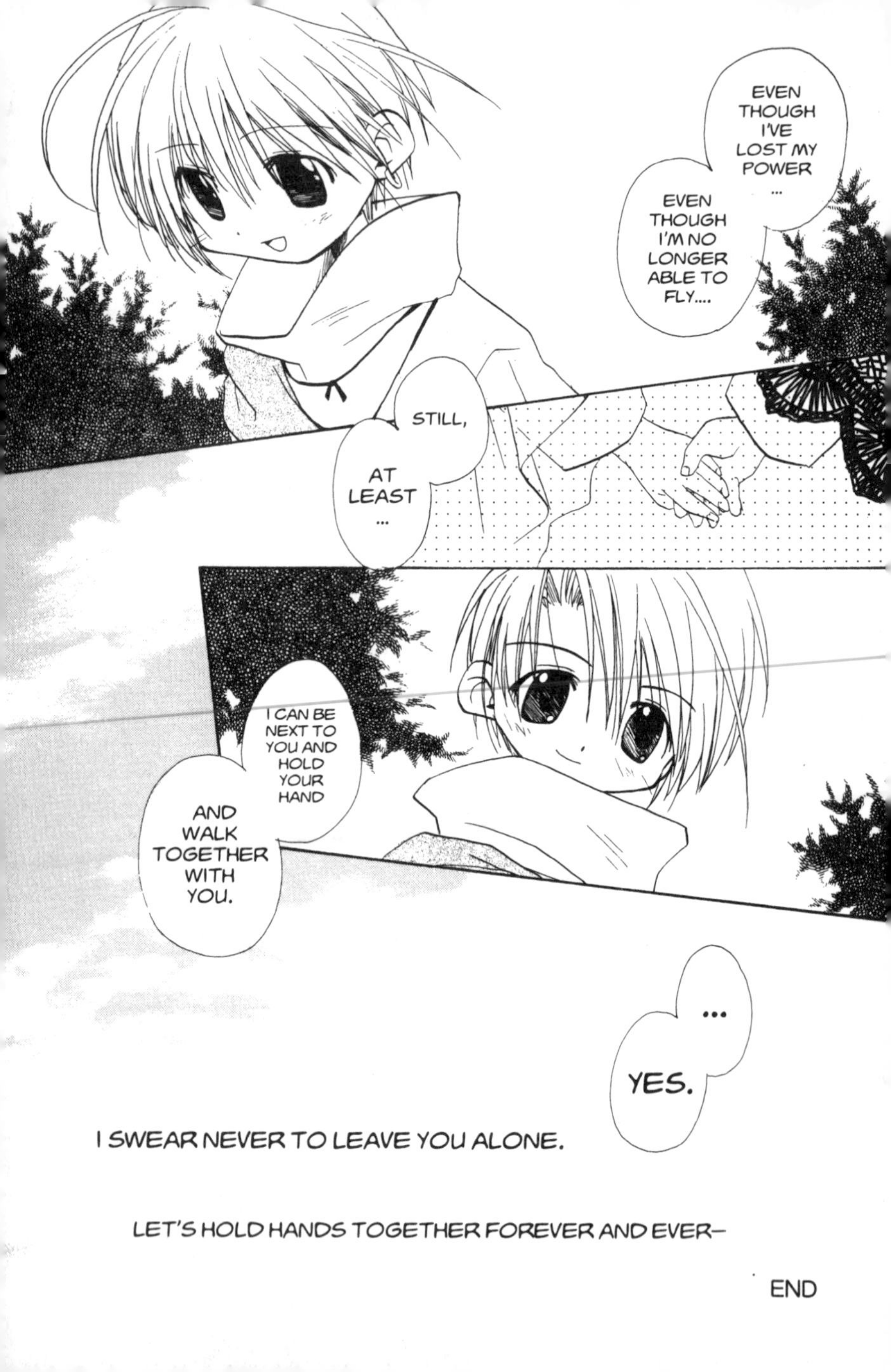
EVEN THOUGH I'VE LOST MY POWER ...
EVEN THOUGH I'M NO LONGER ABLE TO FLY....
STILL,
AT LEAST ...
I CAN BE NEXT TO YOU AND HOLD YOUR HAND
AND WALK TOGETHER WITH YOU.
...
YES.
I SWEAR NEVER TO LEAVE YOU ALONE.
LET'S HOLD HANDS TOGETHER FOREVER AND EVER–
END

RIBBON

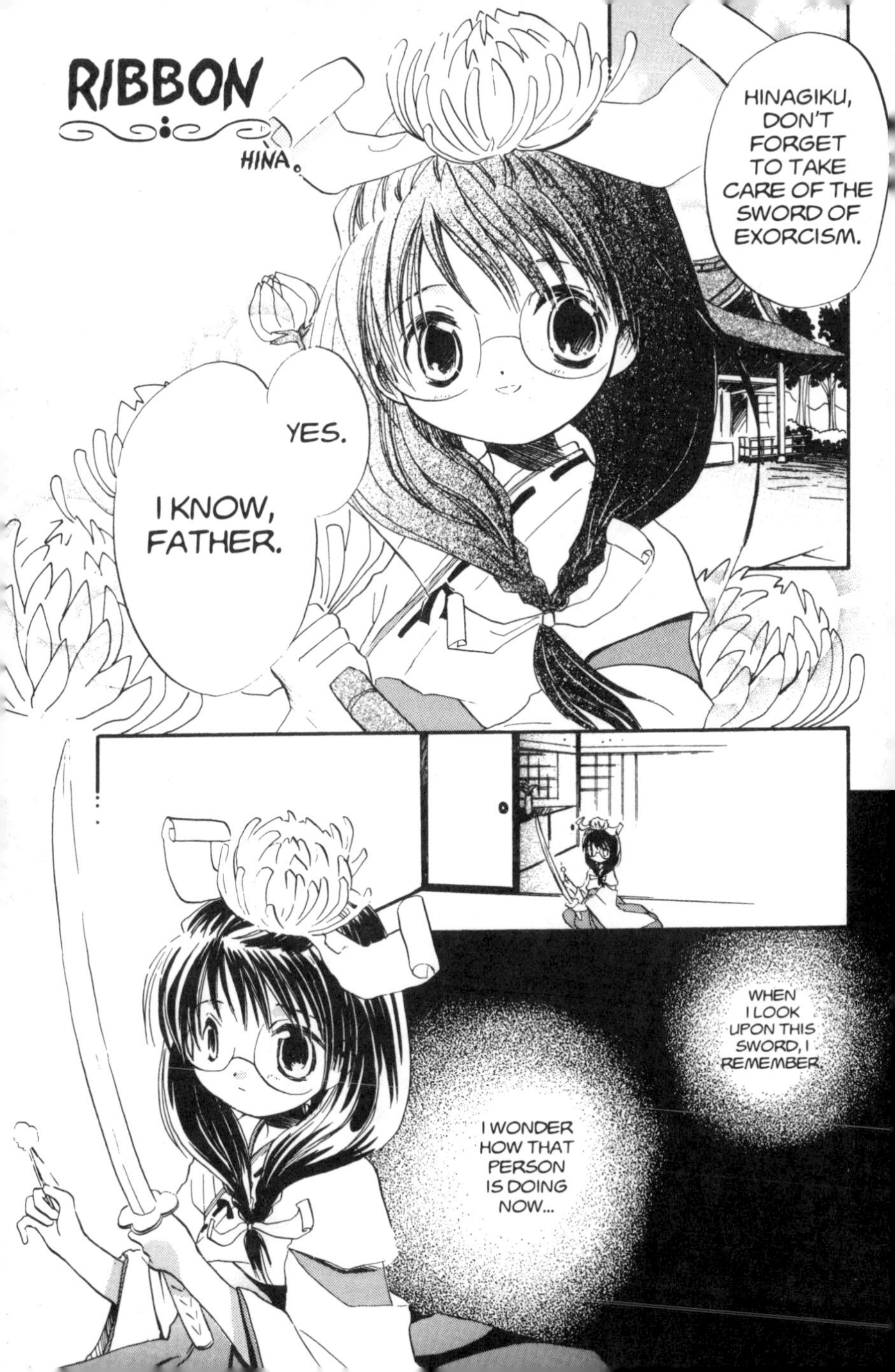
HINA.
HINAGIKU, DON'T FORGET TO TAKE CARE OF THE SWORD OF EXORCISM.
YES.
I KNOW, FATHER.
WHEN I LOOK UPON THIS SWORD, I REMEMBER.
I WONDER HOW THAT PERSON IS DOING NOW...

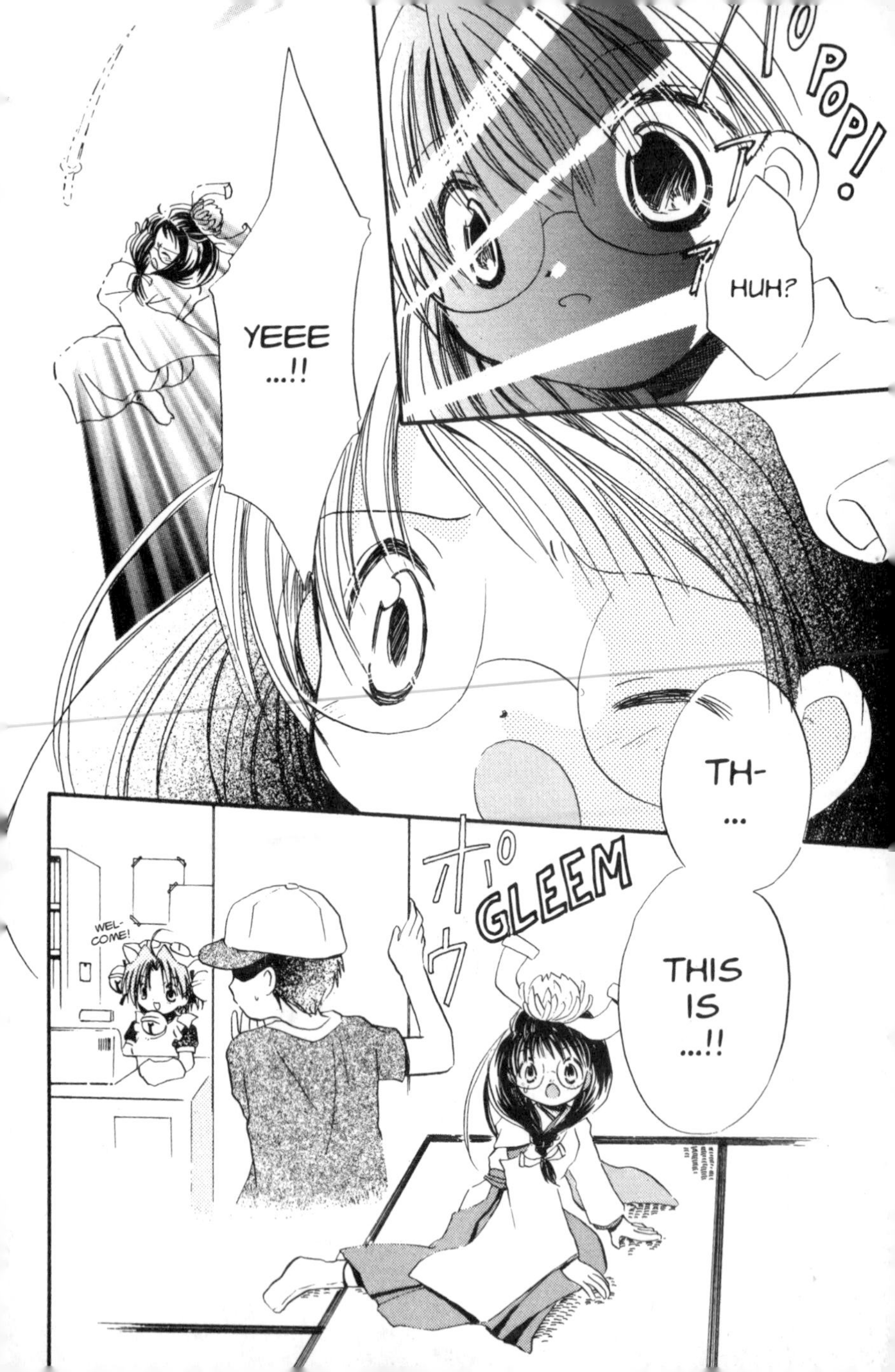
POPI!
HUH?
YEEE ...!!
TH- ...
THIS IS ...!!
GLEEM
WEL-COME!

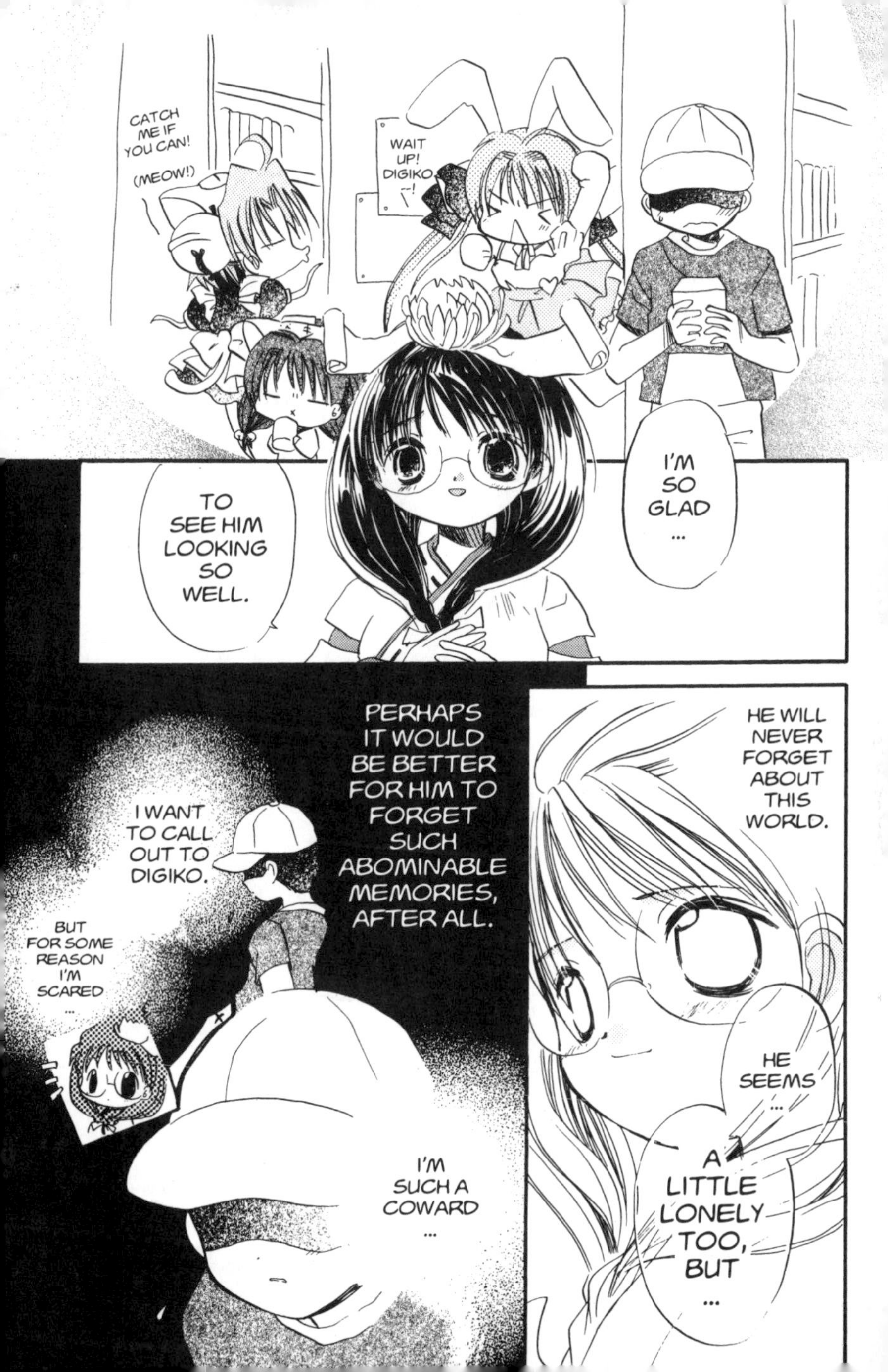
WAIT UP! DIGIKO--!
CATCH ME IF YOU CAN!
(MEOW!)
I'M SO GLAD ...
TO SEE HIM LOOKING SO WELL.
HE WILL NEVER FORGET ABOUT THIS WORLD.
HE SEEMS ...
A LITTLE LONELY TOO, BUT ...
PERHAPS IT WOULD BE BETTER FOR HIM TO FORGET SUCH ABOMINABLE MEMORIES, AFTER ALL.
I WANT TO CALL OUT TO DIGIKO.
BUT FOR SOME REASON I'M SCARED ...
I'M SUCH A COWARD ...

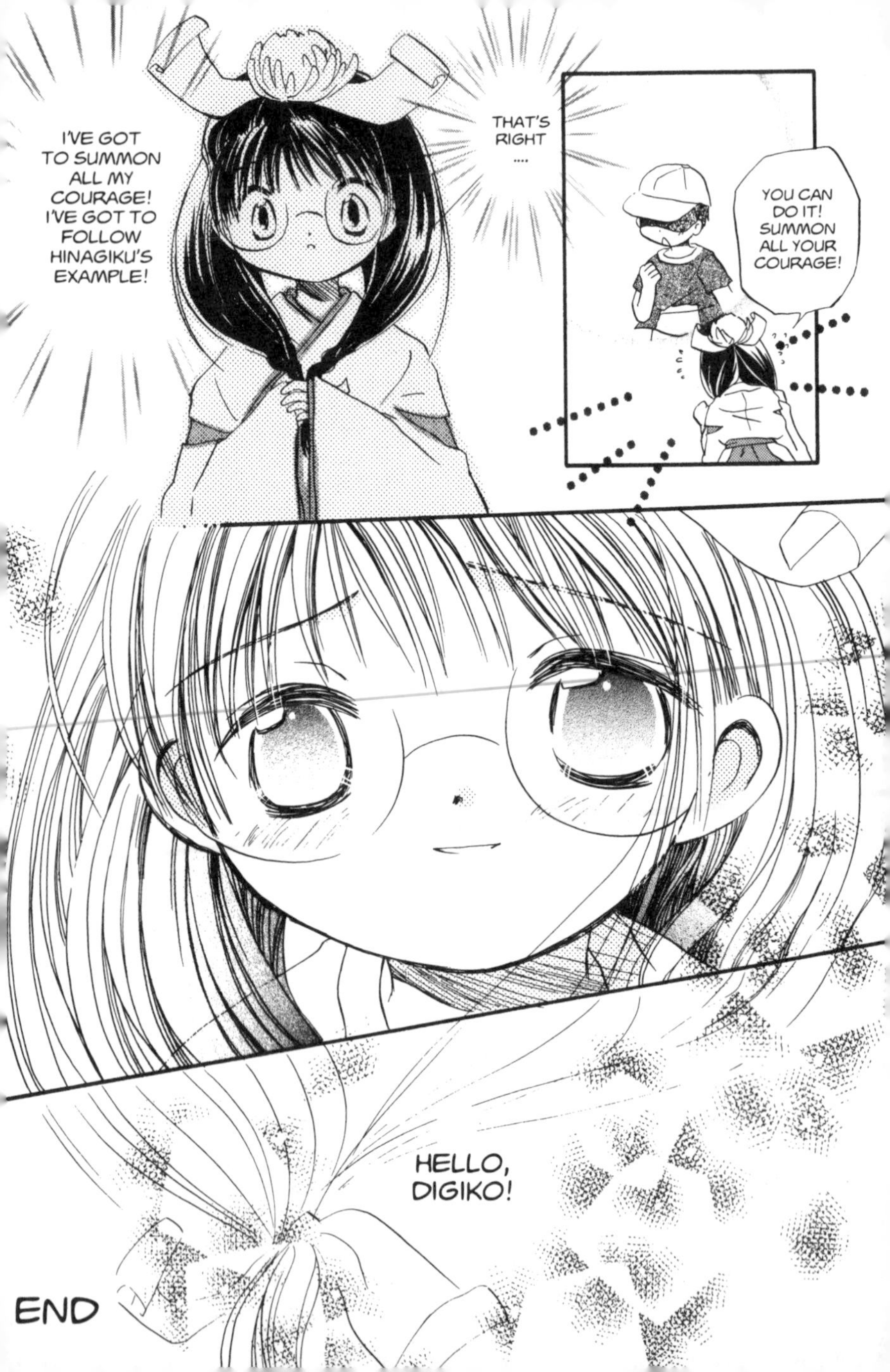
YOU CAN DO IT! SUMMON ALL YOUR COURAGE!
THAT'S RIGHT ....
I'VE GOT TO SUMMON ALL MY COURAGE! I'VE GOT TO FOLLOW HINAGIKU'S EXAMPLE!
HELLO, DIGIKO!
END

A WORD ABOUT "DI-GI-CHARAT"!

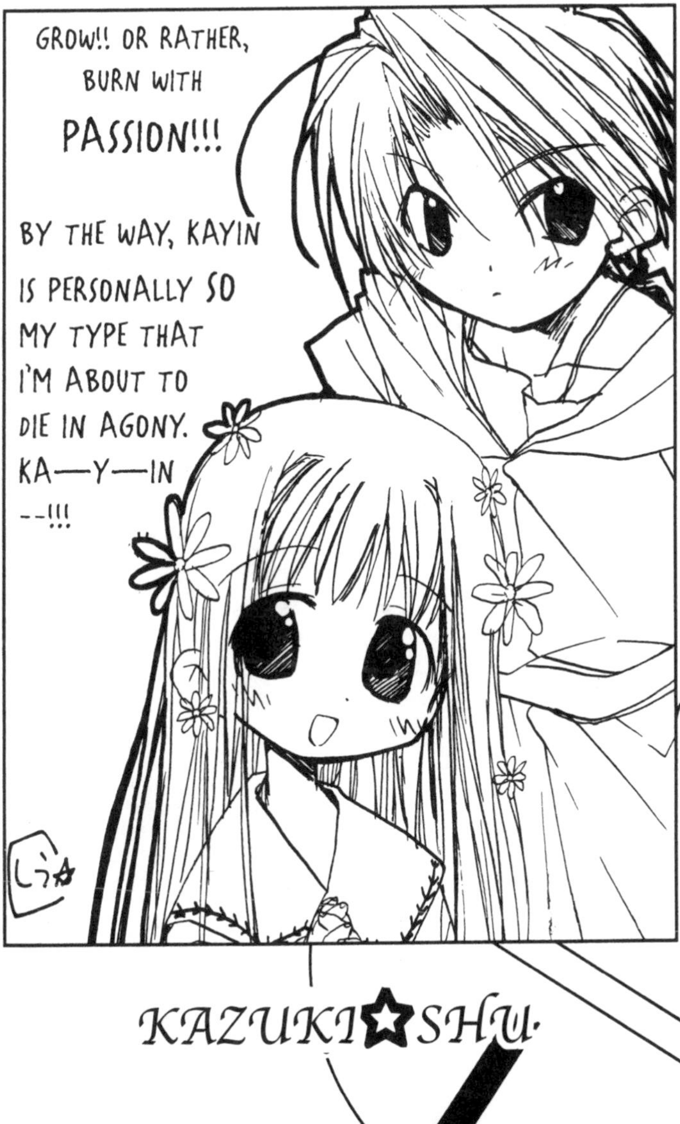
GROW!! OR RATHER, BURN WITH PASSION!!!
BY THE WAY, KAYIN IS PERSONALLY SO MY TYPE THAT I'M ABOUT TO DIE IN AGONY. KA—Y—IN --!!!

KAZUKI☆SHU

A WORD ABOUT "DI-GI-CHARAT"!

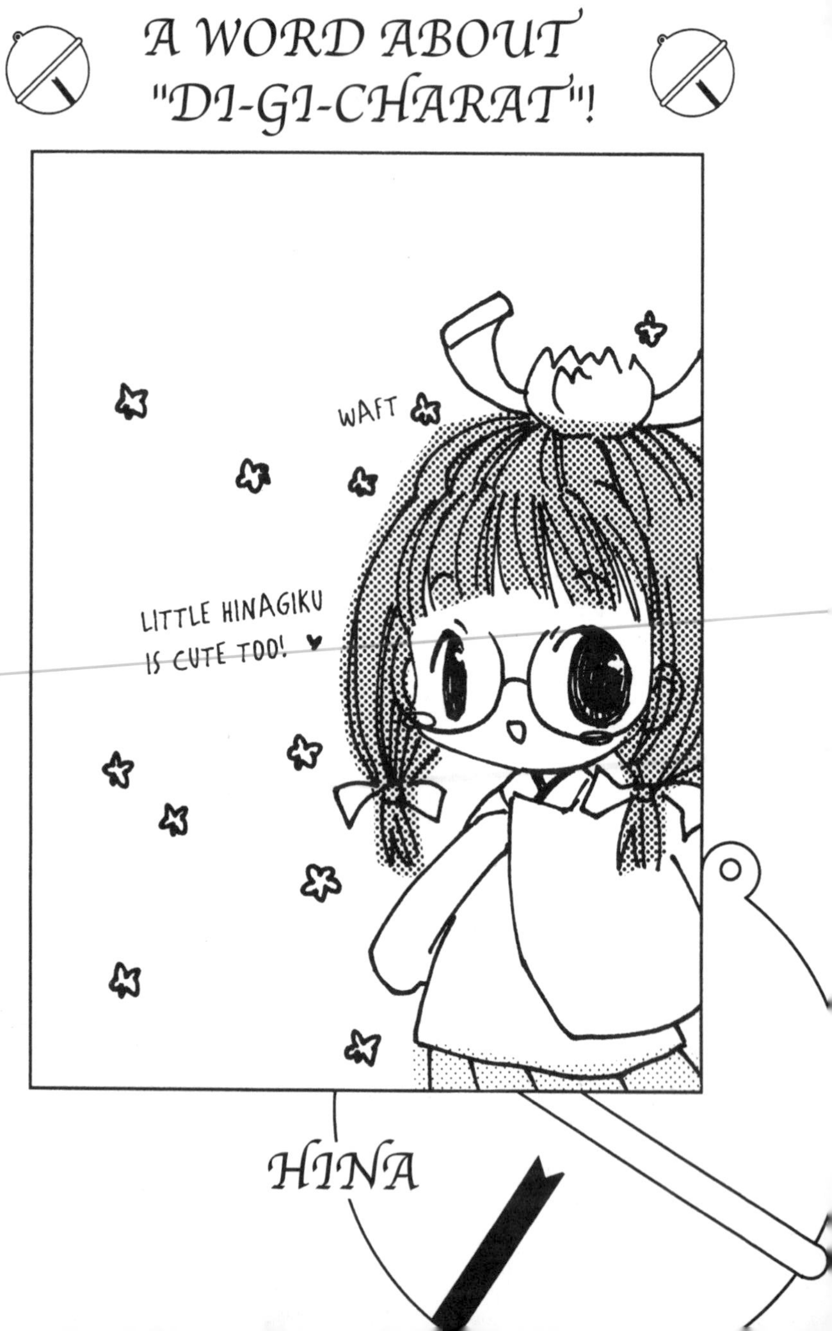
WAFT
LITTLE HINAGIKU IS CUTE TOO! ♥

HINA

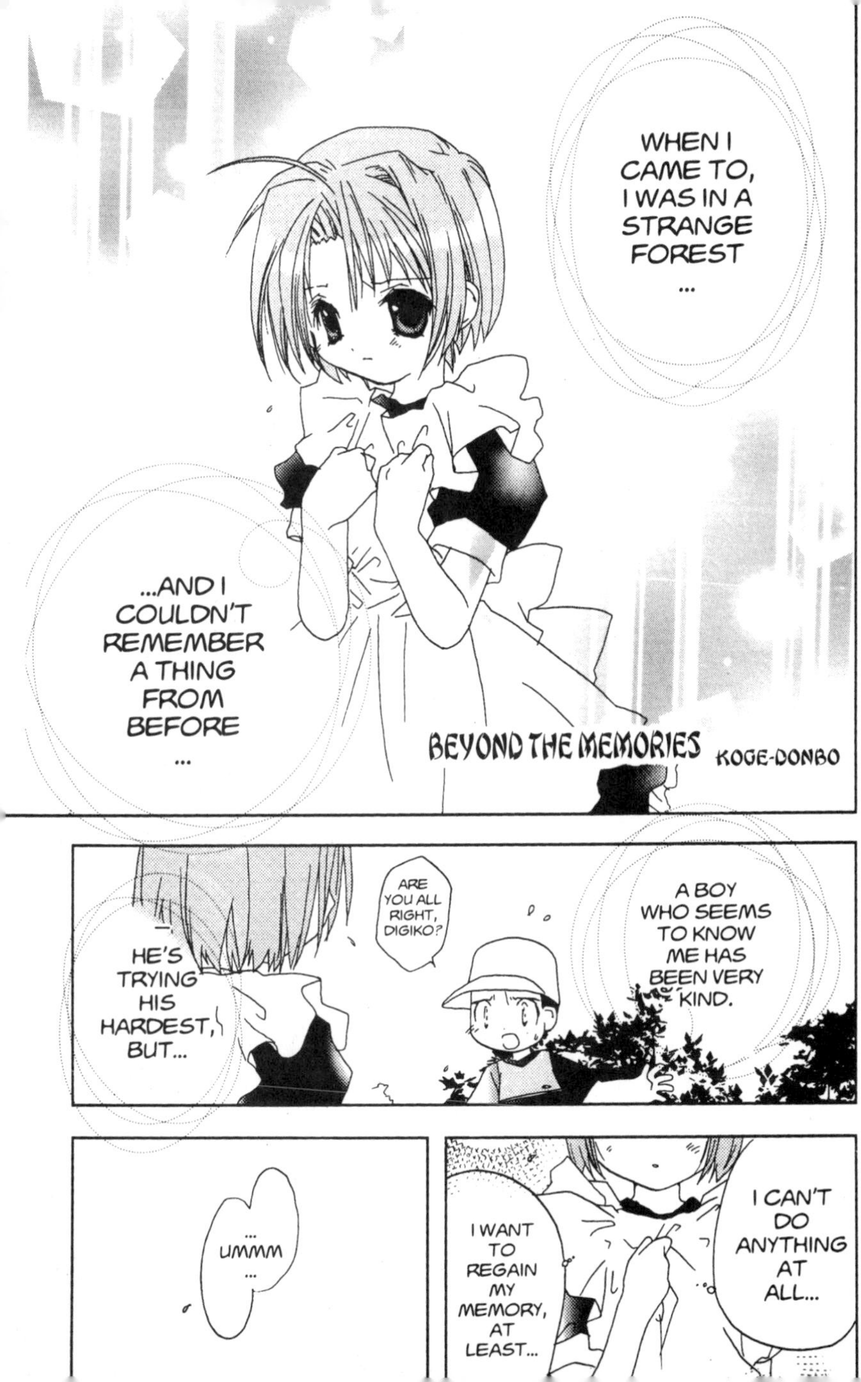
WHEN I CAME TO, I WAS IN A STRANGE FOREST ...
...AND I COULDN'T REMEMBER A THING FROM BEFORE ...
BEYOND THE MEMORIES
KOGE-DONBO
A BOY WHO SEEMS TO KNOW ME HAS BEEN VERY KIND.
ARE YOU ALL RIGHT, DIGIKO?
—. HE'S TRYING HIS HARDEST, BUT...
I CAN'T DO ANYTHING AT ALL...
I WANT TO REGAIN MY MEMORY, AT LEAST...
... UMMM ...

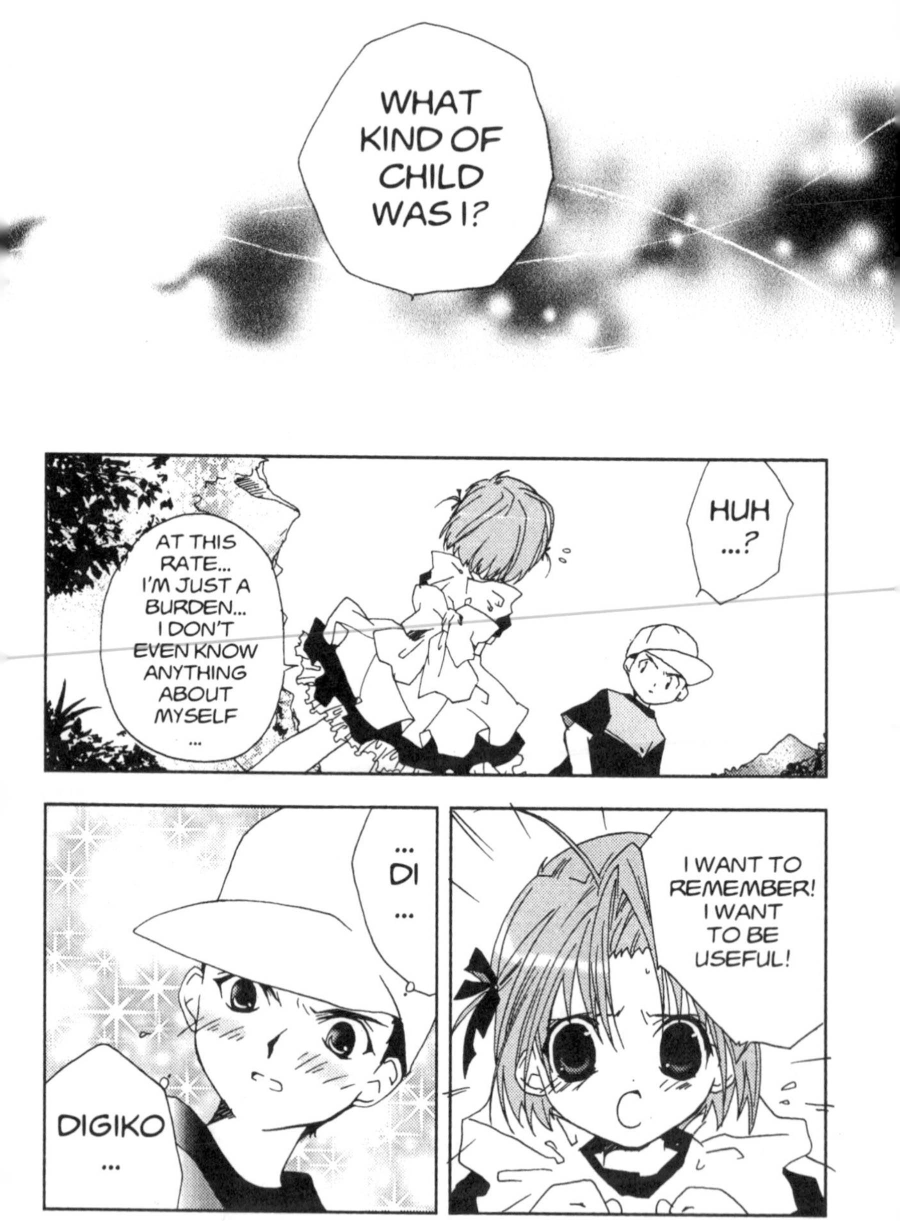
WHAT KIND OF CHILD WAS I?
HUH ...?
AT THIS RATE... I'M JUST A BURDEN... I DON'T EVEN KNOW ANYTHING ABOUT MYSELF ...
I WANT TO REMEMBER! I WANT TO BE USEFUL!
... DI ...
DIGIKO ...

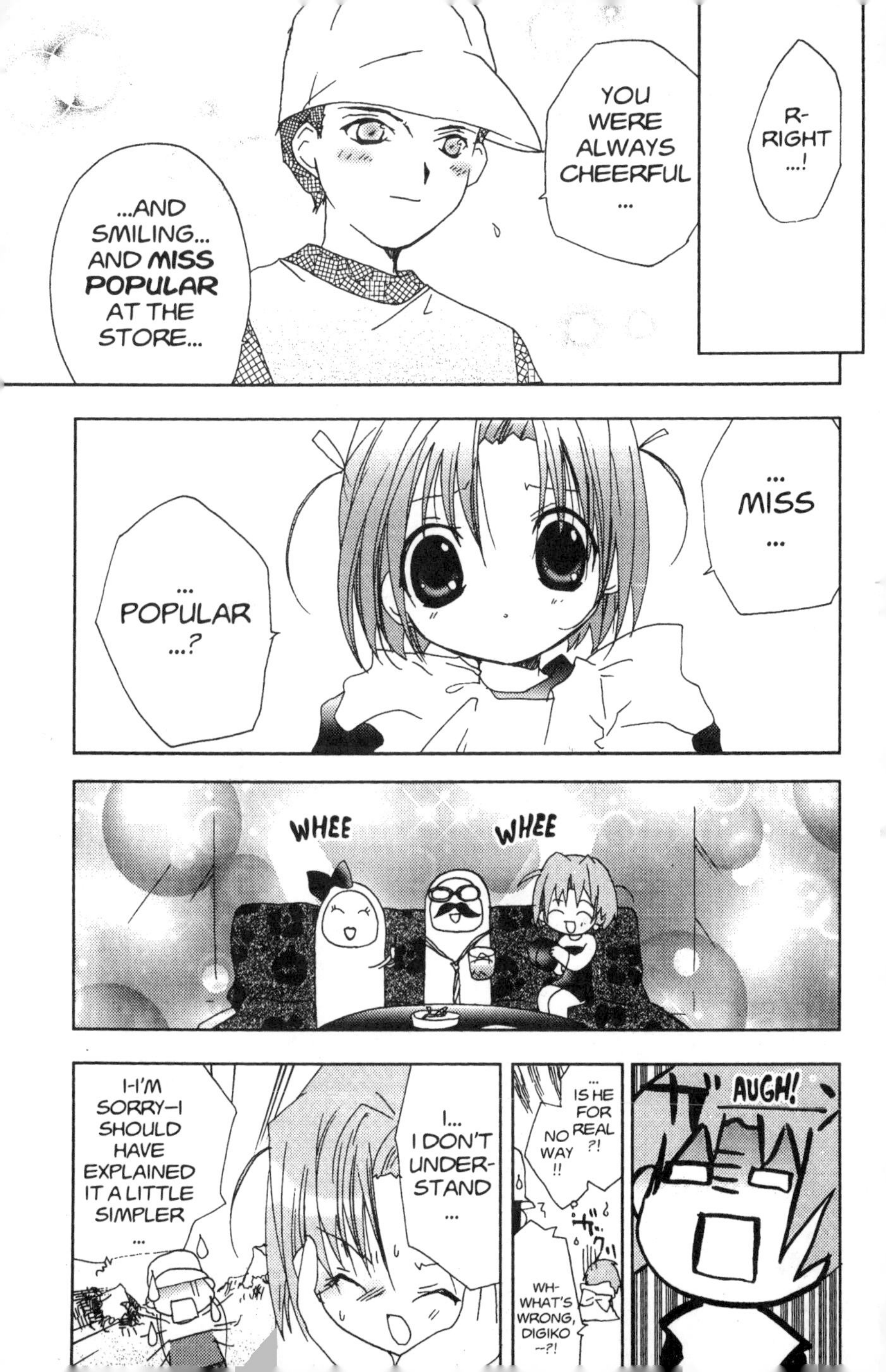
R- RIGHT ...!
YOU WERE ALWAYS CHEERFUL ...
...AND SMILING... AND **MISS POPULAR** AT THE STORE...
... MISS ...
... POPULAR ...?
WHEE
WHEE
AUGH!
... IS HE FOR REAL ?!
NO WAY !!
WH- WHAT'S WRONG, DIGIKO --?!
I... I DON'T UNDER-STAND ...
I-I'M SORRY—I SHOULD HAVE EXPLAINED IT A LITTLE SIMPLER ...

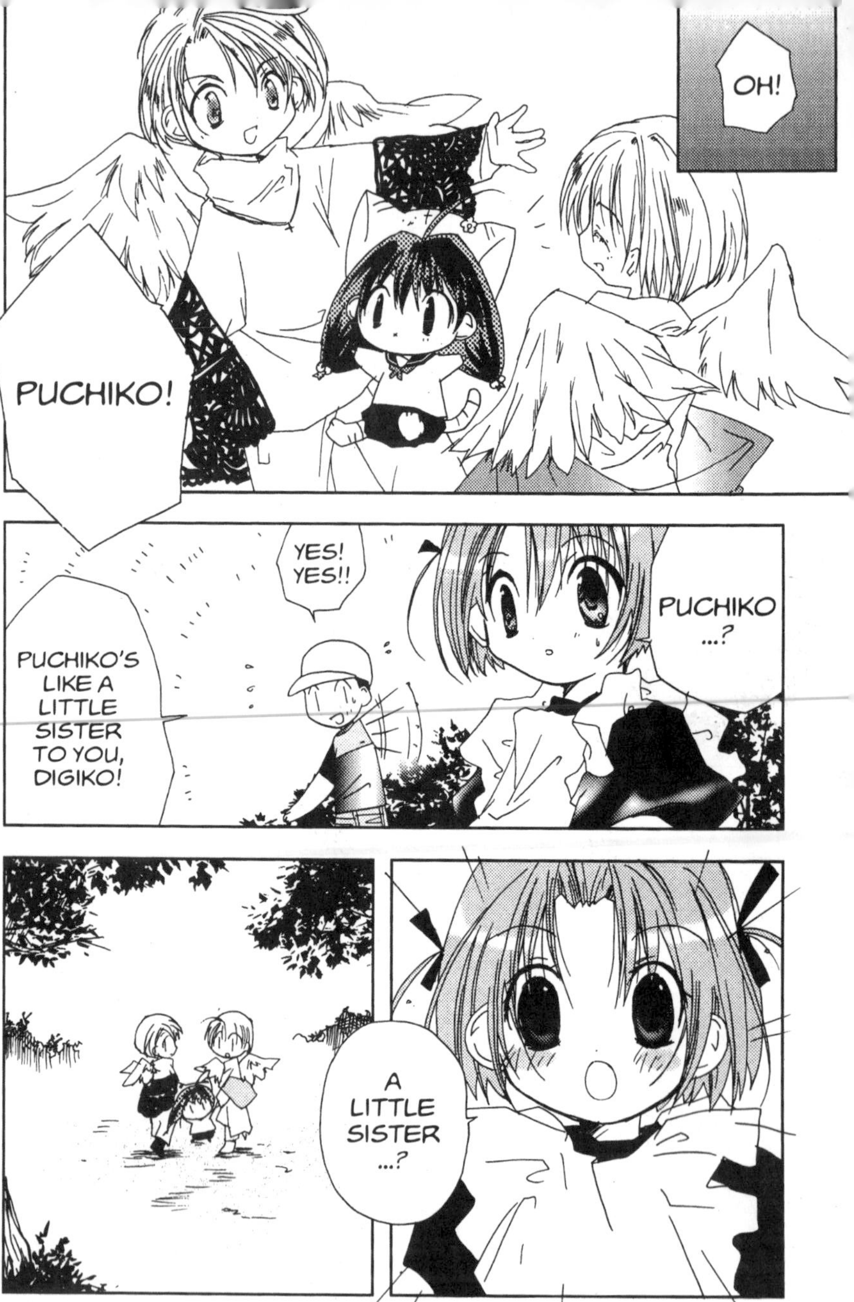
OH!
PUCHIKO!
PUCHIKO ...?
YES! YES!!
PUCHIKO'S LIKE A LITTLE SISTER TO YOU, DIGIKO!
A LITTLE SISTER ...?

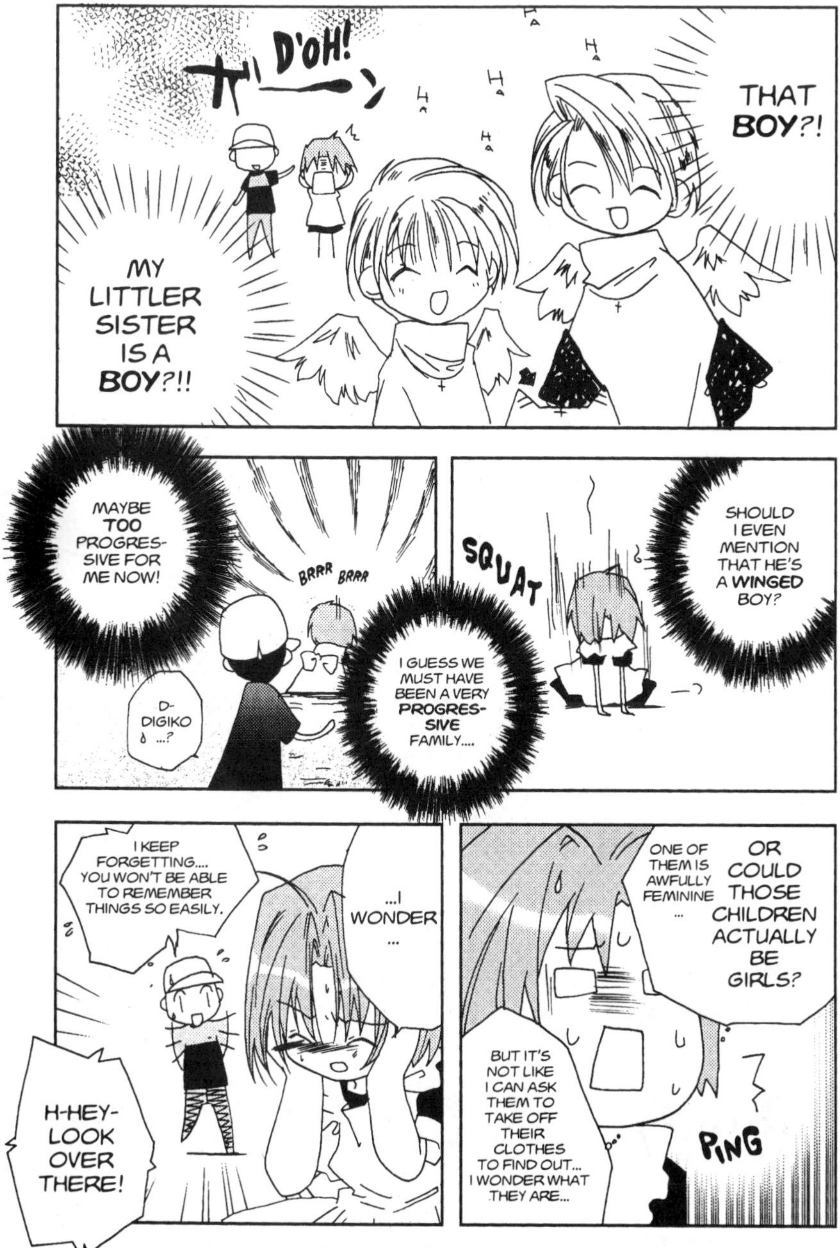
THAT BOY?!
HA HA HA HA HA
ガーン
D'OH!
MY LITTLER SISTER IS A BOY?!!
SHOULD I EVEN MENTION THAT HE'S A WINGED BOY?
SQUAT
I GUESS WE MUST HAVE BEEN A VERY PROGRES-SIVE FAMILY....
MAYBE TOO PROGRES-SIVE FOR ME NOW!
BRRR BRRR
D-DIGIKO ...?
OR COULD THOSE CHILDREN ACTUALLY BE GIRLS?
ONE OF THEM IS AWFULLY FEMININE ...
BUT IT'S NOT LIKE I CAN ASK THEM TO TAKE OFF THEIR CLOTHES TO FIND OUT... I WONDER WHAT THEY ARE...
PING
...I WONDER ...
I KEEP FORGETTING.... YOU WON'T BE ABLE TO REMEMBER THINGS SO EASILY.
H-HEY-LOOK OVER THERE!

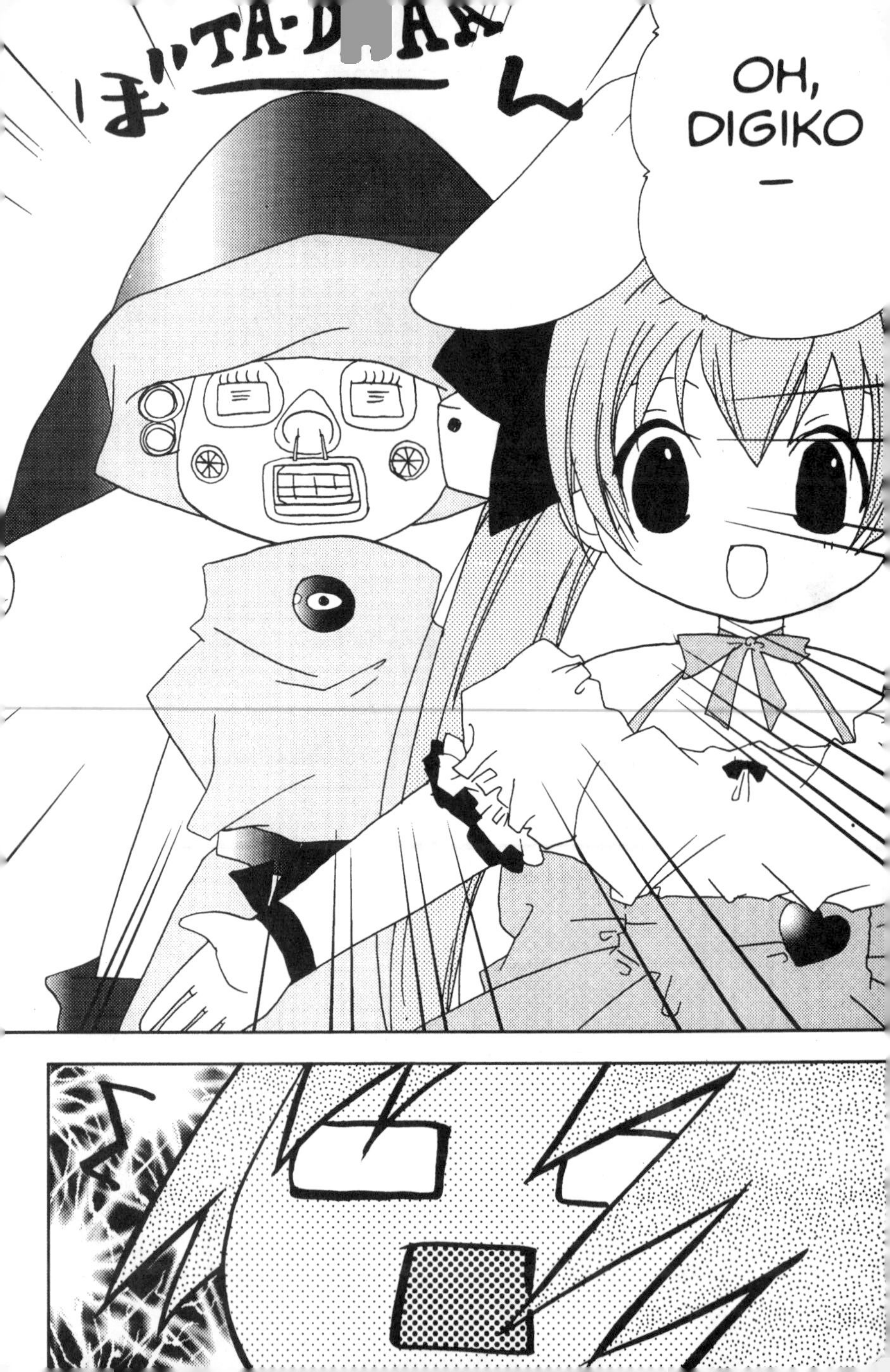
ほ TA-DAA ん
OH, DIGIKO —
ふ

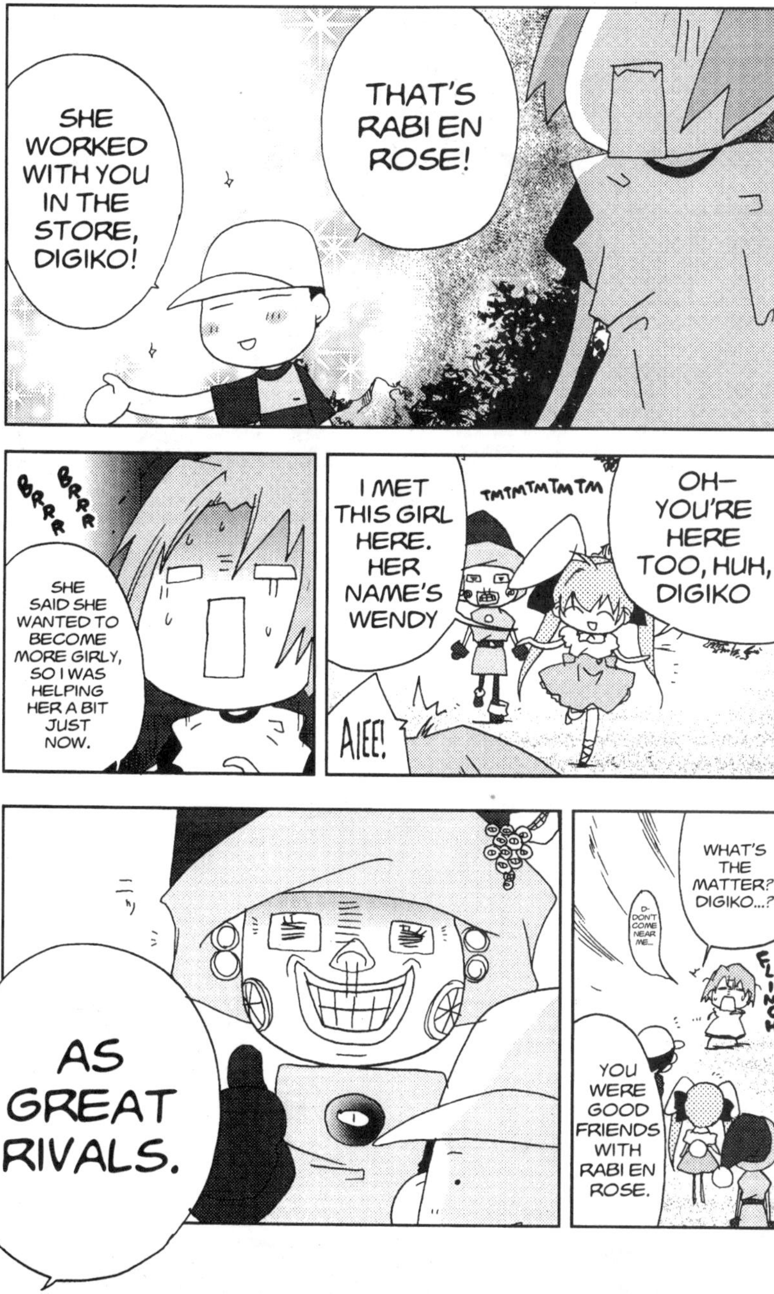
THAT'S RABI EN ROSE!
SHE WORKED WITH YOU IN THE STORE, DIGIKO!
OH— YOU'RE HERE TOO, HUH, DIGIKO
TMTMTMTMTM
I MET THIS GIRL HERE. HER NAME'S WENDY
AIEE!
BRRR BRRR
SHE SAID SHE WANTED TO BECOME MORE GIRLY, SO I WAS HELPING HER A BIT JUST NOW.
WHAT'S THE MATTER? DIGIKO...?
D-DON'T COME NEAR ME...
FLINCH
YOU WERE GOOD FRIENDS WITH RABI EN ROSE.
AS GREAT RIVALS.

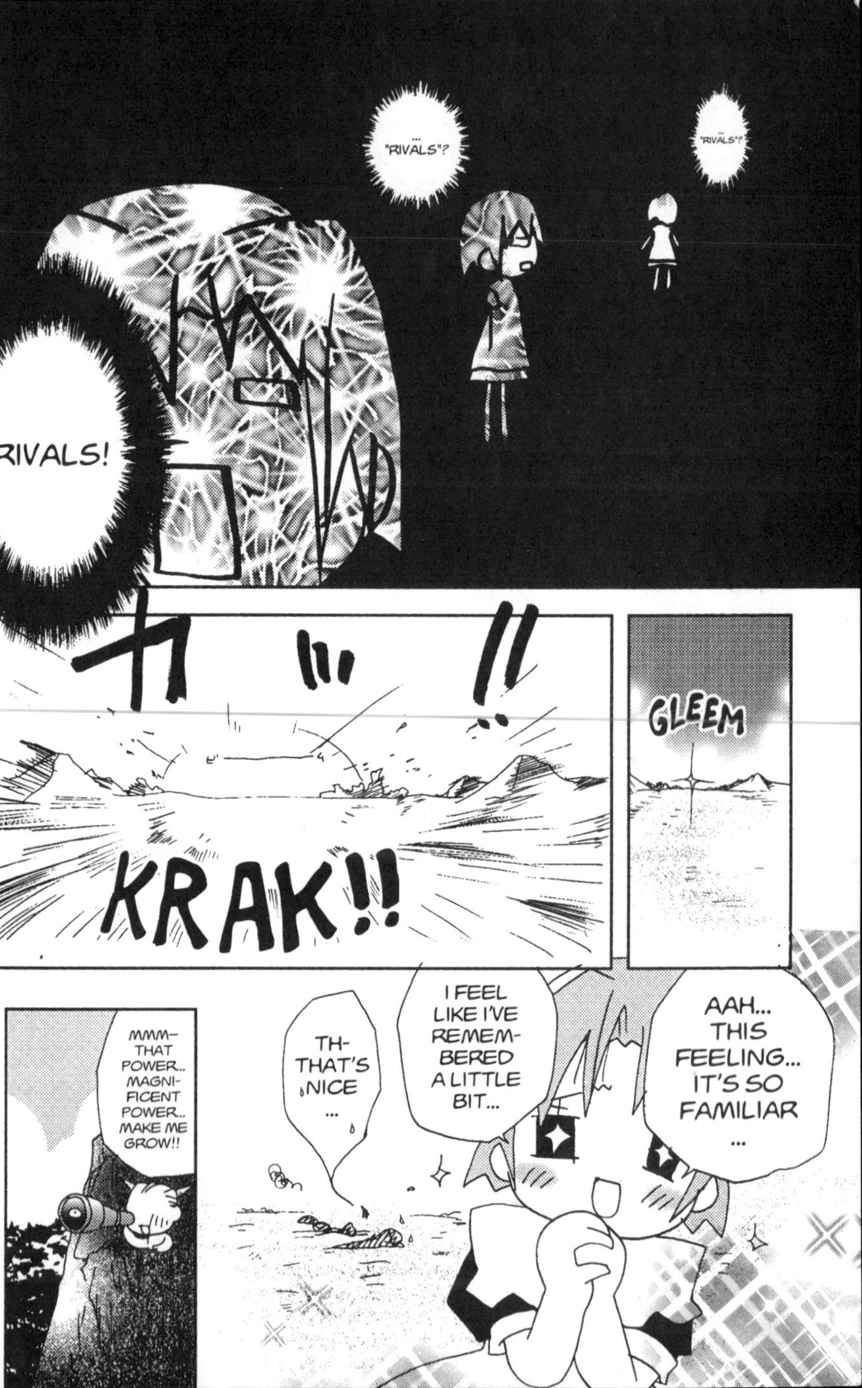

... "RIVALS"?
... "RIVALS"?
RIVALS!
GLEEM
カッ!!
KRAK!!
AAH... THIS FEELING... IT'S SO FAMILIAR ...
I FEEL LIKE I'VE REMEMBERED A LITTLE BIT...
TH-THAT'S NICE ...
MMM— THAT POWER.. MAGNIFICENT POWER.. MAKE ME GROW!!

END

A WORD ABOUT "DI-GI-CHARAT"!

I SURE DREW A LOT, DIDN'T I?
I WOULD LIKE TO CONTINUE WORKING ON IT.

AS LONG AS WORK KEEPS COMING IN--.

SO... I HOPE FOR YOUR
CONTINUED SUPPORT!

2001, 10
KOGE

KOGE-DONBO

A WORD ABOUT "DI-GI-CHARAT"!

FOR THE CAT-LOVER THAT I AM, CAT EARS ARE THE MOST POWERFUL APPEAL! (HA!) PUCHIKO ESPECIALLY... ❤

KAWAKU

KAWAKU

The Di Gi Charat Guide to Sound Effects!

As you've undoubtedly noticed, most of the sound effects in *Di Gi Charat* are in Japanese. Seeing the various explosions, tantrums and incidental dialogue jump off the page in a foreign language offers a unique experience for readers familiar only with American comics.

Fans of Digiko, Usada and the rest of the gang may applaud our respect for the original source material. Others, however, may be confused by the wildly expressive koukaon.

Thus, in an attempt to satisfy everyone, we've compiled this handy glossary. On the following pages you'll find a panel-by-panel account of every Digiko burp and Gema hiccup. In the process, maybe you'll pick up a little bit of Japanese, as well.

59.4	FX: FUN FUN [hum hum]
8.3	FX: ZUBO [smother]
9.1	FX: GABA- [jump-]
10.1	FX: BONN [boof]
11.2	FX: GASA [rustle]
11.4	FX: NIKO NIKO [grin grin]
12.4.1	FX: BAA [leap]
12.4.2	FX: BIKUU [flinch]
13.2	FX: FUE... [wilt...]
16.3	FX: WAKU WAKU WAKU [sounds of anticipation]

16.4 FX: FUFUU [chuckle]

18.3 FX: KUSUU [giggle]

19.1 FX: JITABATA [stomp]

21.1 FX: GAA [clench]
21.3 APRON: MANAGER

22.1 APRON: MANAGER

23.2 BOXES: AQUARIAN
23.4 FX: TEKIPAKI TEKIPAKI [quickly quickly]

24.1 BOXES: OX EXPRESS
24.2 BOXES: AQUARIAN
24.3 FX: DA- [dash-]
24.4.1 FX: DA- [dash-]
24.4.2 BOXES: AQUARIAN

25.1.1 FX: NIKO NIKO [grin grin]
25.1.2 APRON: MANAGER

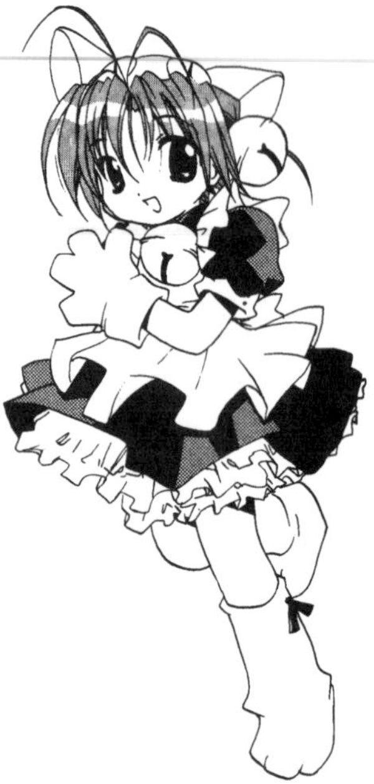

25.2 APRON: MANAGER
25.3 FX: TEKIPAKI TEKIPAKI TEKIPAKI [quickly quickly quickly]

26.1 FX: ZE-HA- ZE-HA- [heave pant heave pant]
26.3 BOX: AQUARIAN

27.3 FX: GYUU [squeeze]

28.2 FX: DOKII [d'oh]

31.2 FX: MI-N MI-N [sound of cicadas]
31.3 FX: PU-N [waft of awful stench]
31.4 FX: KUN KUN [sniff sniff]
31.5 FX: BAA [snatch]
31.6 FX: BOYOYO-N [hurl]

33.4 FX: BENN [whap]

34.2 FX: PII [point]
34.3 FX: GOGOGO NGOGO [rumble rumble]
34.5 FX: NO [pop]
34.8 FX: CHUDO-N [kabloom]

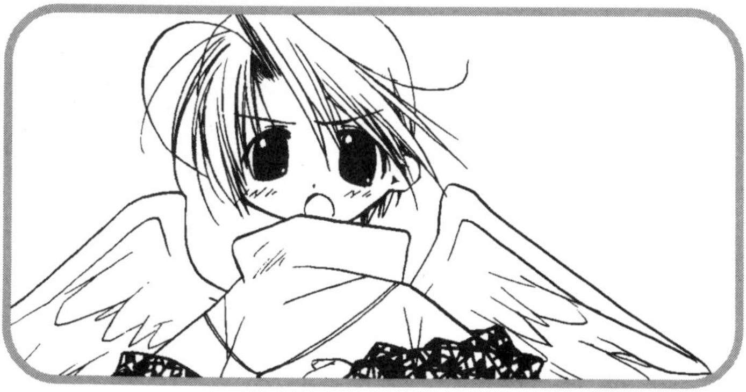

36.2 FX: MU-N [ponder]
36.3 SIDE OF BOX: XX FAMOUS PRODUCT

37.2 FX: SUU [pop]
37.3 FX: DODODODODO [stampede]

38.3.1 BOX: BEAN PASTE BUNS
38.3.2 SIDE OF BOX: XX FAMOUS PRODUCT

39.2 BOX: BEAN PASTE BUNS
39.4.1 BOX: BEAN PASTE BUNS
39.4.2 SIDE OF BOX: XX FAMOUS PRODUCT

40.4 FX: GA-N [gape]

41.1 FX: PIKII [jab]

42.1.1 FX: ITATATA [oww]
42.1.2 FX: U-N [moan]
42.4 FX: GORO GORO [rumble rumble]

47.1 FX: BAN [ta-daa]

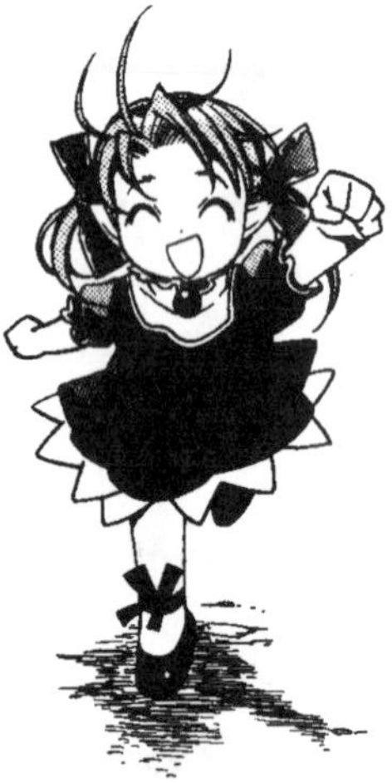

53.6 FX: ZUKI [sting]

54.3 FX: GACHAA GACHAA [clatter clatter]

55.7 FX: JYABU JYABU [splash splash]

56.5 FX: NUU [peer]
56.6 FX: NO!

57.1.1 FX: YORO... [stagger...]
57.1.2 FX: CACHAA [click]

59.4 FX: TEH-HEE

69.4 FX: IKKUZO—[here I come]

70.1 FX: KA-N [clank]
70.3 FX: ZAA [crunch]
70.4 FX: TATATA [dash]

71.3 FX: SHI... [silence...]

74.1 FX: YOJI YOJI [crawl crawl]

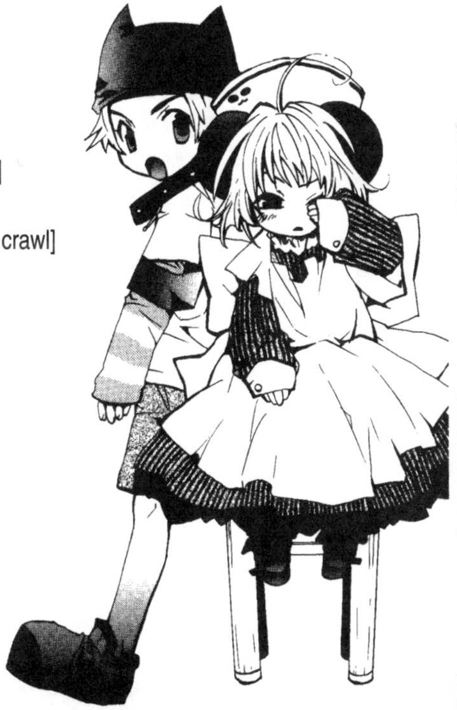

75.4   FX: ZAZAZAZA [fall]

75.5   FX: DOZA [crash]

75.7   FX: FUWA [waft]

76.7   FX: AWA AWA AWA [tremble tremble tremble]

82.3   FX: GABAA [sit up]

84.6   FX: KA- [blush-]

86.4   FX: GUO- [roar-]

87.3   FX: SURU... [slip...]

87.4   FX: KYUU... [twinge...]

94.2   FX: ZUN [funk]

94.3   FX: ARA [oh]

104.3   FX: BUGYURU [belch]

107.3   FX: MUKI- [irk-]

109.2 FX: POWAA... [gleam...]
109.3 FX: PAA... [flash...]

113.3 FX: HA... [sigh...]
113.4 FX: BO... [spaced out...]

115.1 FX: PONN [pat]

116.4 FX: PA- [brighten-]

118.6 FX: DOKII [thump]

124.2 FX: GEHOO GEHOO [cough cough]

153.6 FX: GAKKURI [slump]

156.2 FX: BO-N [ta-daa]

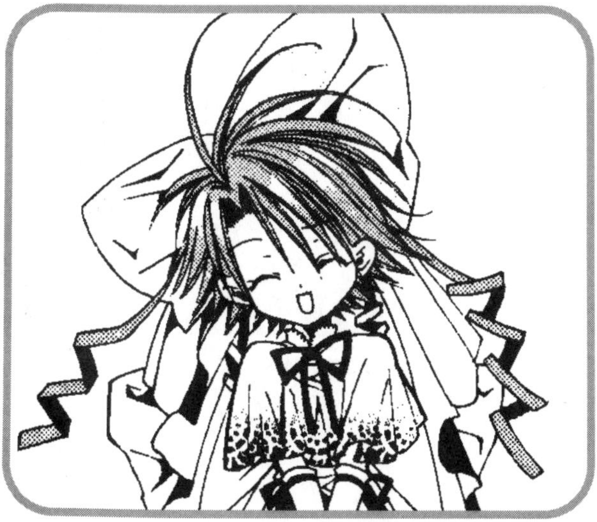

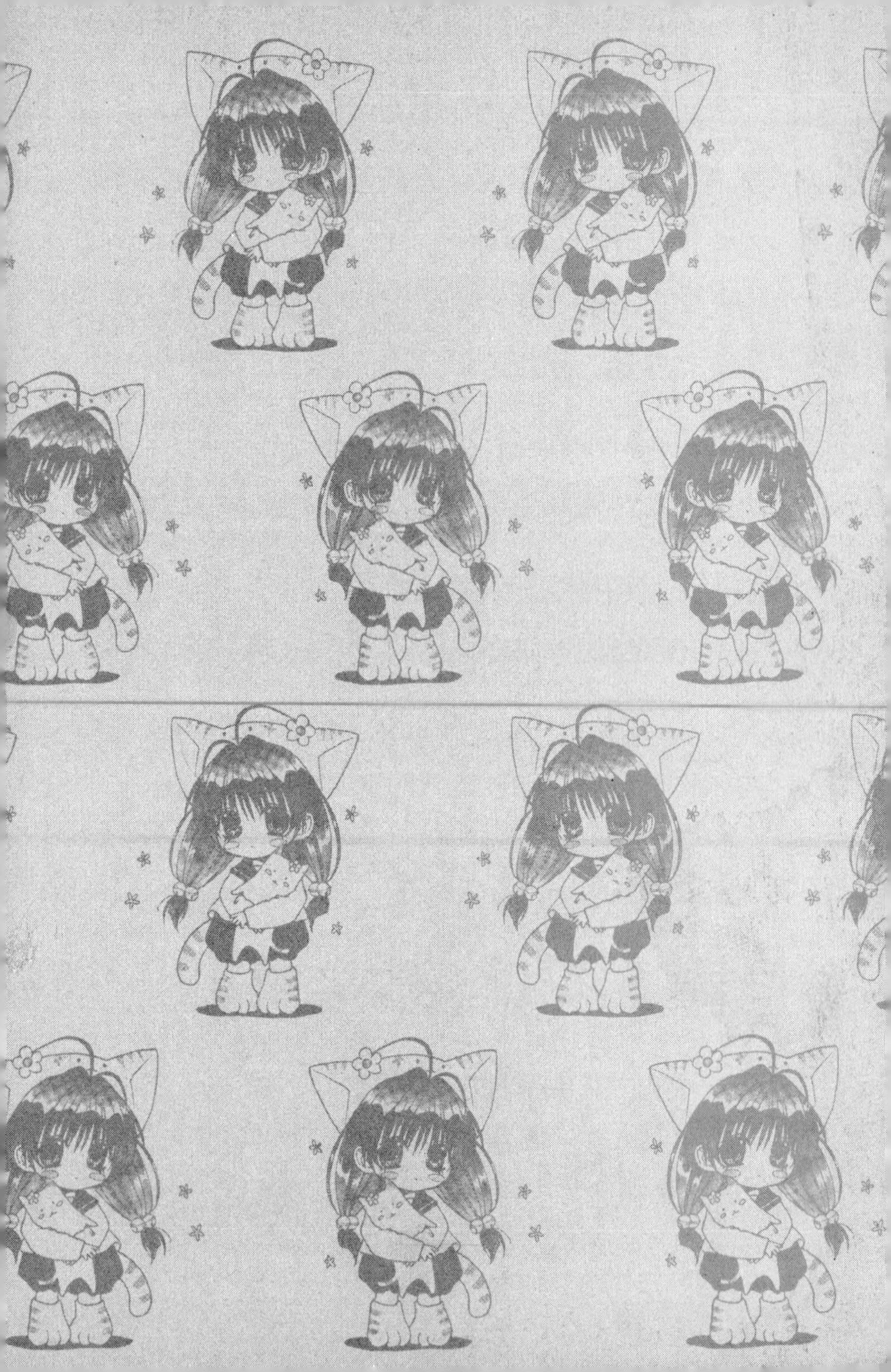